# PEARSON LONGMAN

## CORNERSTONE

**5**

PEARSON English Learning System

**Anna Uhl Chamot**

**Jim Cummins**

**Sharroky Hollie**

PEARSON

Upper Saddle River, New Jersey • Boston, Massachusetts • Chandler, Arizona • Glenview, Illinois

**Pearson Longman Cornerstone 5**

# PEARSON English Learning System

**Staff credits:** The people who made up the Longman Cornerstone team, representing editorial, production, design, manufacturing, and marketing, are John Ade, Rhea Banker, Virginia Bernard, Daniel Comstock, David Dickey, Gina Dillilo, Johnnie Farmer, Nancy Flaggman, Charles Green, Karen Kawaguchi, Ed Lamprich, Niki Lee, Jaime Leiber, Chris Leonowicz, Tara Maceyak, Linda Moser, Laurie Neaman, Leslie Patterson, Sherri Pemberton, Liza Pleva, Susan Saslow, Chris Siley, Loretta Steeves, Kim Steiner, and Lauren Weidenman.

**Text design and composition:** The Quarasan Group, Inc.
**Illustration and photo credits appear on page 427, which constitute an extension of this copyright page.**

**Library of Congress Cataloging-in-Publication Data**
Chamot, Anna Uhl.
   Longman Cornerstone / Anna Uhl Chamot, Jim Cummins, Sharroky Hollie.
   p. cm. — (Longman Cornerstone)
   Includes index.
   Contents: 1. Level 1. — 2. Level 2. — A. Level 3. — B. Level 4. — C. Level 5.
   1. English language—Textbooks for foreign speakers. (1. English language—Textbooks for foreign speakers. 2. Readers.) I. Cummins, Jim. II. Hollie, Sharroky. III. Title.

ISBN-13: 978-1-4284-347
ISBN-10: 1-4284-347

Printed in the United States of Amer
1 2 3 4 5 6 7 8 9 10 V063 16 15 14 13

**Anna Uhl Chamot** is a professor of secondary education and a faculty advisor for ESL in George Washington University's Department of Teacher Preparation. She has been a researcher and teacher trainer in content-based, second-language learning and language-learning strategies. She co-designed and has written extensively about the Cognitive Academic Language Learning Approach (CALLA) and spent seven years implementing the CALLA model in the Arlington Public Schools in Virginia.

**Jim Cummins** is the Canada Research Chair in the Department of Curriculum, Teaching, and Learning of the Ontario Institute for Studies in Education at the University of Toronto. His research focuses on literacy development in multilingual school contexts, as well as on the potential roles of technology in promoting language and literacy development. His recent publications include: *The International Handbook of English Language Teaching* (co-edited with Chris Davison) and *Literacy, Technology, and Diversity: Teaching for Success in Changing Times* (with Kristin Brown and Dennis Sayers).

**Sharroky Hollie** is an assistant professor in teacher education at California State University, Dominguez Hills. His expertise is in the field of professional development, African-American education, and second-language methodology. He is an urban literacy visiting professor at Webster University, St. Louis. Sharroky is the Executive Director of the Center for Culturally Responsive Teaching and Learning (CCRTL) and the co-founding director of the nationally-acclaimed Culture and Language Academy of Success (CLAS).

**Rebecca Anselmo**
Sunrise Acres Elementary School
Las Vegas, NV

**Ana Applegate**
Redlands School District
Redlands, CA

**Terri Armstrong**
Houston ISD
Houston, TX

**Jacqueline Avritt**
Riverside County Office of Ed.
Hemet, CA

**Mitchell Bobrick**
Palm Beach County School
West Palm Beach, FL

**Victoria Brioso-Saldala**
Broward County Schools
Fort Lauderdale, FL

**Brenda Cabarga Schubert**
Creekside Elementary School
Salinas, CA

**Joshua Ezekiel**
Bardin Elementary School
Salinas, CA

**Veneshia Gonzalez**
Seminole Elementary School
Okeechobee, FL

**Carolyn Grigsby**
San Francisco Unified School District
San Francisco, CA

**Julie Grubbe**
Plainfield Consolidated Schools
Chicago, IL

**Yasmin Hernandez-Manno**
Newark Public Schools
Newark, NJ

**Janina Kusielewicz**
Clifton Public Schools/Bilingual Ed.
& Basic Skills Instruction Dept.
Clifton, NJ

**Mary Helen Lechuga**
El Paso ISD
El Paso, TX

**Gayle P. Malloy**
Randolph School District
Randolph, MA

**Randy Payne**
Patterson/Taft Elementaries
Mesa, AZ

**Marcie L. Schnegelberger**
Alisal Union SD
Salinas, CA

**Lorraine Smith**
Collier County Schools
Naples, FL

**Shawna Stoltenborg**
Glendale Elementary School
Glen Burnie, MD

**Denise Tiffany**
West High School
Iowa City, IO

## Dear Student,

### Welcome to Longman Cornerstone!

We wrote *Longman Cornerstone* to help you succeed in all your school studies. This program will help you learn the English language you need to study language arts, social studies, math, and science. You will learn how to speak to family members, classmates, and teachers in English.

*Cornerstone* includes a mix of many subjects. Each unit has four different readings that include some fiction (made-up) and nonfiction (true) articles, stories, songs, and poems. The readings will give you some of the tools you need to do well in all your subjects in school.

As you use this program, you will build on what you already know, learn new words, new information and facts, and take part in creative activities. The activities will help you improve your English skills.

Learning a language takes time, but just like learning to skateboard or learning to swim, it is fun!

We hope you enjoy *Longman Cornerstone* as much as we enjoyed writing it for you!

Good luck!

Anna Uhl Chamot
Jim Cummins
Sharroky Hollie

# Contents

**Helping Others**

# Heroes and Their Journeys

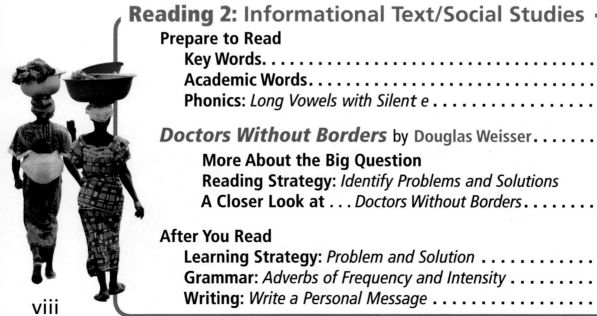

## Reading 3: Literature/Myth

THE BIG QUESTION

# Building a New Country

## Reading 3: Literature/Play

# Your Environment

# Reading 3: Informational Text/Magazine Article

# Sounds and Music

## Reading 3: Informational Text/Social Studies

# Visiting National Parks

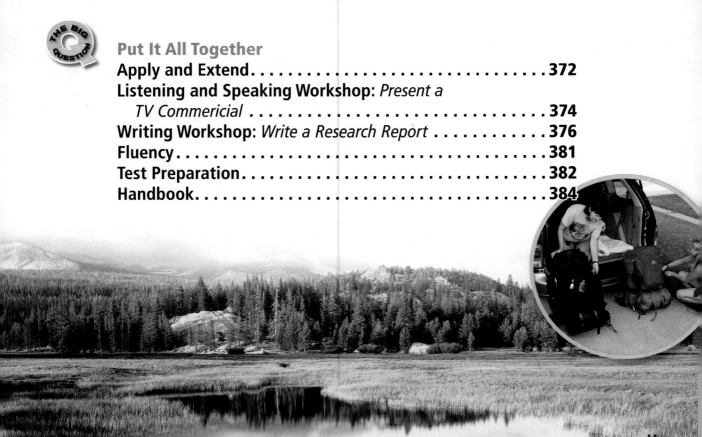

# Helping Others

Teamwork can be hard sometimes, but when everyone pitches in, the results can be amazing.

## Reading

**1 | Short Story**

**The Three Gifts**

**2 | Folktale**

**Stone Soup**

**3 | Biography**

**The Flying Schoolgirl**

## Listening and Speaking

You will discuss how sharing and helping others can make the world a better place. In the Listening and Speaking Workshop, you will make a presentation.

## Writing

You will practice descriptive writing. In the Writing Workshop, you will write a descriptive essay.

**Quick Write**

Tell about the last time you helped someone. How did it benefit both the other person and yourself?

**DVD** **VIEW AND RESPOND**
*Talk about the poster for this unit. Then watch and listen to the video and answer the questions at LongmanCornerstone.com.*

# What do you know about helping others?

## Words to Know

Listen and repeat. Use these words to talk about helping at home.

 set the
table

 make my
bed

 vacuum

 take
out the
garbage

 sweep

 run
errands

## Practice

Work with a partner. Ask and answer questions about chores.

| | | |
|---|---|---|
| the bathroom | my bedroom | the dining room |
| the kitchen | the living room | our neighborhood |

**Example:** A: What chores do you do?

B: I set the table in the kitchen.

## Write

Read the question. Write your response in your notebook.

What chores do you do to help at home?

## Make Connections

Copy the sentences below into your notebook. Complete the sentences with the following words.

**clean the carpet**

**clean the floor**

**recycle**

**put away the groceries**

1. I need to _____ in the kitchen, so I am going to sweep it and then mop it.

2. My mom says it is important to _____, so I never put cans in the garbage.

3. We need to _____ before our grandparents come over, so I am going to vacuum.

4. My dad stopped at the supermarket, so when he got home, he asked us to _____.

## What about you?

Talk with a partner. Talk about who usually does the different types of chores at your home.

# Kids' Stories from around the World

Texas, U.S.A.

Spain

**Charlie**

On my street in Dallas, we celebrate Thanksgiving every year with a potluck picnic. Every family brings a different dish, and we all share each other's food. There is always plenty of food to eat. We have a lot of fun.

**Clara**

I live in Spain. There was a huge oil spill a few years ago. The beaches were full of oil sludge. Many birds were covered with oil and were dying. People from all over the world came to help clean up after the oil spill.

**Russia**

**Egypt**

**Sergei**

An astronaut from my town of Batumi, Russia, has worked on the International Space Station. There, astronauts and engineers from many countries do research together to find out about Earth and the solar system. What they learn will help us make plans for a better future.

**Mert**

Archaeologists from all over the world have come to Egypt to participate in archaeological digs in the Valley of the Kings. A team of experts working together uncovered a tomb near the tomb of King Tutankhamen. By helping each other, experts learn more about ancient history.

## What about you?

1. When have you worked with others?

2. Do you know a story about people helping each other? Share your story.

**Prepare to Read**

## What You Will Learn

**Reading**

■ Vocabulary building: *Context, phonics*

■ Reading strategy: *Identify characters and plot*

■ Text type: *Literature (short story)*

**Grammar**
Future: *will* and *be going to*

**Writing**
Describe a future event

These words will help you understand the reading.

### Key Words

cooperate

bore

marvelous

grain

virtue

grateful

# Key Words

*The Three Gifts* is a short story about how an African leader and his children learn the gift of giving.

## Words in Context  Audio

**1** A job gets done much faster when people cooperate, or work together.

**2** The apple tree bore a lot of fruit.

**3** Lisa and her friends had a marvelous time at the party.

**④** Have you ever tasted millet? It is a grain, like wheat or oats.

**⑤** A virtue is something that is good about a person. Some people think neatness is a virtue.

**⑥** People often show that they are grateful, or thankful, when having a feast with family and friends.

### Practice

**Create a vocabulary notebook.**

- Divide your page into three columns: the new words, their definitions, and a sentence using each word.
- Test yourself by covering one of the columns.

## Make Connections

Think of a time you were grateful that someone helped you. Why did you feel grateful? How did you thank the person? Discuss.

W B

3

These words will help you talk about the reading.

### Academic Words

**assist**
help someone

**benefit**
be useful or helpful for someone or something

**motive**
reason for doing something

WB

4

# Academic Words

## Words in Context

JoAnna liked to **assist** people with their problems.

The bake sale will **benefit** the hurricane victims.

The police are trying to find out the **motive** for the crime.

### Practice

**Write the sentences in your notebook. Choose an academic word to complete each sentence.**

1. When you see somebody carrying a heavy load, you should offer to _____ him.

2. Juanita's _____ for joining the team was to make some new friends.

3. If our class cleans up the park, our work will _____ everybody in town.

### Apply

**Write the answers in your notebook. Use the academic words. Then ask and answer with a partner.**

1. What do you do to **assist** your neighbors?

2. How can helping others **benefit** you?

3. What is your teacher's **motive** for giving homework?

# Phonics

## Long Vowel Pairs

Long vowel sounds can be spelled in different ways. Listen. Then read each word aloud.

| Long Vowel Pairs | | | | |
|---|---|---|---|---|
| **Long a** | **Long e** | **Long i** | **Long o** | **Long u** |
| day | meet | lie | oats | cue |
| grain | seat | | doe | fruit |

Did you notice that each word has two vowels together? Which one of the vowels says its name?

### Rule

When there are two vowels together, the first vowel is usually long, and the second vowel is silent. The vowel pairs below usually have long vowel sounds.

| | | | | |
|---|---|---|---|---|
| ay, ai | ee, ea | ie | oa, oe | ue, ui |

### Practice

**Work with a partner. Take turns sounding out the words in the box.**

| | | |
|---|---|---|
| need | pay | three |
| tried | coast | say |
| fail | tie | plain |
| road | due | fruit |
| clue | | |

1. Make a chart like the one above.

2. List the words from this box in the chart.

3. Add two more words for each long vowel sound.

5

### LITERATURE
### Short Story

**More About**

How can giving to others **benefit** the giver?

 **Listen to the Audio.**
Listen for the general meaning. Raise your hand if you need help understanding.

### Reading Strategy

#### Identify Characters and Plot

Stories have a plot, or story line, that is usually a sequence of events. Stories also have characters, which are people or animals. As you read, think about these questions:

- Who are the main, or most important, characters?
- What events occur in the plot?

Listen as your teacher models the reading strategy.

# The Three Gifts

## by Shannon Doyne
## illustrated by Soud

In Africa, there once was a leader named Jelani. He was a **just** leader and cared about his people very much. The people in his village were happy, healthy, and peaceful.

Jelani had three daughters and four sons. At school, Jelani's children learned about other places in Africa. In some villages, people were hungry because crops did not grow well and trees bore no fruit. In other villages, groups of people did not cooperate, but fought **fiercely** with each other.

Jelani's oldest daughter was named Ada. One night she said, "People in this village have marvelous lives. I want to travel to other places and do what I can to help others."

Jelani looked at her proudly and said, "Finish school. Then you can help others."

That is just what Ada did.

---

**just** treating people the same, no matter who they are
**fiercely** hard

When Ada finished school, she went to other villages where she worked hard to help people. Ada's brothers and sisters **admired** her. She sent drawings of the school she helped to build. Ada wrote that it was a big job, but lots of fun.

One by one, Ada's brothers and sisters finished school. They all asked Jelani if they could go and help people. Jelani's eyes filled with joy each time, and he said, "Yes, you can help people."

In time, only the youngest son remained at home. His name was Kofi. Kofi loved to receive his **siblings'** letters. One brother helped dig wells for fresh water. Another brother helped farmers plant better crops. A sister helped a village hold an **election** to choose a better leader.

All of the letters were alike in one way. All of his brothers and sisters invited Kofi and Jelani to visit their villages.

> ## Reading Skill
>
> Boldfaced words are defined at the bottom of the page. Key words are highlighted. Academic words are in blue.

---

**admired**   looked up to

**siblings**   brothers and sisters

**election**   contest won by the person who gets the most votes

**Before You Go On**   What was Jelani's children's **motive** for helping people?

Kofi and Jelani decided to visit their family. Early one morning, they set out on their horses. They brought with them many of Jelani's **advisors**.

Late in the first day, they stopped at a village to rest. Some people came out to meet them. They took a great interest in the horses, but their eyes looked sad. "What's wrong?" Kofi asked.

A woman replied, "We have horses, too, but we can't grow the right grains for them. Our horses' health is poor."

"Bring some sacks of millet," Jelani called to his men. "We can feed your horses and leave some sacks for you."

"We are so grateful," the people said. "Someday, we will repay this **favor**. Just call on us."

---

**advisors**   people who help others decide what to do

**favor**   kind or helpful act

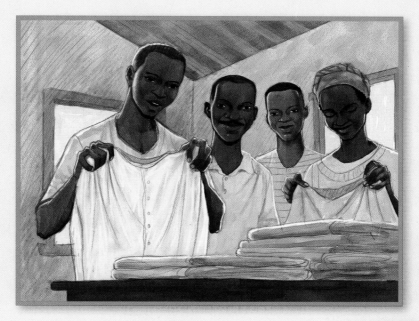

The next day, the group went to the village of Kofi's older brother. His name was Sekou. Sekou hugged Jelani and Kofi tightly. "I have missed you so much!" he said.

Sekou showed Jelani and Kofi the **well** he had helped to dig. "Another problem is the **harsh** sun," Sekou said. "Many people do not have the right clothing to protect them. I gave away all of my extra clothes, but so many people still need clothes."

When Jelani and Kofi **departed** a few days later, they left behind all the extra clothing they had. The villagers told Sekou, "One day, we will find a way to thank them. Please tell this to your father and brother. All they have to do is ask."

**Reading Skill**

Ask your classmates or teacher when you don't understand a word, phrase, or language structure.

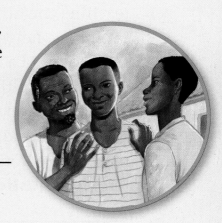

---

**well**   deep hole in the ground where water is found

**harsh**   strong or painful

**departed**   left

**Before You Go On**   How did Kofi and Jelani **assist** the people they met?

The next day, Kofi told his father, "I want to help people, too." Once again, Jelani felt great joy. He was proud that all of his children shared the virtue of caring for others.

Just then, they passed several people. They were building a house with wood, but they were having a difficult time. "Father," Kofi asked, "many of our men have learned how to **construct** with wood. Don't you think we should help them?"

Jelani called out, "Stop, everyone!" Jelani's advisors were soon teaching the others how to build a wood house. The people said, "You have helped us with this house, and now we can use these skills to build a whole village. One day, you will call on us, and we will return this favor."

The last stop was Ada's village. But something seemed very wrong. Kofi and Jelani saw there were piles of wood and mud and rocks where houses had once been. Kofi found Ada. "We had a terrible **mudslide**," Ada said. "Everyone's homes are **destroyed**."

---

**construct**   build

**mudslide**   a lot of very wet dirt falling down a hill

**destroyed**   completely broken

Kofi, Jelani, Ada, the advisors, and people from the village started to work. They rebuilt houses. Everyone was very tired and hot. They were also out of **supplies**. Jelani sent his advisors for help.

Soon, 20 horses appeared. All of the horses had riders, and many of the horses carried bags of supplies.

"You helped us when we had no food for our horses," one of the riders said. "We came to help you get supplies."

Many more people appeared. One called out, "You taught us to build houses. Now we can help you."

People from Sekou's village put up a large tent. "You gave us your extra clothes. We **stitched** them together. You can live in this tent until the new houses are ready."

And together, they rebuilt Ada's village.

---

**supplies**   things that are needed
**stitched**   sewed

6–8

## Reading Strategy

### Identify Characters and Plot

- Who are the main characters in the story?
- What are three events in the plot?

## Think It Over

1. **Recall**   What did Jelani's children learn in school?

2. **Comprehend**   What were the "three gifts" of the title?

3. **Analyze**   How did **assisting** others **benefit** Jelani's family?

# Learning Strategies

## Characters and Plot

Every story has **characters**. The characters are the people, or sometimes animals, in the story. Every story also has a **plot**. The plot is the series of events that take place in the story.

**Practice**  G.O. 152

**Work with a partner. Make a chart like the one below.**

1. Reread the story. Pay attention to the characters and events.

2. List characters and events in the chart. Follow the examples given.

| Character | What Happens | The Result |
|-----------|--------------|------------|
| Jelani | Ada asks him if she can leave. | Jelani tells her to finish school. |
| Kofi | Gets letters from siblings | Visits his siblings with Jelani |
| Sekou | | |
| | | |

# Use a Cause and Effect Chart

When one thing happens, it causes other things to happen. A Cause and Effect Chart helps you see how events in a plot are related.

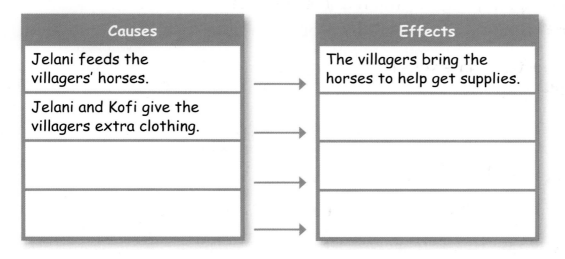

  G.O. 148

**Work with a partner. Copy this Cause and Effect Chart.**

1. Add one more effect to the chart.

2. List two more causes.

3. Show what effects those events caused.

| Causes | Effects |
|---|---|
| Jelani feeds the villagers' horses. | The villagers bring the horses to help get supplies. |
| Jelani and Kofi give the villagers extra clothing. | |
| | |
| | |

W B
9

**Using the pictures in the reading, retell the story to a partner.**

## Extension

**Utilize** Some people say it is better to give than to receive. Think about causes and effects in terms of something you have done for someone else. Why did you decide to do what you did? What was the effect of what you did? Present your experience to the class using a visual aid.

# Grammar

## Future: *will* and *be going to*

Use *will* or *be going* to talk about the future.

Use *will* and the plain form of a verb to express an action that you choose to do, a prediction, or a promise. To make the **negative**, use *will not* (or *won't*).

|  | **Subject + *will* + verb** |
|---|---|
| **Voluntary action** | I will **ride** my bike to school. |
| **Prediction** | You will **win** the race. |
| **Promise** | I will **call** you later. |
| **Promise (negative)** | I will not **talk** during class. |

> will = **'ll**
> will not = **won't**

Use *be going to* plus the plain form of the verb to talk about predictions or plans. The *be* verb must agree with the subject. Add *not* after *be* to form a negative.

| | **Subject + *be going to* + verb** | |
|---|---|---|
| **Prediction** | I | am going to **win** the lottery soon. |
| **Plan** | You, We, They | are going to **have** a party next week. |
| **Plan (negative)** | He, She | is not going to **study** tonight. |

For questions, put *will* or the *be* verb before the subject.

> Will you **help** me clean up?   Will they **bring** presents?
> Where are you going to **stay**?   Who is she going to **call**?

## Practice

**Use the words in parentheses to complete the sentences. Use *will* or *be going to*. (More than one answer may be possible.)**

**Example:** We <u>are going to go</u> to Africa. (go)

**1.** I _____ the moon someday. (visit)

**2.** Evan _____ late. (not be)

**3.** Who _____ the next election? (win)

**4.** You _____ the next test. (not fail)

**5.** They _____ their teacher with the decorations. (**assist**)

**6.** We _____ with them on the project. (cooperate)

## Apply

**Work with a partner. Ask and answer questions about what you are going to do next weekend. Use question words from the list below.**

| | | |
|---|---|---|
| What...? | Where...? | How...? |
| When...? | Who...? | Why...? |

**Example:** A: What are you going to do next weekend?

B: Let's see. On Saturday, we're going to have a party for my uncle.

A: Really? Who's going to be there?

B: Well, my uncle will be there, and his wife and my cousins. And...

**W B**
10

### Grammar Check ✓

Which word is usually used to tell about a future plan, *will* or *be going to*?

# Writing

## Describe a Future Event

*Ongoing Writing Skills Practice*

When you describe an event, choose adjectives or adverbs that appeal to the senses. Describe the sight, sound, smell, taste, and feel of things.

### Writing Prompt

Write a paragraph that describes an event you are planning to go on. It might be a vacation, a day trip, or a visit to the mall. Be sure to use *will* and *be going to* correctly.

## ❶ Prewrite  G.O. 141

Choose an event to write about. List the event and the activities you have planned in a graphic organizer.

A student named Nelli listed her ideas like this:

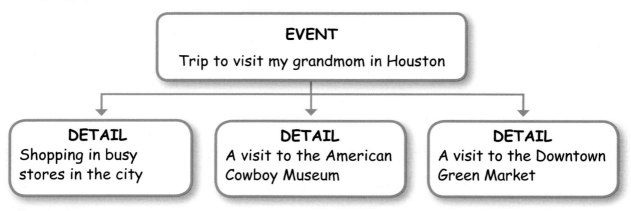

EVENT
Trip to visit my grandmom in Houston

DETAIL
Shopping in busy stores in the city

DETAIL
A visit to the American Cowboy Museum

DETAIL
A visit to the Downtown Green Market

## ❷ Draft

Use your graphic organizer to help you write a draft. Include an opening that catches the reader's interest. Include details that help the reader picture the event.

## ❸ Revise

Read your draft. Look for places where the writing needs improvement. Use the Writing Checklist to help you identify problems. Then revise your draft.

## ❹ Edit

Check your work for errors in grammar, usage, mechanics, and spelling. Trade papers with a partner to get feedback. Use the Peer Review Checklist on page 404.

## ❺ Publish

Prepare a clean copy of your final draft. Share your paragraph with the class. Save your work. You will need to refer to it in the Writing Workshop.

Here is Nelli's paragraph:

### Writing Checklist

**Ideas**

✔ I included details to help readers picture the event.

**Word Choice**

✔ I chose specific adjectives and adverbs.

**Conventions**

✔ I used *will* and *be going to* correctly.

Nelli Perez

My family is going to visit my grandmom in Houston. We are going to leave a few days after Labor Day. It is exciting to visit a big city. I'll go with my mom and grandmom to the stores downtown. It is interesting to see so many people in the shops. You don't see that in my small town! We will also visit the American Cowboy Museum. You can learn all about cowboys and Texas history there. After that, we are going to go to the Downtown Green Market. The farmers there have all kinds of foods. I love the smell of the baked goods they sell.

11–12

## What You Will Learn

**Reading**

- Vocabulary building: *Context, word study*

- Reading strategy: *Identify events in a plot*

- Text type: *Literature (folktale)*

**Grammar**

Simple past: regular and *be* verbs

**Writing**

Describe a memorable day

These words will help you understand the reading.

### Key Words

- carry
- scarce
- share
- peeked
- cottage
- charge

# Key Words

*Stone Soup* is about a boy who finds a clever way to feed some hungry villagers.

## Words in Context  Audio

**1** I helped Mom and Dad carry the groceries when we got back from the store.

**2** When it gets cold in the winter, flowers growing outside become scarce .

**3** It's always nice to share !

**④** Jeffrey peeked out of the window to see if his mom's car was in the street.

**⑤** The cottage was small but very cozy.

**⑥** The elephants charge the lions at the watering hole.

## Practice

**Make flashcards to help you memorize the words.**

- Write a key word on the front.
- On the back, draw a picture to help you remember the word.

## Make Connections

The next story shows how everyone wins when people share. Do you have a story about sharing? Tell your story to a partner.

**Speaking Skills**

When you don't know the right word to use, ask a classmate or your teacher.

13

These words will help you talk about the reading.

### Academic Words

**identify**
tell what something or someone is

**occur**
take place or happen

**major**
big or important

# Academic Words

## Words in Context

We could not **identify** the kind of spices they used on the meat.

When many people work together on a project, amazin things can **occur**.

The **major** ingredients in the soup were fresh vegetable

 **Practice**

**Write the sentences in your notebook. Choose an academic word to complete each sentence.**

1. I can ____ my notebook because it is blue and red.

2. Snowstorms usually ____ in winter.

3. My ____ goal is to save enough for a new bike.

**Apply**

**Write the answers in your notebook. Use the academic words. Then ask and answer with a partner.**

1. Can you **identify** the names of the president and vice president?

2. How often do lightning storms **occur** in your area?

3. What **major** attractions should visitors see in your city or town?

# Word Study

## Multiple-Meaning Words

Some words have more than one meaning.

> John could hardly wait to eat every **drop** of the soup.
> He waited for the water to boil to **drop** the stone into the pot.

A dictionary lists all the different meanings of a word.

### Rule

You can look at how a word is used in a sentence to help you understand what it means.

- A drop of soup is a small amount of soup.
- Drop the stone means to let the stone fall.

### Practice

**Look up each word in the dictionary.**
**Write two different definitions for each word.**

1. trade

2. charge

3. stone

4. fill

5. carry

**More About**

What are the pros and cons of sharing?

 **Listen to the Audio.**
Listen for the general meaning.
Raise your hand if you need help understanding.

### Reading Strategy

### Identify Events in a Plot

A plot is made up of the **major** events that **occur** in a story. **Identifying** these can help you understand and remember the plot. As you read, think about these questions:

- What are the events that take place in the story?
- Which events are the most important?

Listen as your teacher models the reading strategy.

# Stone Soup

**by P. J. Perkins**
**illustrated by Julie Downing**

One of John's favorite things was a big iron pot. The pot had once **belonged** to his moth[er].

As much as he loved the pot, John was hungry. He decided to **trade** the pot for something to eat.

"I'm sorry," said the farmer's wife from her cottage door. "Food is scarce these days. I only have enough for my own family."

"Thank you, anyway," John said. "I will carry my pot to the next village."

John walked many miles.

"May I trade this nice iron pot for something to eat?" he asked everyone he saw.

But the people in this village were just as poor and hungry as John was.

---

**belonged**   was owned

**trade**   to give away for something else

As John started to leave the village, he saw a smooth, round stone in the road. If only this stone were something good to eat, he thought.

Then John got an idea. He filled his iron pot with water. He **gathered** sticks and dry wood and then built a **blazing** fire all around his pot.

As he waited for the water to get hot, he thought about how good his soup would taste. "This stone soup will be **delicious**!" he said to himself. "I can hardly wait to eat every drop!"

When the water began to bubble and boil, he dropped the stone into the pot.

---

**gathered**   collected

**blazing**   very bright

**delicious**   tastes or smells very good

**Before You Go On**   What **major** event **occurs** on this page?

"What are you doing?" asked a little girl, who had been watching him from a nearby garden.

"I'm making stone soup," John told her.

"Stone soup!" she cried. "Is it good?"

"You've never had stone soup?" he asked. "Stone soup is delicious!"

The little girl peeked into the pot of water. She saw the stone at the bottom of the pot.

"I have some extra potatoes," she told him. "Would potatoes be good in stone soup?"

"I like stone soup just as it is," John said. "But I think potatoes will make it even better."

The little girl smiled. "Let's put them in!" she said as she dropped the potatoes into the boiling water.

**Reading Skill**

Ask your classmates or teacher when you don't understand a word, phrase, or language structure.

As the potatoes began to cook, wonderful smells **floated** through the village from cottage to cottage.

A young boy came over with some carrots. "Your soup smells so good," the boy said. "Would these carrots be good in the soup?"

"This stone soup will be delicious," John told him. "But carrots will make it even better."

The boy dropped the carrots into the pot.

John sniffed the delicious **aroma** coming from the pot. "This will be the best stone soup ever," he said to the boy and girl.

That's when John saw how hungry the children looked.

"Will you stay and share this soup with me?" he asked them.

"Will there be enough?" the little girl asked.

"More than enough!" John said.

---

**floated**   traveled over air or water

**aroma**   odor

**Before You Go On**   What **major** events **occur** on this page?

Soon, other people in the village began to charge toward John and his pot of stone soup.

"I've never heard of stone soup, but here is some meat," said a woman. "You may use it if you think it will be good in the soup."

"I have some onions," said another woman as she dropped them into the pot.

As the stone soup **simmered**, more and more people **lined up** to add something good to the pot.

John said to each person, "Please bring a bowl and spoon and share this soup with me. This is too much soup for me to eat alone."

Each person hurried home to get a bowl and spoon.

---

**simmered**   cooked slowly

**lined up**   stood one behind the other

When the soup had cooked, John looked at all the people who had gathered. Each person stood by the pot with a bowl and spoon. He wondered if there would be enough soup for everyone.

John looked into the pot of soup and saw the potatoes, carrots, onions, meat, and other good things. The pot was full!

John spooned the soup into everyone's bowls.

"This is the best soup ever!" exclaimed one person.

"I didn't know that stone soup could be so delicious!" said someone else.

After John finished his third bowl of soup, he called to the little girl who had given him potatoes. "This stone is for you," he said to her. "Now your village will never be hungry again."

16–18

## Reading Strategy

### Identify Events in a Plot

- What **major** events **occur** at the beginning of the story?

- What major events occur in the middle?

- What major events occur at the end?

## Think It Over

1. **Recall** What was one of John's favorite things?

2. **Comprehend** What problem did John and all of the villagers share?

3. **Analyze** What is the moral, or main message, of this story?

# Learning Strategies

## Events in a Plot

The **plot** tells the events that happen in a story. The **events** are the **major** actions that **occur**.

**Practice**

**Read this list of events and details from *Stone Soup*. Identify which ones are major events in the plot. Identify which ones are details.**

a. John is hungry. He has a pot but no food.

b. John meets a farmer's wife. She lives in a cottage.

c. John finds a smooth, round stone. The stone gives him an idea.

d. John's pot is big and made of iron. It once belonged to his mother.

e. John fills his pot with water and drops the stone in when the water is boiling.

f. John has to find sticks and dry wood to build a fire. The fire takes a long time to heat the water.

# Use a Sequence Chart

Events in a story usually occur in order. That order is called the **sequence**. A Sequence Chart can help you put the events in order, from what happened first to what happened last.

**Create a Sequence Chart for *Stone Soup*.**

- Use the three major events you found on page 46.
- Add other events from the list below.
- Then answer the questions at the bottom.

> John shares his soup with the villagers.
> The villagers bring small bits of food to add to the soup.
> A little girl sees John and offers to add potatoes to the stone soup.

| Sequence Chart |
| --- |
| 1. |
| 2. |
| 3. |
| 4. |
| 5. |
| 6. |

**1.** What event in the story occurs before line 1?

**2.** What event in the story occurs after line 6?

**Using the pictures in the reading, retell the story to a partner.**

WB
19

# Grammar

## Simple Past: Regular and *be* Verbs

Use **simple past verbs** for actions that happened already. You can make the simple past tense of **regular verbs** by adding *-ed*.

**Present**
Volunteers **help** people. ⟶ **Past**
Volunteers **helped** people.

| | |
|---|---|
| Add *-d* to verbs ending in *-e*. | save ⟶ **saved** |
| Change the *y* to *i* and add *-ed* to verbs ending in a consonant and *-y*. | try ⟶ **tried** |
| Add *-ed* to verbs ending in a vowel and *–y*. | play ⟶ **played** |
| Double the consonant and add *-ed* for verbs with a stressed CVC ending. | permit ⟶ **permitted** |

Remember to make sure that **past *be* verbs** agree with the subject.

| Subject | Simple Past *be* | |
|---|---|---|
| I / He / She / It | **was** | hungry. |
| You / They / We | **were** | |

You can use the following **contractions** in negative sentences.

did not = **didn't**      was not = **wasn't**      were not = **weren't**

To make **questions** with regular verbs, use *did* and the plain form of the verb. When asking questions with *be* verbs, use the correct past form.

**Did** your brother **help**?      How **was** the book?

Change each regular or *be* verb to its simple past form. Write the sentences.

**Example:** She offers to add onions to the pot.

She offered to add onions to the pot.

1. The idea **occurs** to her on the road.

2. We stay in a cottage one night.

3. The horse carry the load up the hill.

4. They **identify** many birds on the hike.

5. We share a tent on the camping trip.

6. He is not on time for the movie.

7. You peek at your birthday present.

8. They do not have enough for everyone.

**Apply**

Work with a partner. Ask and answer questions about what you did last weekend. Use question words from the list below.

| What...? | Where...? | How...? | When...? | |
|---|---|---|---|---|
| Who...? | Why...? | Did...? | Were...? | Was...? |

**Example:** A: What did you do last weekend?

B: Well, on Saturday I played in a soccer game.

A: Really? Where did you play?

B: We played at a park near my house. It was a good game.

A: Who did you play with?

20

## Grammar Check ✓

How do you form questions with regular past verbs?

# Writing

## Describe a Memorable Day

Ongoing Writing Skills Practice

When you describe something that happened to you, you want your reader to experience it the way you did. Include details about why the event was important or memorable.

### Writing Prompt

Write a paragraph that describes a memorable day from your past. It might be a day in which you won a prize, learned how to do something, or overcame a fear. Be sure to use the simple past correctly.

## ❶ Prewrite  G.O. 141

Choose a day from your past to write about. Think about why it was important. List what happened and the details that made it memorable in a graphic organizer.

A student named Martina listed her ideas like this:

**EVENT**
First day at a new school

**DETAIL**
I was worried I could not make friends.

**DETAIL**
When my teacher introduced me to the class, I was too scared to speak.

**DETAIL**
At recess some girls invited me to play softball with them.

## ❷ Draft

Use your graphic organizer to help you write a draft. Include an opening statement that draws the reader into the essay.

## ❸ Revise

Read over your draft. Look for places where the writing needs improvement. Use the Writing Checklist to help you identify problems. Then revise your draft.

## ❹ Edit

Check your work for errors. Trade papers with a partner to get feedback. Use the Peer Review Checklist on page 404.

## ❺ Publish

Prepare a clean copy of your final draft. Share your paragraph with the class. Save your work for the Writing Workshop.

Here is Martina's paragraph:

## Writing Checklist

**Ideas**

✓ I included details telling why the day was important.

✓ I told how I felt about the day.

**Conventions**

✓ I used the simple past correctly.

Martina Alvarado

It was my first day at a new school. I was entering mid-year, and I was afraid I couldn't make friends. Ms. Ling, my teacher, introduced me to the class. I was too nervous to speak. I just smiled. Everybody stared at me as I took my seat. At recess, I watched some girls playing softball. They didn't notice me. Suddenly, the ball rolled over to me. I threw it back to them. "Hey, you've got a great arm!" one of them said. "You're Martina, right?" she asked. I nodded. "I'm Cassie," she said. "Why don't you join us?" I was so grateful to make friends on my very first day.

21–22

## What You Will Learn

**Reading**
- Vocabulary building: *Context, phonics*
- Reading strategy: *Preview and predict*
- Text type: *Informational text (biography)*

**Grammar**
Past irregular verbs

**Writing**
Describe a person from history

**These words will help you understand the reading.**

### Key Words

pilot

solo

mechanic

damage

skywrite

tradition

# Key Words

*The Flying Schoolgirl* is about Katherine Stinson, a woman who achieved many firsts in flying.

## Words in Context
Audio

**1** A pilot needs to train for many hours to learn how to fly.

**2** She sang her song solo, or alone, up on the stage.

**3** My dad was glad when the mechanic fixed our car.

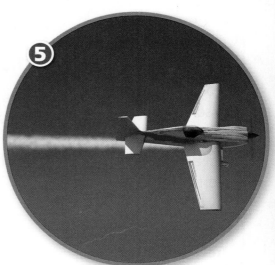

**4** There was a lot of damage to our house after the tree fell on it.

**5** Watching a plane skywrite a message in the sky is very exciting.

**6** One family tradition we have is that we all eat dinner together on Sundays.

Make flashcards to help you memorize the words.

- Write a key word on the front.
- On the back, write a sentence, but leave a blank where the key word should be.

## Make Connections

Would you like to be a stunt pilot? Why or why not? Write your answer using some of the key words. Then discuss your response with a partner.

23

These words will help you talk about the reading.

## Academic Words

**affected**
produced a change in someone or something

**establish**
start or set up a company, system, situation, rules, etc.

**license**
official document giving the right to do something, such as drive

24

# Academic Words

## Words in Context

The book **affected** me so much that I could not sleep.

The school wants to **establish** a fund to help students attend college.

A pilot needs to fly for many hours to get a **license**.

## Practice

**Write the sentences in your notebook. Choose an academic word to complete each sentence.**

1. Roman did not have his driver's _____ yet.

2. We should _____ some rules before we begin playing this game.

3. Shin's lack of study _____ her grade on the exam.

## Apply

**Write the answers in your notebook. Use the academic words. Then ask and answer with a partner.**

1. What book or movie **affected** the way you think?

2. What kind of company would you like to **establish**? Why?

3. When do you think you will get your driver's **license**?

# Phonics

## Short Vowels

Each word in the chart has one vowel. Listen.
Then read each word aloud.

| Short Vowels | | | | |
|---|---|---|---|---|
| **a** | **e** | **i** | **o** | **u** |
| am | Ed | if | on | up |
| flag | get | win | job | shut |

### Rule

When a word has a single vowel, the vowel sound is usually short.

### Practice

**Read the sentences with a partner. Look for short vowels.**

- I bet you will start a fan club.
- There is a cup in the bag.
- It was a hit at the dance.
- Pat has the best plan.
- Let's stop to sit and rest.

1. Make a short vowel chart like the one above.
2. Add the short vowel words you found to the chart.
3. Add one more word for each short vowel.

25

**INFORMATIONAL TEXT**

### Biography

**More About**

How can you help others by doing what you love?

**Listen to the Audio.**

Listen for the general meaning. Raise your hand if you need help understanding.

### Reading Strategy

#### Preview and Predict

Before you read, try to guess, or predict, what the text will be about. To predict, follow these steps:

- Read the title.
- Look at the illustrations and photos. Read the captions.
- Predict what the text will be about.
- As you read, check to see if your predictions are correct.

Listen as your teacher models the reading strategy.

# The Flying Schoolgirl

by Nancy Diehl

Katherine Stinson was a flight pioneer. Although her career as a pilot lasted just eight years, she achieved many firsts.

Stinson was born on February 14, 1891, in Fort Payne, Alabama. She grew up in Mississippi, where she **developed** a love of music. In a plan to raise money to study music, she talked her parents into letting her take flying lessons. At that time, there were very few women pilots. In fact, she had a hard time talking the teacher into letting her try to fly. Once he agreed to teach her, he was amazed at how fast Stinson learned. She flew solo after just four hours!

---

**developed**   had a feeling or interest that became stronger

Stinson **obtained** her pilot's license on July 24, 1912. She was just the fourth American woman to do so. Stinson found that she enjoyed flying so much that she gave up her plans for a musical career.

A year later, Stinson began performing as a stunt pilot. She traveled around the country. Because she looked so young, she was **billed** as "The Flying Schoolgirl." She was the first woman to perform the dangerous loop-the-loop trick. Over her career, she performed it over 500 times. And she did it in a plane she built herself! She was also the very first pilot to fly at night. Later, she was also the first pilot to **skywrite** at night. Using flares, she spelled out CAL in the skies over Los Angeles in 1915.

---

**obtained**   got something through skill and hard work

**billed**   advertised or described as

**Before You Go On**   What did Katherine Stinson do after getting her pilot's **license**?

**Katherine was a huge hit in Japan. Huge crowds turned out to watch her fly.**

Stinson became the first woman to fly a plane in Asia. She took her plane apart to ship it. Then she put it back together when she got there! People loved her air shows. Fans in Japan and China turned out in huge numbers. Japanese women even set up fan clubs.

Stinson was the first woman **commissioned** to fly the U.S. mail. She was also the first woman in the U.S. **Aviation Reserve Corps**. To top it off, in 1915 she set a record for long distance flight. Later, she broke her own record!

---

**commissioned**    asked to do a special job

**Aviation Reserve Corps**    a group of pilots that can be called on by the government if needed

Stinson's younger sister, Marjorie, also became a pilot. The sisters wanted to help others learn to fly. So, with their airplane mechanic brother Eddie, they moved to San Antonio, Texas, in 1913 and set up a flying school. They named it The Stinson School of Flying. They taught many people to fly over the years. Even Canadian Air Force pilots trained there. Sadly, the school closed in 1917.

Then the United States entered World War I. Stinson volunteered for military flying duty twice. She was **rejected** twice, simply because she was a woman. But she still wanted to help with the war effort.

---

**rejected**   not wanted or accepted

**Katherine, Eddie, and Marjorie Stinson shared a love of airplanes and flying. Together, they opened The Stinson School of Flying.**

**Before You Go On**   **What did Katherine Stinson have in common with her brother and her sister?**

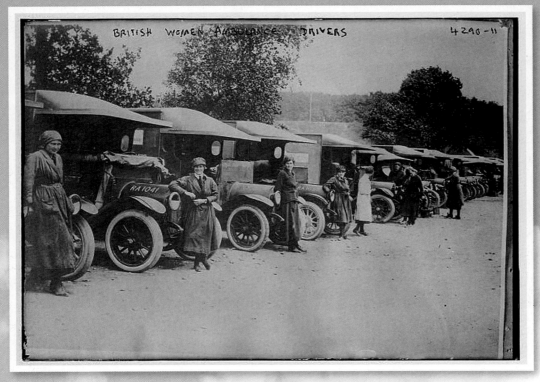

**Like many women who wanted to help with the war effort, Katherine became an ambulance driver.**

First, Stinson raised money for the Red Cross. She raised over 2 million dollars at flying shows. But she wanted to do more. So Katherine became an ambulance driver serving soldiers in Europe. While doing this job, she contracted **pneumonia**. Later, she came down with **tuberculosis**. This disease did damage to her lungs, which forced her to stop flying.

After the war, Stinson moved to Santa Fe, New Mexico. She married an airman named Miguel Otero. She also became a successful **architect** and won awards for her designs. She lived in Santa Fe until her death in 1977.

---

**pneumonia**    a serious illness that affects the lungs and makes it hard to breathe

**tuberculosis**    a disease that affects many parts of your body, especially the lungs

**architect**    someone who designs buildings

The Stinson family tradition lives on in San Antonio. The flight school location is now Stinson **Municipal** Airport. It is a thriving general aviation airfield on the south side of the city. Two flight schools operate there today, along with an aviation museum. Katherine Stinson would surely be pleased.

---

**municipal**  belonging to a town or city

## Important Dates in Katherine Stinson's Life

| born on February 14 in Fort Payne, Alabama | opens the Stinson School of Flying in San Antonio, Texas | raises money for the Red Cross with flying exhibitions | retires from flying due to lung damage caused by tuberculosis | dies in Santa Fe, New Mexico, after a successful career as an architect |
|---|---|---|---|---|

| **1891** | **1912** | **1913** | **1915** | **1917** | **1918** | **1920** | **1928** | **1977** |
|---|---|---|---|---|---|---|---|---|

|  | obtains her pilot's license on July 12 | becomes the first woman pilot to execute the loop-the-loop and becomes the first pilot to skywrite at night |  | becomes an ambulance driver in Europe |  | marries Miguel Otero, an airman, in Santa Fe |
|---|---|---|---|---|---|---|

WB
26–28

### Reading Strategy

**Preview and Predict**

Before reading, you predicted what the text would be about.

- What did you predict the selection would be about?
- Were your predictions correct?

## Think It Over

1. **Recall**  What made Stinson give up flying?

2. **Comprehend**  How did Stinson **establish** herself as a successful pilot?

3. **Analyze**  How do you think Stinson's flying achievements **affected** young women of the time?

# Learning Strategies

## Preview and Predict

After previewing, you can predict what you think a reading selection will be about.

**Answer the questions.**

1. When previewing, what did you look at to **establish** what the reading was about?
2. What did you learn about the pilot from previewing the selection?
3. What did you predict the story was about? Were you right?
4. Did making predictions before reading the selection help you to understand the story? How was your understanding **affected** by previewing?

# Use a Problem and Solution Chart

Writers often present problems and solutions in stories.
Identifying these will help you better understand the selection.

 **Practice**

**Copy this Problem and Solution Chart. Complete it to show
problems and solutions from the story.**

| Problem | | Solution |
|---------|---|----------|
| Katherine needed money to study music. | → | |
| Katherine and Marjorie wanted to teach others to fly. | → | |
| Katherine wanted to help with the war effort. | → | |
| | → | |

**Apply**

**Using the pictures in the reading, retell the selection to
a partner.**

29

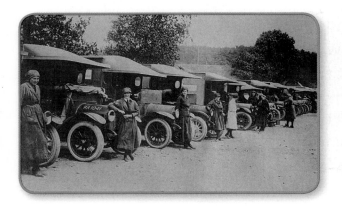

## Extension

**Utilize**   Talk with your partner
about the things that each of
you are good at. How could
you use those skills to help
others? Present your ideas to
the class.

# Grammar

## Past Irregular Verbs

**Past tense irregular verbs** are not formed by adding *-ed*.
Instead, irregular verbs have a different past tense form.

| Present Tense | Past Tense |
|---|---|
| She **takes** flying lessons. ⟶ | She **took** flying lessons. |

Review these **common irregular verbs** from the reading. Notice how some don't change, some change the vowel, and others change completely.

| | | |
|---|---|---|
| break ⟶ broke | fly ⟶ flew | set ⟶ set |
| become ⟶ became | give ⟶ gave | stand ⟶ stood |
| come ⟶ came | grow ⟶ grew | take ⟶ took |
| find ⟶ found | put ⟶ put | teach ⟶ taught |

Make the past **negative** form of irregular verbs with *did not* (or *didn't*) and the plain form of the verb.

| Affirmative Past Tense | Negative Past Tense |
|---|---|
| She **flew** with the military. ⟶ | She **didn't fly** with the military. |

Make *Yes-No* **questions** with *did* and the plain form of the verb.
Make *Wh*-**questions** the same way when there is a subject. When there is no subject in a *Wh-question,* use just the past form of the verb.

> **Did** they **break** the record?
> When **did** he **become** an architect?
> Who **flew** at night for the first time?

**Practice**

**Change each irregular verb to the past tense. Write the sentences.**

**Example:** Stinson began her flying career as a stunt pilot.

1. She flies solo and builds a plane herself.

2. Stinson gets her pilot's **license** in 1912.

3. The sisters teach people to fly in San Antonio.

4. Later, Stinson becomes an ambulance driver.

5. Katherine Stinson sets a lot of records.

6. Stinson grows up in Mississippi.

**Apply**

**Work with a partner. Take turns making statements using the past tense of the verbs below. You can talk about the life of Katherine Stinson or yourself.**

**Example:** A: Katherine Stinson broke a lot of records.

B: I came to school by bus today.

| become | fly | set |
|--------|------|-------|
| break | give | stand |
| come | grow | take |
| find | put | teach |

30

**Grammar Check ✓**

How do you form the past tense of irregular verbs?

# Writing

## Describe a Person from History

Ongoing Writing Skills Practice

When you describe a person from history, tell about the major events or achievements in the person's life. Include important dates, facts, and background information.

### Writing Prompt

Write a paragraph that describes a person from history. It could be a famous leader, explorer, writer, or artist from the past. Do research to find information. Be sure to use irregular past verbs correctly.

## ❶ Prewrite  G.O. 144

Choose a person from history to write about. Do research to find out what made this person a historical figure. List the information you find in a graphic organizer.

A student named Chin listed his ideas like this:

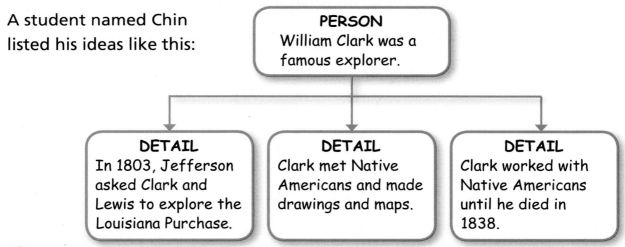

**PERSON**
William Clark was a famous explorer.

**DETAIL**
In 1803, Jefferson asked Clark and Lewis to explore the Louisiana Purchase.

**DETAIL**
Clark met Native Americans and made drawings and maps.

**DETAIL**
Clark worked with Native Americans until he died in 1838.

## ❷ Draft

Use your graphic organizer to write a draft. Include important dates, facts, and background information.

# ❸ Revise

Read over your draft. Look for places where the writing needs improvement. Use the Writing Checklist to help you identify problems. Then revise your draft.

# ❹ Edit

Check your work for errors in grammar, usage, mechanics, and spelling. Trade papers with a partner to get feedback. Use the Peer Review Checklist on page 404.

# ❺ Publish

Prepare a clean copy of your final draft. Share your paragraph with the class. Save your work.

## Writing Checklist

**Ideas**

✓ I told about major events and achievements.

✓ I included important dates, facts, and background information.

**Conventions**

✓ I used simple past correctly.

Here is Chin's paragraph about William Clark:

Chin Sung

William Clark was a famous American explorer. In 1803, President Thomas Jefferson asked Clark and his friend, Meriwether Lewis, to take an important trip. He wanted them to explore a large area of land called the Louisiana Purchase. The United States had bought this land from France.

On their trip, Lewis and Clark met many Native American tribes. Clark made drawings of the people he met. He also drew many maps. Their trip was a great success. President Jefferson was very pleased with their work. He gave Clark a job working with the Native Americans in the Louisiana Territory. He worked with them until his death in 1838.

31–32

# Apply and Extend

## Link the Readings

Copy the chart into your notebook. Read the words on the top row. For each text selection, put an X under words related to that reading.

|  | Informational text | Literature | Sharing | Teaching |
|---|---|---|---|---|
| *The Three Gifts* |  |  |  |  |
| *Stone Soup* |  |  |  |  |
| *The Flying Schoolgirl* |  |  |  |  |

## Discussion

1. What **motive** did Katherine Stinson have for helping during World War I?

2. In *The Three Gifts*, how did Kofi and Jelani **assist** their family members?

3. How did sharing **benefit** the African villagers? How did it benefit the villagers in *Stone Soup*?

THE BIG QUESTION In what ways can people help others?

**Listening Skills**

If you want to hear something again, you can ask "Would you repeat that, please?"

# Projects

**Your teacher will help you choose one of these projects.**

|  Written |  Oral |  Visual/Active |
|---|---|---|
| **Top Ten List** | **Interview** | **Poster** |
| Write a list of 5 activities you can do to help people. Present the ideas on your list to a partner or group. | Interview someone who helps others. Use the 5W questions for ideas. Share with a partner or group. | Create a poster about a group that helps people in your community. Tell what the group does. |
| **Letter** | **News Watch** | **Event Collage** |
| Write a letter to a group that helps people in your area. Ask how young people can help the group make life better for the people it serves. | Watch or listen to news programs for a few days. Jot down information about events or programs that help people. Present what you learned to the class. | Attend an event where people help others, such as a park cleanup. Make a poster or collage about the event. |

# Further Reading

 **For more projects visit**
_LongmanCornerstone.com_

 *A Monkey's Tale*

In this Penguin Young Reader®, two communities of monkeys have been divided for centuries—and they really don't trust one another. Can they work things out and come together?

*Sam and the Lucky Money,* Karen Chin

For Chinese New Year, Sam receives the traditional gift of "lucky money." Now, with his four dollars, he hopes to buy something special in Chinatown.

33–34

# Listening and Speaking Workshop

## Give a Presentation

You are going to give a presentation about a hobby or interest. You will listen as your classmates talk about their hobbies and interests.

### ❶ Prepare

**A.** Choose a hobby or interest that you'd like to share with the class. You will write and give a presentation about it. Then your classmates will ask you questions.

**B.** Think about what you want to say and what is important to tell your classmates. Now write your presentation. Describe your hobby or interest and explain why you do it. Find props and other visuals to use in your presentation.

Books and reading are interests of mine. Today I am going to tell you about volunteering at the public library.

I volunteer at the library two days a week. Each day is different. On Wednesday afternoons, I go to the library after school. I help the librarians check books back in. It's really fun. I use a computer to record the return of each book.

I also go the library on Saturday mornings. I read to a group of young children. They're four and five years

### ❷ Practice

Practice your presentation with your props. Practice in front of your family or friends. If possible, record your presentation. Then listen to yourself. How do you sound? Record yourself again and try to improve.

# ❸ Present

**As you speak,** do the following:
- Speak loudly so that your classmates can hear you.
- Use your props to help show what you are talking about.
- After your presentation, answer the questions your classmates ask.

**As you listen,** do the following:
- Think about what you already know.
- Take notes.
- Think of questions to ask the speaker after the presentation.

**Speaking Skills**

Presentations are formal situations. Use formal language. Use complete sentences without slang.

**Listening Skills**

Listen carefully for information and ideas that aren't stated directly.

# ❹ Evaluate

**After you speak,** answer these questions:
- ✔ Did you describe your hobby or interest well?
- ✔ Did you explain why you do it?

**After you listen,** answer these questions:
- ✔ Did you understand the general meaning, the main points, and the important details?
- ✔ Did you take notes?
- ✔ Did you ask questions?

# Writing Workshop

## Write a Descriptive Essay

### Writing Prompt

Write an essay in which you describe a trip you have taken,
a place that is special to you, or an experience you have had.
To help readers imagine the scene, use adjectives and adverbs
that appeal to the five senses.

### ❶ Prewrite

Review your previous work in this unit. Now
choose a topic. Think about something you
experienced that you would like to describe in
an essay. List details about the experience in a
graphic organizer.

**Listening Skills**

Writing an essay is a
process. Listen carefully
and follow your teacher's
directions and requests.

A student named Raul listed his ideas in this graphic organizer:

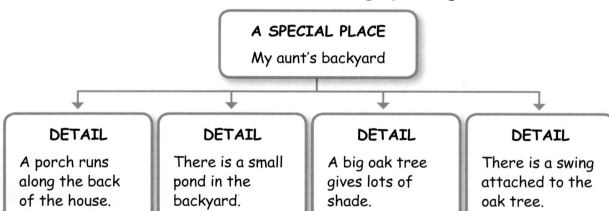

A SPECIAL PLACE
My aunt's backyard

DETAIL
A porch runs along the back of the house.

DETAIL
There is a small pond in the backyard.

DETAIL
A big oak tree gives lots of shade.

DETAIL
There is a swing attached to the oak tree.

### ❷ Draft

Use your graphic organizer to write a draft. Keep in mind your
purpose for writing—to describe a place or experience that is
special to you. Use adjectives and adverbs that appeal to the senses.
This will help readers to picture what you are describing.

## ❸ Revise

Read your draft. Look for places where the writing needs improvement. Use the Writing Checklist to help you identify problems. Then revise your draft.

Here is how Raul revised his essay:

## Six Traits of Writing Checklist

✔ **Ideas**
Did I focus my essay on one topic?

✔ **Organization**
Does my introduction draw the reader in?

✔ **Voice**
Does my writing show how I feel?

✔ **Word Choice**
Did I use adjectives that appeal to the five senses?

✔ **Sentence Fluency**
Did I vary my sentence lengths?

✔ **Conventions**
Did I use punctuation correctly?

---

Raul Mendoza

### A Special Place

The whole family enjoy*s* getting together at my aunt's house. My aunt's backyard is a very special place. A wide porch overlooks the yard. There is a small pond with frogs and a few small fish. In the summer, the surface of the pond sparkles in the *bright* sunlight. At night, you can sit on the porch and listen to the frogs as they softly call to one another. In the winter, the pond is sometimes covered with a thin coat of ice.

Near the pond there is a large oak tree. The tree's large branches reach for the sky. A swing is attached to *one of* the tree's branches. My sister and I love to push each other on the swing. Even on a hot day, the tree provides cool shade. Sometimes my aunt makes a picnic lunch and we all eat under the tree. I ~~am~~ never ~~getting~~ tired of visiting my aunt's house. Her yard is one of my favorite places in the world

**Revised** to correct verb agreement.

**Revised** to include more adjectives.

**Revised** to correct error in punctuation.

**Revised** to make the meaning clearer.

**Revised** to correct error in grammar.

## ❹ Edit

Check your work for errors. Trade papers with a partner. Use the Peer Review Checklist to give each other feedback. Edit your final draft in response to feedback from your partner and your teacher.

## ❺ Publish

Make a clean copy of your final draft. Share your essay with the class.

35–36

**Listen to the sentences. Pay attention to the groups of words. Read aloud.** Audio

1. Sometimes when you help others, they will help you in return.

2. When people share what they have, everyone benefits.

3. Flight pioneer Katherine Stinson raised money for the Red Cross and drove an ambulance in World War I.

**Work in pairs. Take turns reading the passage below aloud for one minute. Count the number of words you read.**

| | |
|---|---|
| "What are you doing?" asked a little girl, who had been | 11 |
| watching him from a nearby garden. | 17 |
| "I'm making stone soup," John told her. | 24 |
| "Stone soup!" she cried. "Is it good?" | 31 |
| "You've never had stone soup?" he asked. "Stone soup is | 41 |
| delicious!" | 42 |
| The little girl peeked into the pot of water. She saw the | 54 |
| stone at the bottom of the pot. | 61 |
| "I have some extra potatoes," she told him. "Would potatoes | 71 |
| be good in stone soup?" | 76 |
| "I like stone soup just as it is," John said. "But I think | 89 |
| potatoes will make it even better." | 95 |
| The little girl smiled. "Let's put them in!" she said as | 106 |
| she dropped the potatoes into the boiling water. | 114 |
| As the potatoes began to cook, wonderful smells floated | 123 |
| through the village from cottage to cottage. | 130 |

**With your partner, find the words that slowed each of you down.**

37–38

- Practice saying each word.
- Then take turns reading the text again.

## Taking Tests

You will often take tests that help show what you know. Follow these tips to improve your test-taking skills.

## Coaching Corner

### Answering Test Items That Are Cloze Passages

- Cloze items will ask you to fill in a blank.

- Sometimes you will be asked to complete a sentence. Other times you will be given a selection with some words left out.

- First read the questions and answer choices. Sometimes there is no question, just a list of words.

- Read the whole selection carefully. Try to think of words that might fit as you read.

- If you don't know what a word means, use the words around it to help you.

- In your head, read the sentence with each answer choice. Then choose the answer that makes the most sense.

Read the following test sample. Study the tips in the box.

39–40

**Read the selection. Then choose the correct words to fill in the blanks.**

The Wildcats practiced hard for their first soccer game. They really worked hard to play as a team and __1__. Coach Wong and the girls were very excited about the game. But there was so much to do to get ready. The coach asked the girls to __2__ her. Donna and Mei made sure everyone had their uniforms and equipment. Wanda and Erin made sure the team had enough __3__ to drink and enough fruit snacks. Everyone arrived on time to the game. Afterwards, the girls cheered, "We are a great team!"

1   **A**   fail
    **B**   argue
    **C**   cooperate
    **D**   cheer

2   **F**   assist
    **G**   carry
    **H**   benefit
    **J**   charge

3   **A**   water
    **B**   shoes
    **C**   apples
    **D**   time

**Tips**

✔ Reread the sentence to make sure your answer makes sense.

✔ Make sure you read the entire selection before you choose your answers.

# Heroes and Their Journeys

There are many kinds of heroes.
They always have interesting stories.

## Reading

**1** | Short Story

**The Elephant Shepherd**

**2** | Social Studies

**Doctors Without Borders**

**3** | Myths

**The Origin of Fire**
**Water Spider Gets the Fire**

**THE BIG QUESTION**

What does it take to be a hero?

## Listening and Speaking

You will talk about what makes someone a hero. In the Listening and Speaking Workshop, you will make a presentation.

## Writing

You will practice narrative writing. In the Writing Workshop, you will write a story.

*Quick Write*

What does being a hero mean to you? Write down your ideas and share them with a partner.

**VIEW AND RESPOND**
*Talk about the poster for this unit. Then watch and listen to the video and answer the questions at LongmanCornerstone.com.*

# What do you know about community heroes?

## Words to Know

Listen and repeat. Use these words to talk about people and animals who help the community.

**a paramedic**

**a firefighter**

**a service animal**

**a volunteer**

**a physician**

**a police officer**

Work with a partner. Ask questions using the words above in the plural form. Answer using the words in the box or your own ideas.

| aiding others | fighting fires | helping their owners |
| protecting people | providing medical care | |

**Example:** A: How do <u>physicians</u> help others in a community?

B: <u>Physicians</u> help others by <u>providing medical care</u>.

Read the question. Write your response in your notebook.

What people help in your community?

## Make Connections

Copy the sentences below into your notebook. Complete the sentences with the following words.

rescue cats

save lives

guide their owners

comfort the sick

1. Service dogs can _____ to places like the supermarket, the post office, and the bank.

2. Firefighters sometimes _____ that climb into trees and can't get down.

3. Volunteers provide many services to the community. Some _____ at hospitals.

4. Paramedics _____ every day by providing emergency medical care to patients on their way to the hospital.

## What about you?

Talk with a partner. Which community helpers do you respect the most? Would you like to do any of these jobs? Why or why not?

# Kids' Stories from around the World

Audio

Illinois, U.S.A.

**Charlene**

My hero is Binti. Binti is a female gorilla who lives in a zoo in Illinois. She rescued a three-year-old boy who fell from the railing into the zoo's gorilla exhibit. She carried the boy to an area where humans could take care of him. Binti is a very caring animal!

**Sophie**

My hero is Ryan Hreljac. Ryan wanted to help people in Africa get clean water. He saved enough money to build a well in Uganda. He was so happy with the result that he decided to help build more wells. His organization, Ryan's Well, raises money to build wells all over Africa.

China

Indonesia

**Dai**

My hero is Jackie Chan. He stars in martial arts movies. We were both born in Hong Kong, an administrative region of China. He started the Jackie Chan Charitable Foundation in Hong Kong and Japan. This organization gives scholarships to needy students. He also has organizations to help the elderly and to give coats to homeless people. Jackie Chan is a great guy!

anut

My hero is a woman from my country, Indonesia. Butet Manurung wanted to educate children who lived in the Jambi Forest. She volunteered to teach the Anak Dalam people how to read and write. Now Butet lives in the Jambi Forest. Butet's new goal is to teach people from other tribes, too.

## What about you?

1. Who is a hero to you? Why?

2. Do you have a story about your hero? Share your story.

## What You Will Learn

**Reading**

- Vocabulary building: *Context, phonics*

- Reading strategy: *Make connections*

- Text type: *Literature (short story)*

**Grammar**

Quotations

**Writing**

Write a dialogue

These words will help you understand the reading.

### Key Words

related

cattle

herd

tend

pasture

survive

# Key Words

***The Elephant Shepherd*** is about an African boy who tries to help protect elephants.

## Words in Context

**1** This mother and daughter are related. They are part of the same family.

**2** People keep cattle for their meat or milk. A group of animals, such as cattle, is called a herd.

**3** A shepherd <mark>tends</mark>, or takes care of, sheep or cattle.

**4** A <mark>pasture</mark> is covered with grass for sheep or cattle to eat.

**5** All animals need food and water to <mark>survive</mark>, or stay alive.

## Practice

Draw a picture of a pasture with a shepherd and a herd of cattle eating grass. Label the picture with sentences using five of the key words.

## Make Connections

Would you like to be a shepherd? Why or why not? Write your response in your notebook using some of the key words. Discuss your answer with a partner.

These words will help you talk about the reading.

## Academic Words

**aware**
know about or have knowledge of

**motivate**
make someone want to do something

**similar**
almost the same, but not exactly

# Academic Words

## Words in Context

I am **aware** that elephants live a long time.

Seeing elephants at a zoo might **motivate** you to learn more about them.

Elephants and people are **similar** because both elephants and people have long lives.

### Practice

**Write the sentences in your notebook. Choose an academic word to complete each sentence.**

1. I was _____ that cows eat grass, but I didn't know that elephants eat leaves.

2. A dog is _____ to a wolf, but wolves are bigger and more dangerous.

3. Hearing a great musician might _____ you to try playing an instrument.

### Apply

**Ask and answer with a partner.**

1. What is a new fact you recently became **aware** of?

2. What **motivates** you to study for a test?

3. How are cats and dogs **similar**?

# Phonics

## Vowel Pair: *ea*

The vowel pair *ea* can stand for two sounds.
Each word in the chart has the vowel pair *ea*.
Listen. Then read each word aloud.

| Vowel Pair *ea* | | | |
|---|---|---|---|
| **Long** *e* | | **Short** *e* | |
| eat | plead | head | sweat |
| sea | speak | bread | death |
| teach | | spread | |

## Rule

The vowel pair *ea* can have the long e sound, as in **eat,** or
the short e sound, as in **head.** If you come across a word
you do not know, try reading it both ways!

## Practice

**Read the sentences in the box with a partner.**

1.  List the words in which *ea* has the long e sound.

2.  List the words in which *ea* has the short e sound.

3.  Add two more words to each list.

- I can read about heroes.
- Some heroes reach out to others.
- Some heroes work hard to get ahead.
- Some heroes fight in deadly battles.

43

### LITERATURE
#### Short Story

**More About**

Can anyone be a hero?

 **Listen to the Audio.**
Listen for the general meaning. Use the pictures to help you understand the selection.

### Reading Strategy

#### Make Connections

As you read the story, think of moments in your life when something **similar** happened to you. Ask yourself:

- How did you feel?
- What did you do?

Listen as your teacher models the reading strategy.

# The Elephant Shepherd

**retold by Abdoul Tafari**
**illustrated by Gary Torrisi**

Ousmane was finally old enough to watch the cattle by himself. He loved spending his days on top of the hill looking over the pasture. He knew he had an important job to do. Ousmane's father, Amadou, told him that the family needed the cattle to survive.

One hot, sunny day, Ousmane was standing on the hill watching the cattle. The cattle were **grazing** calmly when Ousmane heard loud **stomping** noises. He thought a giant was coming. The cattle looked up.

Ousmane saw what was making the noise. It was a herd of elephants. Ousmane was so excited. His father had told him about elephants, but he had never seen one. Ousmane liked watching the baby elepha with its mother the best.

---

**grazing**   eating grass
**stomping**   walking with very heavy steps

"Ousmane!"

Suddenly, Ousmane saw his father, Amadou, running toward the elephants. "Shoo!" "Shoo!" Amadou yelled at the elephants. The elephants started to move away. The baby elephant looked scared and walked close to its mother.

"Why did you scare the elephants away?" asked Ousmane.

"I like the elephants, but we need the grass for our cattle," Amadou replied. "If the elephants stomp on the grass, the cattle will have nothing to eat."

Ousmane was sad. That night at supper, Ousmane told Amadou that he hoped the mother and baby elephant would come back to visit when there was more grass for the cattle.

Ousmane dreamed about the mother and baby elephant that night.

**Before You Go On**   Why did Amadou scare away the elephants?

Early the next day, Ousmane and Amadou set out to find good grass for their cattle. They came across an elephant on the ground. They were shocked to see that the elephant's **tusks** had been **sawed** off.

"**Poachers**," said Amadou. "They take the tusks and sell them for money. It is against the law, but some people don't care."

"Why would someone want to hurt the elephants?" Ousmane asked sadly.

Ousmane and Amadou walked on and came upon the rest of the elephant herd. They watched the elephants for a little while and then went back to tend their cattle.

Ousmane thought about the elephants all day. He wished he could stop the poachers.

---

**tusks**   two very long teeth on an elephant

**sawed**   cut with a saw

**poachers**   people who take, kill, or hurt animals not belonging to them

Ousmane and Amadou took their cattle to a pasture near the elephants the next day. The elephants were eating leaves off some trees, and Ousmane and Amadou stopped to watch.

"They are such beautiful, strong creatures," Amadou said. "Look how nicely the baby elephant and the adults are getting along."

"Do you think they are related?" Ousmane asked.

"Probably," replied Amadou. "Elephants have families like we do."

When he returned to school the following week, Ousmane decided to ask his teacher if his classmates could do something to protect the elephants. After school the next day, Ousmane and his classmates started to tell the other villagers why it was important to protect the elephants from poachers.

## Reading Strategy

### Make Connections

- Which parts of the story reminded you of a situation in your own life?

- How was your situation **similar** to the situation in the story?

## Think It Over

44–46

1. **Recall** What did Ousmane do to help protect the elephants?

2. **Comprehend** How did Ousmane become **aware** of the poachers?

3. **Analyze** What **motivated** Ousmane to want to protect the elephants?

# Learning Strategies

## Make Connections

One way to understand a text is to **make connections** between what happens in the text and your life.

**Practice**

- Read the first column. It tells about situations in the story.
- Work with a partner. Answer the questions in the second column and tell about **similar** situations in your life.

| Situations in the Story | Situations in Your Life |
|---|---|
| 1. Ousmane was excited to see the elephants. | 1. What's something you were excited to see? |
| 2. He was sad when the mother and baby elephant left. | 2. What's something that made you sad? |
| 3. He learned poachers took an elephant's tusks. | 3. What's something shocking or sad you learned? |
| 4. He and his classmates talked to the villagers about poachers. | 4. When have you tried to protect a person or animal? |

# Use a Story Map

You can use a Story Map to help you better understand a story.

 G.O. 151

Copy this Story Map. Complete it to show the main characters, the setting, and what happens in *The Elephant Shepherd*.

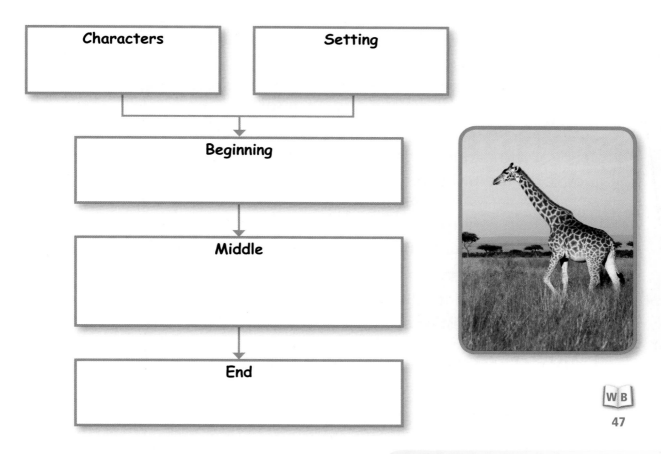

Characters

Setting

Beginning

Middle

End

W B
47

Close your book and retell the story to a partner. Use some of the key words.

## Extension

**Utilize**   Take turns talking about good deeds you have done with a partner. Then describe something that happened as a result of your good deed.

# Grammar

## Quotations

**Quotations** show the exact words, spoken or written, that someone used. Follow these rules when quoting what someone said.

Always use **quotation marks** in pairs. Use one at the beginning and one at the end of the quoted words.

> He looked at me and said, "I'm sorry."

Use a **capital** with a quote that is a complete sentence, even if the quote appears in the middle of the sentence.

> "Clean your room," she said.
> The ranger said, "Don't scare the elephants."

If the sentence quoted is split, use a **lower-case** letter for the second part of the question.

> "Don't," said the ranger, "feed the lions."
> "Where," Mrs. Hill asked, "is the key to this door?"

Use proper punctuation with quotations. Look at the examples above. Notice how:

- we set off a quote with a **comma**.
- the **final period, comma,** or **question mark** occurs inside the quotation mark.
- a **split quotation** has **commas** after the first part of the quote and before the rest of the quote.

**Rewrite the sentences using proper capitalization and punctuation.**

**Example:** we're over here we yelled

"We're over here," we yelled.

1. it's my job to tend the cattle he replied

2. he said Africa is wonderful place to visit

3. are you related she asked

4. I'm not **aware** of any problem he said

5. if the calf gets separated from the herd he said it may not survive

6. why she asked are poachers taking the tusks

 Apply

**Work with a partner. Ask your partner the questions below. Write your partner's answers as quotations.**

**Example:** What is your name?

"My name," he said, "is Lorenzo."

- What is your name?
- What is your favorite food?
- What do you usually do after school?
- What did you do on Saturday?
- Will you ask me a question?

48

**Grammar Check ✓**

In a quotation, where does the final punctuation go?

# Writing

## Write a Dialogue

*Ongoing Writing Skills Practice*

A dialogue is a written conversation between two or more characters. Writers use dialogue to show the exact words the character uses. Dialogue can show what a character is like and how he or she interacts with others.

### Writing Prompt

Write a dialogue between two characters. The dialogue could show two friends having a conversation, arguing, or sharing a joke. Be sure to use quotation marks correctly.

## ❶ Prewriten

Think about a dialogue that two characters could have. Remember that dialogue can give information about a character's thoughts and feelings.

A student named Lorenzo listed his ideas like this:

## ❷ Draft

Use your graphic organizer to help you write a draft. Include information in your dialogue that tells how the characters are feeling. Use a variety of sentence patterns.

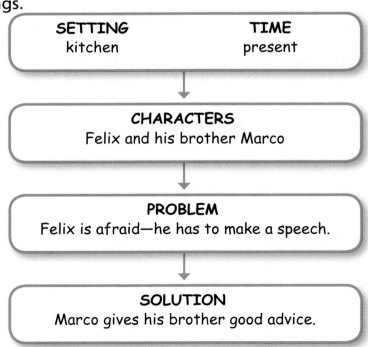

| SETTING | TIME |
|---|---|
| kitchen | present |

**CHARACTERS**
Felix and his brother Marco

**PROBLEM**
Felix is afraid—he has to make a speech.

**SOLUTION**
Marco gives his brother good advice.

## ❸ Revise

Read your draft. Look for places where the writing is needs improvement. Use the Writing Checklist to help you identify problems. Then revise your draft.

## ❹ Edit

Check your work for errors. Trade papers with a partner to get feedback. Use the Peer Review Checklist on page 404.

## ❺ Publish

Prepare a clean copy of your final draft. Share your dialogue with the class. Save your work for the Writing Workshop.

Here is Lorenzo's paragraph:

## Writing Checklist

**Ideas**

✔ My dialogue shows how the characters feel.

**Sentence Fluency**

✔ I used a variety of sentence patterns.

**Conventions**

✔ I used quotation marks correctly.

---

Lorenzo Vargas

Felix sat down for breakfast. "Are you excited about your speech today?" his brother Marco asked.

"I don't know," said Felix. "It's in front of the whole school. What if I'm terrible?"

"You'll be great!" Marco said. "You practiced your speech at least 50 times."

"I know," replied Felix. "But what if I lose my place while I'm talking? I'll be so embarrassed." He reached for some cereal.

Marco thought for a moment. Then he smiled. "Maybe you should picture the people in the audience as clowns wearing big red noses!"

Felix grinned. "And green hair and big glasses too! Thanks, Marco. I feel less nervous already."

WB

49–50

**Prepare to Read**

## What You Will Learn

**Reading**

- Vocabulary building: *Context, phonics*

- Reading strategy: *Identify problems and solutions*

- Text type: *Informational text (social studies)*

**Grammar**

Adverbs of frequency and intensity

**Writing**

Write a personal message

These words will help you understand the reading.

### Key Words

**emergency**

**courageous**

**teamwork**

**training**

**intervene**

**refugees**

# Key Words

*Doctors Without Borders* is about an organization that sends doctors to help people in need all over the world.

## Words in Context

**1** These operators answer the telephone when people call 911 to report an **emergency**.

**2** Firefighters have to be **courageous**. They put their lives in danger so that we can be safe. They often work together to put out a fire. That is real **teamwork**.

**3** The local community center offers training to show people how to care for others who are sick or hurt.

**4** Sometimes an adult has to intervene when students have problems.

**5** Refugees are people who have to leave their countries because of war or food shortages.

## Practice

**Make flashcards for the words.**
- Write a key word on the front.
- On the back, write a sentence, but leave a blank where the key word should be.

## Make Connections

Suppose you were asked to help others in another country. What help would you like to give? What supplies would you need to bring with you? Use some of the key words in your response.

### Speaking Skills
When you don't know the right word to use, explain or describe the idea using words you know.

51

These words will help you talk about the reading.

### Academic Words

**aid**
help
**commit**
use time, money, etc., to do something
**sufficient**
enough

# Academic Words

## Words in Context

Doctors and nurses **aid** people who have health problems.

Doctors **commit** a lot of time and effort to helping people.

After a natural disaster, it is important to have **sufficient** food and water.

### Practice

**Write the sentences in your notebook. Choose an academic word to complete each sentence.**

1. Our class decided to _____ the refugees by donating food and clothing.

2. If you _____ a lot of time to practicing, you will become better.

3. I didn't have _____ time to study, so I didn't do well on the test.

### Apply

**Ask and answer with a partner.**

1. How could your class **aid** earthquake victims?

2. How much time do you **commit** to doing homework each day?

3. Did you set aside **sufficient** time to study for your last test?

52

# Phonics

## Long Vowels with Silent *e*

Listen. Then read each word aloud. Which vowels say their names?

| a_e | i_e | o_e | u_e |
|-----|-----|-----|-----|
| age | ice | woke | use |
| take | fine | globe | cube |

### Rule

When the first vowel (**V**) in a one-syllable word is followed by a consonant (**C**) and an **e,** the vowel is usually long. The final **e** is silent. This is the "silent **e** rule."

Some words that have a *v*, *m*, or *n* after the first vowel are exceptions to the rule.

### Practice

**With a partner, take turns sounding out the words in the box.**

| | |
|------|------|
| like | safe |
| gave | give |
| ate | line |
| gone | plane |
| make | move |

1. Use the words to make two lists.
   - Words that follow the silent *e* rule.
   - Exceptions to the silent *e* rule.

2. Read your list of words that follow the silent *e* rule to your partner. Point to and say the name of the long vowel in each word.

53

## INFORMATIONAL TEXT
### Social Studies

**More About**

When is a doctor a hero?

 **Listen to the Audio.**
Listen for the general meaning. Use the pictures to help you understand the selection.

## Reading Strategy

### Identify Problems and Solutions

As you read this article, look for problems and solutions. Ask yourself:

- What problems does the article tell about?
- What solutions does Doctors Without Borders provide?

Listen as your teacher models the reading strategy.

# Doctors Without Borders

### by Douglas Weisser

When we are sick or hurt, we go to the doctor. Some places in the world do not have enough doctors or **supplies** to help people. This is really true when there is a crisis in that place.

A group called Doctors Without Borders works to help people in need. If there is an emergency, these doctors volunteer to go where they are needed. The group gives medical care and other services. Doctors Without Borders has been helping people since 1971.

---

**supplies**   things that people want or need

**A member of Doctors Without Borders with refugees in Ethiopia.**

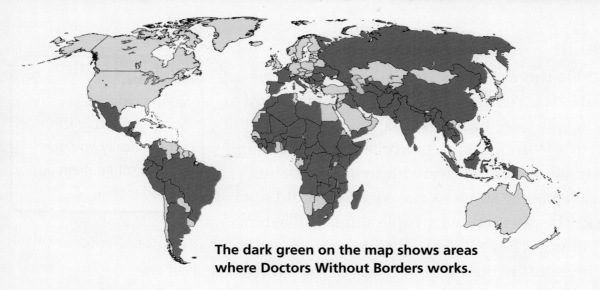

The dark green on the map shows areas where Doctors Without Borders works.

## Bringing Help Where It Is Needed

The doctors bring their medical **skills** to places where they are needed. They also bring supplies like blankets and drinking water. Sometimes the doctors train other people so they can help, too.

This doctor helped a child in Sri Lanka.

Doctors Without Borders has worked in countries all over the world. If there is a war in a country, the people there need help. Refugees are people who have to leave their homes. They leave because there is no food or because fighting has made their homes unsafe.

Doctors Without Borders can intervene to help refugees. Sometimes, refugees do not even have clean water. The volunteers come with water and **medicine**. They teach refugees how to eat better and stay **healthy**. They can show refugees how to make water safe for drinking.

---

**skills**   something a person does well

**medicine**   a substance used to treat sickness

**healthy**   not sick

**Before You Go On**   Where might Doctors Without Borders have gone recently to help?

## Tsunami!

In 2004 there was a **tsunami**, or tidal wave, in South Asia. The tsunami **destroyed** many towns. Many people were hurt or killed.

Doctors Without Borders worked for more than a year in countries that were hit by the tsunami. They gave people shots to make sure they did not get sick. The doctors gave people supplies like tents and clothing. They talked to people about what had happened. Sometimes just being there to listen to the **victims** helped the most.

**Reading Skill**

Sight words are words you recognize automatically. You don't have to sound them out to read them.

---

**tsunami**   huge wave that causes great destruction on land

**destroyed**   damaged so that it cannot be used

**victims**   people who have been affected by something bad

**Workers unload supplies that doctors used to help the 2004 tsunami victims.**

A doctor helps a boy in Sri Lanka after the 2004 tsunami.

## Helping Others Help Themselves

Sometimes the volunteers help people in a town build new hospitals. That involves real teamwork!

Sometimes the best help the volunteers can give is training. It can be better for Doctors Without Borders to help train local doctors to take care of people after a crisis. The local doctors can give care to sick and hurt people after Doctors Without Borders leaves the area.

The volunteers who work for Doctors Without Borders travel all over the world to help people after emergencies. They are courageous, and borders do not stop them.

54–56

### Reading Strategy

**Identify Problems and Solutions**

- What problems did you read about in this article?

- What solutions do Doctors Without Borders provide?

- How did identifying problems and solutions help you understand the article?

## Think It Over

1. **Recall** How do Doctors Without Borders **aid** people who don't have **sufficient** clean drinking water?

2. **Comprehend** Why is training local doctors sometimes the best help?

3. **Analyze** Why did Doctors Without Borders **commit** so much time to countries hit by the tsunami?

# Doctors Without Borders

▲ **Angola**
Doctors Without Borders sets up centers to feed people who don't have **sufficient** food.

▲ **Tibet**
Doctors Without Borders works to help people in rural Tibet get clean drinking water.

▲ **Afghanistan**
This volunteer is training women in Afghanistan to provide care for the people in their village.

▲ This doctor is giving a child a checkup.

▲ **Chad**
**This volunteer is vaccinating a refugee's child.**

## Activity to Do

These pages use pictures and words to tell where Doctors Without Borders works.

• Work with a partner. Research any country that interests you. Share information and work collaboratively.

• Create two pages, using pictures and words, to tell about that country.

# Learning Strategies

## Problem and Solution

A **problem** is a major difficulty. A **solution** is how the problem is solved. Look at the following example:

> **Country**: Angola
>
> **Problem:** Some people don't have **sufficient** food.
>
> **Solution:** Doctors Without Borders sets up centers to feed people.

**Practice**

**Reread pages 94 and 95. Identify two problems and how Doctors Without Borders helps solve them.**

1. Country: _____
   Problem: _____
   Solution: _____

2. Country: _____
   Problem: _____
   Solution: _____

# Use a Problem and Solution Chart

You can use a Problem and Solution Chart to help you record problems and solutions in a text.

 **Practice** G.O. 149

Reread how Doctors Without Borders helped people after the 2004 tsunami. Then copy and complete this Problem and Solution Chart.

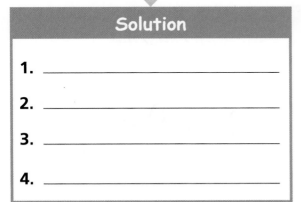

| Problem |
| --- |
| 1. People could get sick easily. |
| 2. People lost their homes. |
| 3. People didn't have sufficient clothing. |
| 4. People were upset. |

| Solution |
| --- |
| 1. _____ |
| 2. _____ |
| 3. _____ |
| 4. _____ |

W B
57

 **Apply**

Close your book and retell the selection to a partner. Use the key words.

## Extension

**Utilize** Find a problem in your classroom. Work with a group to come up with different solutions. Decide which one is best. Present the problem and your solution to the class.

# Grammar

## Adverbs of Frequency and Intensity

**Adverbs** can modify verbs, adjectives, or sentences. Different kinds of adverbs tell *when, where, why* or *how* something is done. Many adverbs end in *-ly*, like *frequently* or *absolutely*, but others do not, such as *never* or *much*.

**Adverbs of frequency** answer the question *How often?* They range from *always* to *never*. Note their position in statements:

| Position | Example |
|---|---|
| After a *be* verb | He **is** always busy after school. |
| Before other verbs | They usually **eat** lunch together. |
| At the end of a sentence | She plays the piano rarely. |
| At the start of a sentence* | Sometimes she practices soccer. |
| * except *always, hardly ever, rarely, never* | |

**Adverbs of intensity** answer the question *How much?* Adverbs of intensity include *very, really, pretty, kind of, almost, barely,* and *just*. Note their position in statements:

| Phrase | Position | Example |
|---|---|---|
| very really pretty kind of | Before an adjective or adverb | They are pretty **happy.** We ran really **quickly.** |
| almost barely just | Before the main verb | He almost **won** the race. I barely **finished** on time. |

Complete the sentences with an adverb of frequency or intensity from the box. Write the sentences. (More than one answer may be possible.)

**Example:** The tsunami <u>completely</u> destroyed the town.

| | | | |
|---|---|---|---|
| just | very | pretty | rarely |
| completely | sometimes | frequently | |

1. The doctors are here—they _____ arrived.

2. Some people were _____ badly hurt.

3. Refugees _____ have enough food to eat.

4. Volunteers _____ help people build houses.

5. The group's teamwork was _____ good.

Work with a partner. Ask and answer questions about your typical week. Be sure to use adverbs of frequency and intensity.

**Example:** A: What do you do in the evenings?

B: Well, I usually study every evening.

58

| | | |
|---|---|---|
| What...? | Where...? | How...? |
| When...? | Who...? | Why...? |
| Did...? | Were...? | Was...? |

**Grammar Check ✓**

What kind of adverb is *really*? What about *usually*? How can you tell?

# Writing

Ongoing Writing Skills Practice

## Write a Personal Message

When writing a personal message, a writer shares his or her personal thoughts and feelings. A personal message includes a greeting and a closing.

### Writing Prompt

Write a personal message to a friend or family member. Write about what is happening in your life. Include your personal thoughts and feelings. You might also include questions about the other person's life or activities. Be sure to use adverbs of frequency and intensity correctly.

## ❶ Prewrite  | G.O. 144 |

Think about who you will write to and what you want to say. List the information in a graphic organizer.

A student named Nestor listed his ideas like this:

## ❷ Draft

Use your graphic organizer to help you write a draft. Include details and events that will make your message interesting and enjoyable to read.

**ITEM:** Reply to Sunita's last message.

↓

**ITEM:** Tell about the big snowstorm.

↓

**ITEM:** Tell about going skiing.

↓

**ITEM:** Include information about the dog show.

## ❸ Revise

Read over your draft. Look for places where the writing needs improvement. Use the Writing Checklist to help you identify problems. Then revise your draft.

## ❹ Edit

Check your work for errors in grammar, usage, mechanics, and spelling. Trade papers with a partner. Use the Peer Review Checklist on Workbook page 404.

## ❺ Publish

Prepare a clean copy of your final draft. Share your letter with the class.

Here is Nestor's message:

## Writing Checklist

**Ideas**

✓ I included a greeting and a closing.

✓ My message contains interesting information about my life.

**Conventions**

✓ I used adverbs of frequency and intensity correctly.

Dear Sunita,

    It was great to hear from you! I'm happy that you like your new school. Are you really still wearing shorts? That's hard to believe, since we have snow here in Illinois!

    You may have heard about our big storm. It was very cold. The news isn't all bad, though. We're going skiing in Wisconsin next weekend. I can't wait!

    Remember the dog show we went to last year? They held it again this year. Just about every dog in town was in the show. I'm trying to talk my folks into getting me a dog!

    Write soon, and tell me all about Florida. I miss you.

Your friend,

Nestor

WB
59–60

## What You Will Learn

**Reading**

- Vocabulary building:
  *Context, word study*

- Reading strategy:
  *Compare and contrast*

- Text type:
  *Literature (myth)*

**Grammar**
Possessives

**Writing**
Write a myth

**These words will help you understand the reading.**

### Key Words

eager

pretended

fastened

clever

punishment

scattered

# Key Words

The two myths you are about to read explain how animals captured fire.

## Words in Context

**1** Juan was so eager to open his birthday present, he could hardly wait!

**2** Scott pretended to be asleep, but he was actually awake.

**3** Sally fastened her seatbelt in the car.

**4** Some dogs are very clever and can easily learn new tricks.

**5** Because Tung did not behave, his punishment was to do the dishes by himself.

**6** The farmer scattered the seeds all over the ground in the spring.

Make flashcards to help you memorize the words.

- Write a key word on the front.
- On the back, write a sentence, but leave a blank where the key word should be.

## Make Connections

Do you know a story about clever animals? What happens in the story? Does the story have a moral or meaning?

These words will help you talk about the reading.

## Academic Words

**attach**
connect one object with another

**challenge**
something difficult that tests strength, skill, or ability

**secure**
get something using a lot of effort

# Academic Words

## Words in Context

Lilly used tape to **attach** her favorite pictures to her bedroom wall.

Putting out a forest fire is a **challenge** on a hot, dry da

A runner has to train for many hours to **secure** a first place prize.

### Practice

**Write the sentences in your notebook. Choose an academic word to complete each sentence.**

1. The prince had to fight many men to _____ the crowr for himself.

2. We used tacks to _____ the poster to the bulletin board.

3. It was a _____ for the climbers to reach the top of the mountain.

### Apply

**Ask and answer with a partner.**

1. What is something you often **attach** to something else?

2. What is something you did that was a **challenge** for you?

3. What is something you would be willing to work hard to **secure**?

# Word Study

## Word Origins

The English word **fire** comes from the Old German word **fiur.** There are many words in English that come from another language.

( **Practice** )

**Read the clues below. Match each clue with a word from the box.**

1. This word is taken from the ancient Greek word **historia.** It means "the study of things from the past."

2. This word comes from Japan. It is spelled the same way it is pronounced in Japanese. It means "a big, dangerous wave."

3. This word is taken from the Spanish word **tronada.** It means "a storm with strong winds that turn very fast."

4. This word is from the Old French word **anoncier.** It means "to tell a lot of people."

5. This word comes from the ancient Latin word **anima. Anima** meant "life."

animal
announce
history
tornado
tsunami

63

**More About**

What characteristics do heroes have?

**Listen to the Audio.**
Listen for the general meaning.
Use the pictures to help you
understand the selection.

### Reading Strategy

**Compare and Contrast**

As you read two stories about
where fire came from, think about
how the stories are alike and
different.

- Where does each story come
  from?
- Who is the hero in each story?
- How is each hero able to
  **secure** the fire?

Listen as your teacher models the
reading strategy.

# The ORIGIN of FIRE

## An Apache Myth • Retold by Susan Martins Miller

*Hundreds of years ago, the Apache in Canada
began to move south. Other tribes called them the
"new people," but they called themselves* Dine
*(DIN-eh), or simply "the people." On the long
journey from Canada, Apache storytellers passed
down this myth about where fire comes from.*

In the beginning of time, animals and
trees talked to each other. At that time, only
**fireflies** had fire. Fox was clever, and he
wanted to get fire for the world. He had to
find a way to steal some from the fireflies.
   One day, Fox asked the geese to teach him
their cry. They answered that he must first learn
to fly with them before they would teach him.

___

**fireflies**   insects that have tails that shine in the dark

The geese tied wings to Fox. "Do not open your eyes when you fly," they warned him.

Fox flew with the geese, keeping his eyes closed. As day turned to darkness, they flew over the village of fireflies. Fox opened his eyes. Right away his wings stopped working. He fell to the ground inside the walls of the fireflies' village. Two kind fireflies came to help Fox. When he asked how he could get over the wall, they showed him a cedar tree. They told him the tree would bend down if he asked it to. This gave Fox an idea.

**Before You Go On** How did Fox trick the geese into helping him get into the village of the fireflies?

That evening, Fox asked the fireflies to dance, so they gathered wood and built a great fire. In secret, Fox tied a piece of cedar **bark** to his tail. Then he made a drum and beat it while the fireflies danced.

After a while, Fox pretended to be tired and gave his drum to the fireflies to beat. When they were not looking, Fox stuck his tail in the fire and set the bark on fire. Then he ran to the cedar tree and cried out, "Bend down for me!"

The cedar tree bent down and Fox climbed on. When the tree stood up again, it carried him over the wall.

---

**bark**   hard skin covering the outside of a tree

Fox ran and ran, and the fireflies chased after him. Everywhere he went, Fox's tail set the bushes and trees along the side of the path on fire.

When Fox found Hawk, he gave the burning bark to the bird. Hawk flew high above the ground and continued to scatter fire sparks everywhere. This is how fire came to the whole world.

When the fireflies caught Fox, they said, "Because you stole our fire, your punishment is that you will never be able to use fire for yourself." And to this day, no fox uses fire.

This was the beginning of fire for the Apaches, however. They learned to use fire to cook food and keep warm.

**Before You Go On** Why would the Apaches think that Fox was a hero?

# WATER SPIDER gets the FIRE

A Cherokee Myth • Retold by Susan Martins Miller

The Cherokee were originally from the American Southeast. They were one of the largest and most advanced tribes in North America when European colonists arrived. After gold was discovered on their land in the 1830s, the Cherokee were forced to leave their homes and march west. Today, they are still one of the largest Native American tribes in the United States with more than 300,000 members. Like all Native American tribes, the Cherokee's stories explain where things came from. This story is about the first fire.

Long, long ago the world was cold because there was no fire to keep it warm. One day the Thunders sent Lightning into the bottom of a sycamore tree. The tree was on an island in the center of a large lake. The animals knew the tree had fire because they could see smoke rising from the branches. They would have to cross the water to get the fire.

Every animal was eager to be the one who would bring fire to the rest. **Raven** was first on the list because he was large and strong. But when he landed on the sycamore tree, the heat burned his feathers black. He went home without the fire.

---

**raven**   a large, shiny black bird

**Before You Go On**   What is the **challenge** that the animals have to face to get the fire?

When Screech Owl went, a **blast** of hot air burned his eyes. When Hooting Owl and Horned Owl went, the burning ashes made rings around their eyes.

Then Black Racer Snake and Climber Snake took their turns, but came back without fire. Now many animals were afraid to try. Only one animal was brave enough to go. Water Spider said she would go to the island. But Water Spider was an insect. How would such a small animal carry the fire back?

The other animals did not think she could do it, but Water Spider had a plan.

---

**blast**   a sudden, strong movement of wind or air

Water Spider spun a thread from her body and **wove** it into a bowl. Then she fastened the bowl on her back.

Water Spider ran on top of the water all the way to the island. She crossed through the grass to find the tree. Then she put one little burning coal in the bowl on her back. Water Spider ran on top of the water again to carry fire back to all the other animals.

Even today, Water Spider still has a little bowl on her back.

---

**wove**   crossed threads under and over each other

WB
64–66

### Reading Strategy

**Compare and Contrast**

- Where does each story come from?
- Who is the hero in each story?
- How is each hero able to **secure** the fire?

## Think It Over

1. **Recall**   Why does Water Spider **attach** a bowl to her back?

2. **Comprehend**   What role does a tree play in each story?

3. **Analyze**   What was it about each of the heroes that made them able to get the fire?

# Learning Strategies

## Compare and Contrast

One way to understand the ideas you read about is to **compare and contrast** them. When you compare, you tell how two or more things are similar. When you contrast, you tell how two or more things are different.

**Practice**

Compare and contrast the items described in each pair of words. Discuss how they are similar and how they are different.

1. a car and a bus
2. fire and ice
3. soccer and football
4. a dog and a fox

# Use a Venn Diagram

You can use a Venn Diagram to compare and contrast two things. In the outer circles, list how each thing is different from the other. In the space where the circles overlap, list how the two things are similar.

 G.O. 142

**Create a Venn Diagram to compare the myths.**

- Circle A represents the myth *The Origin of Fire.*
- Circle B represents the myth *Water Spider Gets the Fire.*

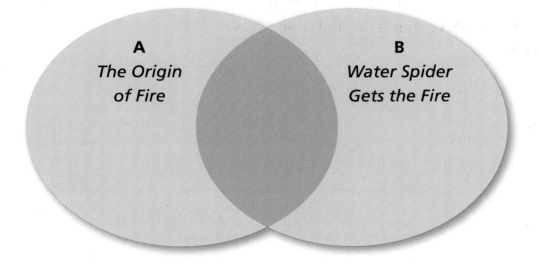

**A**
*The Origin of Fire*

**B**
*Water Spider Gets the Fire*

67

**Close your book and retell the stories to a partner. Use the key words as you speak.**

## Extension

**Utilize** Fire is important in all cultures. What other stories do you know about fire—from folktales, books, plays, or movies? Discuss your response with a partner or small group.

# Grammar

## Possessives

A **possessive** shows ownership. To form a possessive with singular or plural nouns that don't end in -s, we add 's (apostrophe s).

| Singular Noun | Object |
|---|---|
| the boy's | bike |
| the team's | notes |

| Plural Noun | Object |
|---|---|
| the children's | bikes |
| the women's | team |

To form the possessive of common plural nouns that end in -s, add an apostrophe ( ' ) to the end of the word.

| Plural Noun | Object |
|---|---|
| the students' | school |

| Plural Noun | Object |
|---|---|
| the teachers' | house |

To show **shared ownership,** the last noun takes an apostrophe s.

Amy and Claude's party ⟶ *(Both Amy and Claude have a party.)*

To show **separate ownership,** each noun takes an apostrophe s.

Amy's and Claude's party ⟶ *(Amy and Claude each have their own party.)*

**Possessive pronouns** can show possession, too.

| Possessive Pronoun | Object |
|---|---|
| my, your, his, her, its, our, their | books |

## Practice

Rewrite each phrase using possessives.

**Example:** the fire of the fireflies

the fireflies' fire

1. the stories of the Cherokee

2. the punishment of the fox

3. the bowl of the spider

4. the socks of Mr. Rivers

5. the house of Alberto and of Yolanda

6. an uncle of Liz

7. an aunt of ours

8. the games of theirs

## Apply

Work with a partner. Look back through the myths to find who owns what. Then complete the possessive phrases below. Write your answers in your notebook.

**Example:** the Apache's legend

***The Origin of Fire***    ***Water Spider Gets the Fire***

- _____ fire
- _____ cry
- _____ tail

- _____ feathers
- _____ eyes
- _____ bowl

WB
68

### Grammar Check ✓

How do you show ownership for a plural noun that ends in *s*?

# Writing

## Write a Myth

*Ongoing Writing Skills Practice*

Remember that a myth is a story that tells about the beliefs of a group of people. Myths often explain something that happens in nature, and often contain gods or heroes.

### Writing Prompt

Write a myth of your own that explains something that happens in nature. Use characters from a Native American or Greek myth, or create your own characters. Make sure your story is interesting and has a strong conclusion. Remember to use possessives correctly.

## ❶ Prewrite  G.O. 151

Think about what you want to explain in your myth. List the characters and the events in the plot in a graphic organizer.

A student named Maria listed her ideas like this:

> **CHARACTERS:** A Greek girl named Helena and the goddess Athena

> **SETTING:** Ancient Greece

> **BEGINNING:** Helena weaves clothes. She says her clothes make women more beautiful than Athena.

> **MIDDLE:** Athena challenges Helena to a contest. Athena wins.

> **END:** Athena turns Helena into a caterpillar.

## ❷ Draft

Use your graphic organizer to help you write a first draft. Include a variety of sentence lengths.

# ❸ Revise

Read over your draft. Look for places where the writing needs improvement. Use the Writing Checklist to help you identify problems. Then revise your draft.

# ❹ Edit

Check your work for errors in grammar, usage, mechanics, and spelling. Trade papers with a partner. Use the Peer Review Checklist on Workbook page 404.

# ❺ Publish

Prepare a clean copy of your final draft. Share your paragraph with the class. Save your work for the Writing Workshop.

Here is Maria's myth:

## Writing Checklist

**Organization**

✔ I have a strong conclusion.

**Sentence Fluency**

✔ I used some long and some short sentences.

**Conventions**

✔ I used possessives correctly.

---

Maria Pappas

In ancient Greece there lived a girl named Helena. She was a very good weaver and made beautiful clothes. In fact, she told people that in her clothes a woman would look more beautiful than the goddess Athena.

When Athena heard this, she became very angry and went to visit the girl. "I challenge you to a contest! We will both weave a cloak and we'll see whose is the best!"

Athena and the girl both began to weave. Soon the young girl saw that Athena's cloak was far better than her own.

"From now on," Athena said, "you will be an ugly insect. You will weave a cocoon. Only after you come out of the cocoon will you be beautiful."

And with that, the girl turned into a caterpillar.

WB
69–70

# Apply and Extend

## Link the Readings

Copy the chart into your notebook. Read the words in the top row. For each text selection, put an X under words related to that reading.

|  | Informational text | Literature | Helping animals | Volunteering to help |
|---|---|---|---|---|
| **The Elephant Shepherd** | | | | |
| **Doctors Without Borders** | | | | |
| **The Origin of Fire** **Water Spider Gets the Fire** | | | | |

## Discussion

1. In *The Elephant Shepherd*, why is it important for Ousmane to make his classmates **aware** of poachers?

2. What is **similar** about doctors bringing supplies to other countries and animals bringing fire to the world?

3. In these four readings, what **challenges** do the helpers have to face?

**THE BIG QUESTION** What does it take to be a hero?

**Listening Skills**

If you can't hear someon well, you can ask "Coul you speak a little more loudly, please?"

# Projects

**Your teacher will help you choose one of these projects.**

|  Written |  Oral |  Visual/Active |
|---|---|---|
| **Definition** | **Discussion** | **Magazine Cover** |
| Write your own definition for the word *hero*. List five people who would fit your definition. | Have a discussion asking: *What is the most important quality a hero needs?* Give examples to support your choice. | Create a magazine cover that shows one of your heroes and words that describe him or her. Give the magazine a special title. |
| **Survey** | **Reality Show** | **Hero Cards** |
| Write a 10-question survey about heroes. Ask your classmates to complete the survey as it relates to their favorite heroes. Report your results to the class. | Work with a group. Have each student describe a hero from real life or from stories. Ask questions, and vote for the most heroic character. | Create a set of cards about heroes. One set of cards should show pictures of heroes. The set of matching cards should describe what the heroes did. |

# Further Reading

 **For more projects visit**
*LongmanCornerstone.com*

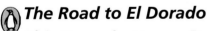

***The Road to El Dorado***
This Penguin Young Reader® tells the story of two adventurers, Tulio and Miguel, who set out to seek fame and fortune. Then fate hands them a map to El Dorado, the city of gold.

***American Tall Tales,*** Mary Pope Osborne This collection of nine adventurous legends includes stories about American folk heroes such as Sally Ann Thunder, Ann Whirlwind, Pecos Bill, and John Henry.

71–72

# Listening and Speaking Workshop

## Perform a Skit

You are going to write and perform a skit based on one of the readings in this unit. You will listen as your classmates perform their skits and then answer your teacher's questions.

### 1 Prepare

**A.** Work with two or more partners. Choose a scene from one of the readings that you find interesting and can use to create a skit.

**B.** Discuss the scene with your partners. Who are the characters? What do they do? What do they say? How do they feel? Now write your skit. Find props and costumes.

| The Elephant Shepherd |
|---|
| **Amadou:** Ousmane! Look! Elephants! (*Ousmane is surprised. Amadou runs toward the elephants.*) |
| **Amadou:** Shoo! Shoo! Shoo! Go away! (*Ousmane is sad as the elephants run away.*) |
| **Ousmane:** Why did you scare the elephants away? |
| **Amadou:** I like the elephants, too. But we need the grass for our cattle. |

### 2 Practice

Practice your skit with your props and costumes. Act it out in front of your family or friends. If possible, record your skit. Then listen to it. How do you and your partners sound? Record it again and try to improve.

# ❸ Present

**As you speak,** do the following:

- Don't read your skit—perform it.
- Speak naturally and with feeling.
- Use gestures and facial expressions.
- Pay attention to your partners so you know when to say your lines.

**As you listen,** do the following:

- Watch the actors' gestures and facial expressions.
- Pay close attention. Your teacher will ask you questions after the skit.

# ❹ Evaluate

**After you speak,** answer these questions:

- ✓ Did you perform your part well?
- ✓ Did you speak naturally and with feeling?
- ✓ Did you use gestures and facial expressions?

**After you listen,** answer these questions:

- ✓ Did you understand the skit?
- ✓ Did the actors use formal or informal language?
- ✓ Did the actors' gestures and facial expressions help?

## Speaking Skills

Skits can be about formal or informal situations. Use formal or informal language based on the story.

## Listening Skills

Listen carefully to make sure you understand the situation and events. This will help you understand each skit.

# Writing Workshop

## Write a Story

### Writing Prompt

Write a story that you create from your imagination.
Include the setting, the time, and the place in which the
action occurs. Include either human or animal characters.
Write a plot that involves a problem that the characters
have to solve.

## ❶ Prewrite

Review your previous work in this unit. Now think about an idea
that would make a good story. Plan the events in your story in a
graphic organizer.

A student named Mariana listed her ideas in this graphic organizer:

> **CHARACTERS**: Carmen,
> Toby, a boy, Carmen's father

> **SETTING**: A winter
> afternoon near a pond

> **BEGINNING**: Carmen and Toby walk by a frozen pond. A boy is in the water.

> **MIDDLE**: Carmen gets her dad. He brings a rope. Together they try to pull
> the boy from the water.

> **END**: They save the boy and he thanks them.

## ❷ Draft  G.O. 151

Use your graphic organizer to write a draft. Keep in mind your
purpose for writing—to write a story that readers will enjoy. If
you use dialogue, remember to make it sound natural.

## ❸ Revise

Read your draft. Look for places where the writing needs improvement. Use the Writing Checklist to help you identify problems. Then revise your draft.

Here is how Mariana revised her story:

## Six Traits of Writing Checklist

✔ **Ideas**
Is my plot interesting and exciting?

✔ **Organization**
Did I create a plot with a beginning, middle, and end?

✔ **Voice**
Do I involve the reader in the story's problem?

✔ **Word Choice**
Does my dialogue sound natural?

✔ **Sentence Fluency**
Did I use a variety of sentence types?

✔ **Conventions**
Do my nouns, pronouns, and verbs agree?

---

Mariana Castillo

The Rescue

It was a cold, clear winter afternoon. Carmen Lopez and her friend Toby were walking near the large frozen pond behind her familys'house.

> **Revised** to correct error in mechanics.

All of a sudden, Carmen saw something moving. "Look, Toby!" Carmen shouted. They saw a boy's head. He was in the pond, holding on to the edge of a broken piece of ice. "I'll go get my dad," Carmen said. "You stay here."

> **Revised** to correct error in mechanics.

Soon Carmen's father was racing to the pond, and Max, the family German shepherd, was close behind. Mr. Lopez had a thick rope in his hand. He threw the end of the rope to the boy. ^

> **Revised** to make the sequence of events clearer.

The boy grabbed the rope. "Pull!" Mr. Lopez shouted. Max barked as Carmen and Toby helped Carmen's father pull the rope. Soon the boy was on solid ground. "You're Your safe now," said Carmen softly. "Thank you," the boy said. "I thought I could walk across the pond. I didn't realize the ice was so thin. You saved my life."

> **Revised** to correct error in spelling.

> **Revised** to correct error in mechanics.

## ❹ Edit

Check your work for errors. Trade papers with a partner. Use the Peer Review Checklist on page 440 to give each other feedback. Edit your final draft in response to feedback from your partner and your teacher.

## ❺ Publish

Make a clean copy of your final draft. Share your essay with the class.

73–74

**Peer Review Checklist**

✓ The plot is exciting.

✓ The grammar and punctuation are correct.

✓ The dialogue sounds natural.

**SPELLING TIP**

When *i* and *e* are together, the *i* usually comes before the *e* except after *c*, or when pronounced as long *a* in words like *neighbor* and *weigh*.

**Listen to the sentences. Pay attention** Audio
**to the groups of words. Read aloud.**

1. A young shepherd becomes a hero when he tries to
   prevent poachers from hurting elephants.
2. Doctors Without Borders is a heroic group that helps people
   in need in different parts of the world.
3. In the myth *The Origin of Fire*, Fox is a hero who brings fire to
   the Apache people.

**Work in pairs. Take turns reading the passage below aloud for
one minute. Count the number of words you read.**

|  |  |
|---|---|
| A group called Doctors Without Borders works to help | 9 |
| people in need. If there is an emergency, these doctors | 19 |
| volunteer to go where they are needed. The group gives | 29 |
| medical care and other services. Doctors Without Borders | 37 |
| has been helping people since 1971. | 43 |
| The doctors bring their medical skills to places where | 52 |
| They are needed. They also bring supplies like blankets | 61 |
| and drinking water. Sometimes the doctors train other | 69 |
| people so they can help, too. | 75 |
| Doctors Without Borders has worked in countries all over | 84 |
| the world. If there is a war in a country, the people | 96 |
| there need help. Refugees are people who have to leave | 106 |
| their homes. They leave because there is no food or | 116 |
| because fighting has made their homes unsafe. Doctors | 124 |
| Without Borders can intervene to help them. | 131 |

**With your partner, find the words that slowed each of you down.**

- Practice saying each word and then say the sentence each
  word is in.
- Take turns reading the text again. Count the number of
  words you read.

**W** **B**
75–76

# Test Preparation

## Taking Tests

You will often take tests that help show what you know. Follow these tips to improve your test-taking skills.

## Coaching Corner

### Answering Questions About Selections

- Many tests ask questions about selections.

- Some selections are short. Other selections are long.

- Preview the questions and answer choices before you read the selection. This will help you focus as you read.

- After reading the selection, try to answer each question in your head. When you read the choices, look for the one that is closest in meaning to the answer in your head.

- After you choose an answer, check the selection again. Make sure you can point to details in the selection that support your choice.

**Read the following test sample. Study the tips in the box.**

77–78

**Read the selection. Then answer the questions.**

1      Cows don't look alike to themselves. But they do look similar to us. How do you think ranchers tell their cows apart? They put brands on them! A brand is a special mark ranchers put on their animals to identify them. Brands show which ranchers own which cows. Today, ranchers brand their cows by putting tattoos on them.

2      The designs that ranchers use are interesting. Each rancher has his or her own brand. Some of the brands have been in the ranchers' families for a long time. Hernando Cortés brought branding from Spain to America in 1541.

**1**  Brands are used for cows _____

    **A**  so ranchers can easily herd them
    **B**  so ranchers know how old they are
    **C**  so ranchers know how many they have
    **D**  so ranchers can easily identify them

**2**  In paragraph 1, the word <u>similar</u> means _____

    **F**  different from
    **G**  interesting
    **H**  unlike
    **J**  almost the same as

> **Tips**
> ✔ Preview the questions and answer choices before you read the passage.
> ✔ Be careful. *Similar* is one of the academic words you learned. Look for the answer choice that asks you to find the same meaning as *similar*.

# Building a New Country

New countries have been created throughout history. When new countries are created, many challenges and opportunities are created, too.

## Reading

**1** | Short Story

**The Real Soldier**

**2** | Social Studies

**One Hot Summer in Philadelphia**

**3** | Social Studies

**One Out of Many**

How do
people create new
countries?

## Listening and Speaking

You will talk about what people have to
do to create a new country or state. In the
Listening and Speaking Workshop, you will
give a speech.

## Writing

You will practice persuasive writing.
In the Writing Workshop, you will write
a persuasive essay.

**Quick Write**

What do you know about the early history of
the United States? Write down five facts.

**DVD**    VIEW AND RESPOND
*Talk about the poster for this unit. Then
watch and listen to the video and answer the
questions at LongmanCornerstone.com.*

# What do you know about your country?

## Words to Know

**Listen and repeat. Use these words to talk about countries.**

currency

national government

flag

national anthem

landmarks

national bird

**Work with a partner. Ask and answer questions about the United States.**

| | | |
|---|---|---|
| in Washington, D.C. | the U.S. dollar | "The Star-Spangled Banner" |
| the bald eagle | the Statue of Liberty | 50 stars and 13 stripes |

**Example:** A: What do you know about the <u>currency</u> of the United States
B: Well, I know the <u>currency</u> is <u>the U.S. dollar</u>.

**Read the question. Write your response in your notebook.**

What are some facts about your country of origin?

## Make Connections

Copy the sentences below into your notebook. Complete the sentences with the following words. Use the correct form of the verb.

**control traffic**

**make laws**

**trade**

**vote**

1. A country needs currency for _____, or the buying and selling of goods.

2. The citizens of the United States _____ to elect the members of the national government.

3. The national government _____, or rules and regulations, for its citizens to follow.

4. State and city governments make many local laws, such as laws to _____.

## What about you?

Talk with a partner. Compare your home country with the United States. How are they similar? How are they different?

# Kids' Stories from around the World

Audio

Pennsylvania, U.S.A.

Mexico

Trinidad & Tobago

### Diego

I live in Mexico City, Mexico. I love to walk around the plazas on El Grito, which is September 16. El Grito is the celebration of Mexico's independence from Spain. People decorate every plaza in Mexico City with beautiful lights. They sell flags, sombreros, and food in the streets.

### Trinidad

I live in Trinidad. My parents named me Trinidad because I was born on August 31. That's the day that my country celebrates its independence from the United Kingdom. There are many parades and street festivals on Independence Day. It feels as if the whole country is celebrating my birthday!

**Greece**

**Ezio**

In Greece, we celebrate Independence Day on March 25. Greece became an independent country on March 25, 1821. I am learning traditional Greek dances at school so that I can join the Independence Day festival in my town next year. I am excited to help my community celebrate this special day!

**Andie**

I live in Philadelphia, Pennsylvania. My city is sometimes called the birthplace of the United States because the U.S. Declaration of Independence was signed here in 1776. Each year on July 4, we have parades and fireworks to celebrate this special day.

## What about you?

1. Does your home country celebrate its independence? How do people celebrate?

2. Do you have a story to tell about your country's independence day? Share your story.

## What You Will Learn

**Reading**

- Vocabulary building: *Context, phonics*

- Reading strategy: *Make inferences*

- Text type: *Literature (short story)*

**Grammar**

Necessity: *should, have to, must*

**Writing**

Write a review

These words will help you understand the reading.

### Key Words

**rule**

**colonies**

**Minutemen**

**militia**

**Redcoats**

# Key Words

*The Real Soldier* tells the story of a boy who helps his village in a fight for independence.

## Words in Context

**1** To **rule** is to have power and control over a country. King George III ruled Britain in 1776.

**2** The first British to arrive in North America lived in **colonies**. The British king ruled the colonies.

**3** The Minutemen were soldiers. They fought for American independence. They were not in a professional army. They fought in groups called militia.

**4** During the American Revolution, British soldiers were called Redcoats.

**Make flashcards to help you memorize the words.**
- Write a key word on the front.
- On the back, write the meaning.

## Make Connections

What do you know about the British colonies and the American Revolution? Write your response in your notebook using the key words. Then discuss what you know with a partner.

WB

79

**These words will help you talk about the reading**

### Academic Words

**infer**
form an opinion based on knowledge or facts you have

**initially**
at the beginning

**inspect**
look at something carefully

# Academic Words

## Words in Context

After hearing about the earthquake, Lynn could **infer** that earthquakes cause serious damage.

**Initially**, the hikers walked fast, but after they walked two miles, they slowed down.

The firefighters wanted to **inspect** the house to make sure it was safe.

### Practice

**Write the sentences in your notebook. Choose an academic word to complete each sentence.**

1. I didn't understand _____, but then I was able to figure it out.

2. Because of her accent, I could _____ that she was British.

3. Farmers usually _____ their crops often to make sure they are healthy.

### Apply

**Ask and answer with a partner.**

1. What might you **infer** from the fact that a musician won an important award?

2. Why might it be surprising to learn that an actor was **initially** very shy in school?

3. How do you **inspect** a bicycle tire?

# Phonics

## R-controlled: *ar, or, ore*

Listen. Then read each pair of words.

| | | |
|---|---|---|
| am | ton | toe |
| arm | torn | tore |

Notice how the letter *r* changes the vowel sound. Here are more words with an *r* after a vowel. Read them aloud.

| | |
|---|---|
| far | or |
| hard | for |
| dark | more |

### Rule

The letters *ar* usually have the vowel sound in *arm*.
The letters *or* and *ore* usually have the vowel sound in *torn*.

### Practice

**Work with a partner. Take turns.**
• Sound out each pair of words.
• Tell whether the words have the same vowel sound.

1. arm, park
2. more, form
3. car, rack
4. care, George
5. sure, soar
6. bore, floor

**More About**

Why do people fight for independence?

**Audio** Listen to the Audio.
Listen for the general meaning. Think about the situation or context. Use this to help you understand the story.

### Reading Strategy

#### Make Inferences

When you make **inferences**, you use clues from the story and think inductively to understand something the author doesn't explain. As you read the story, ask yourself:

- Why did Jacob want to be a soldier?
- What did the other characters think about him?

Listen as your teacher models the reading strategy.

# The Real Soldier

### by Laurie Calkhoven
### illustrations by Doris Ettlinger

"Star, someday we'll ride in front of an army, just like General Washington," Jacob said, rubbing the horse's nose.

"You're too young," said his sister Emily.

"I said someday." Jacob was tired of being told he was too young. He and his father believed the colonies should be free from British rule. Two days ago, Jacob and his father had watched the local militia ride by his family's farm. They were called Minutemen.

Jacob wanted to be a soldier. He wanted to join the Minutemen, like his father. His father and other farmers in the area had promised to join General George Washington if he needed help.

Jacob was getting some wood to bring into the house when his mother **rushed** into the barn.

"Redcoats are here," she whispered.

Jacob was scared. He wondered if the British soldiers knew that his father and the other farmers were Minutemen.

Emily was scared, too. She ran and hid in Star's **stall**. Jacob wanted to hide with her, but his mother needed him. Together, they walked into the yard to face the British soldiers.

Jacob was **relieved** when he heard what the Redcoats wanted. This time, they only wanted food and supplies.

Jacob chose his words carefully. "My father has gone to the market," he said. "We don't have anything here." Jacob didn't tell the soldiers that the "market" was General Washington's camp!

When Jacob's father got home, he was proud. "Good thinking," he said. "You **fooled** them."

---

**rushed**   hurried

**stall**   enclosed area for keeping horses

**relieved**   happy because something bad did not happen

**fooled**   tricked

**CheckUP**   **Why were Jacob and Emily afraid of the Redcoats?**

"I want to help you fight the Redcoats," Jacob said.

"I know," his father said. "But you have work to do here, too. It is important to make sure everything at home looks as if nothing unusual is going on. Your job is to take care of your mother and Emily."

Later that night, Jacob heard a knock at the door. He was scared. What if the British soldiers had come back? He walked slowly to the door.

Jacob opened the door and saw three men carrying guns. Jacob knew the men because they often visited his father. They were some of the Minutemen he had seen two days ago.

"Hi, Jacob," one of the men said.

"My father isn't here," Jacob said.

"We know. Your father said we could meet here. He said you would keep watch and that your mother had food for us."

Jacob kept watch while the men made their plans. Jacob's mother served the men stew and bread.

Jacob listened to their plans, his eyes wide. "May I come with you?" he asked.

"Your job is here," one of the men replied.

"But my father said I was brave today, and I can be brave again," Jacob said. "Star is ready for battle, and so am I."

The men laughed.

"What if the Redcoats come back?" one of the men asked. "We need you here." The men **grabbed** their guns and hats. "Look after your mother and sister," they said as they went out into the night.

There was a loud knock at the door a few hours later.

---

**grabbed**　took hold of quickly

**Before You Go On**　Why did the men laugh at Jacob?

Jacob opened the door a tiny bit, and two British soldiers pushed the door open and **marched** into the room.

"Where is your husband?" a soldier shouted to Jacob's mother.

"He went to the market," she said.

Emily held on to her mother's skirts and hugged her doll tightly.

Jacob knew he had to be brave. He put his hands in his pockets and tried to act calm. He tried to act like a soldier.

"We haven't seen any Minutemen today," Jacob said in a strong voice. Like his mother, he chose his words carefully. The Minutemen left his house a few hours ago.

The soldier **narrowed** his eyes and **stared** at Jacob.

Jacob did not move. He looked directly at the man. "British soldiers were here earlier today," he said. "But no Minutemen."

---

**marched** walked quickly

**narrowed** made small, less wide

**stared** looked at for a long time

The Redcoats **searched** the house, and they did not find any Minutemen. The Redcoats were angry, but they left. Jacob, Emily, and their mother **sighed** with relief. They hoped that they would not see any more British soldiers.

The next morning, Jacob's father came home. He said that the British soldiers had been **driven out** of the area.

"You helped us by fooling the Redcoats," Jacob's father said to him. "We were able to surprise them."

Jacob knew his father had gone to fight the war, but he was a real soldier at home.

---

**searched**   looked carefully to find something

**sighed**   let out a long, deep breath

**driven out**   made to go out

82–84

### Reading Strategy

#### Make Inferences

- Why did Jacob want to be a soldier?
- What did his father, the Minutemen, and the Redcoats think about him?

## Think It Over

1. **Recall**   Why did the Redcoats visit Jacob's family's farm **initially**?

2. **Comprehend**   Why did the Redcoats **inspect** Jacob's house after he said no Minutemen were there?

3. **Analyze**   What can you **infer** that the Minutemen were planning at Jacob's house?

# Learning Strategies

## Make Inferences

When you make inferences, you think inductively and make guesses about things the author does not directly tell you. Thinking about the characters, their situation, and what they say and do can help you make inferences about them. This will help you understand the characters and the story better.

Tell what you can **infer** about the following characters in the story.

1. George Washington
2. Jacob's father
3. Jacob's mother and sister
4. The Redcoats

# Use a 5 W Chart

You can ask the 5 W Questions to help you understand
and remember a story better.

**Who?    What?    Where?    When?    Why?**

  **Practice**   G.O. 146

Copy the 5 W Chart. Write a question for each of the
5 Ws. Have a partner answer your questions.

| **Who?** | Who were the characters in the story? |
|---|---|
| **What?** | |
| **Where?** | |
| **When?** | |
| **Why?** | |

 **Apply**

Close your book and retell the story to a partner. Use
the key words.

85

## Extension

**Utilize**   With a group, make
a list of time capsule objects
that would show people in the
future what life is like today.
Work cooperatively with your
group and listen carefully to
your classmates. Then present
your list to the class.

# Grammar

## Necessity: *should, have to, must*

To strongly say something is necessary, use *have to* or *must*.
Use *should* to say something is advisable, rather than necessary.
*Should, have to,* and *must* are followed by the plain form of the verb.

|  | Past | Present | Future |
|---|---|---|---|
| should | You **should have** taken the bus yesterday. | You **should** take the bus now. | You **should** take the bus tomorrow. |
| have to | You **had to** wear your uniform yesterday. | You **have to** wear your uniform now. | You **will have to** wear your uniform tomorrow. |
| must | (use *had to*) You **had to** show your school ID yesterday. | You **must** show your school ID now. | You **must** show your school ID tomorrow. |

When forming negatives, you can use the contractions *shouldn't, didn't/don't have to,* and *won't*. Note that for the future, you can say either *don't* or *won't have to*.

|  | Past | Present | Future |
|---|---|---|---|
| should | You **shouldn't have** taken the bus yesterday. | You **shouldn't** take the bus today. | You **shouldn't** take the bus tomorrow. |
| have to | You **didn't have to** wear your uniform yesterday. | You **don't have to** wear your uniform today. | You **don't/won't have to** wear your uniform tomorrow. |
| must | (use *didn't have to*) You **didn't have to** show your school ID yesterday. | You **must not** show your school ID now. | (use *don't/won't have to*) You **don't/ won't have to** show your school ID tomorrow. |

Read each phrase. Then respond with a positive or negative statement of necessity using *should*, *have to*, and/or *must*. Write the sentences.

**Example:** told a lie

> You shouldn't have told a lie.

1. study before a test

2. speak loudly in class

3. bring your pet to school

4. done your homework

5. interrupt the teacher

6. edit your writing carefully

7. spread gossip

8. infer the answer to some questions

**Apply**

Work with a partner. Suppose there is a new student in your class. Create a list of ten things that the student should know about your school. Use *have to*, *must*, and *should*.

**Example:** A: You won't have to wear a uniform.

> B: You will have to climb the rope in gym.

> A: You don't have to, but you should join a team or club.

86

**Grammar Check ✓**

What do the verbs *should*, *have to*, and *must* tell us?

# Writing

## Write a Review

When you write a review, you should tell readers if you do or do not recommend the work. You should present reasons to support your opinion.

### Writing Prompt

Write a review of a play or movie you have seen, or a book you have read. Explain why you did or did not like it, and whether you would recommend it. Use words that show necessity in your review.

## ❶ Prewrite

Choose a play, book, or film to review. List what you liked or didn't like about the work. Then list your reasons.

A student named Trang wrote about the book *Little House in the Big Woods* by Laura Ingalls Wilder. She listed her ideas like this:

> **What I Like/Dislike:** I liked finding out about life in the 1800s.
> **Why:** Life was very different from today.

> **What I Like/Dislike:** I liked learning how Laura's family had to work hard to grow and hunt food.
> **Why:** Today we go to the supermarket, but it was different then.

> **What I Like/Dislike:** I liked learning what people did for fun then.
> **Why:** I never knew people could have fun just telling stories.

## ❷ Draft

Use your graphic organizer to help you write a first draft.

## ❸ Revise

Read over your draft. Look for places where the writing needs improvement. Use the Writing Checklist to help you identify problems. Then revise your draft.

## ❹ Edit

Check your work for errors in grammar, usage, mechanics, and spelling. Trade papers with a partner to get feedback. Use the Peer Review Checklist on Workbook page 404.

## ❺ Publish

Prepare a clean copy of your final draft. Share your paragraph with the class.

Here is Trang's review of *Little House in the Big Woods*:

## Writing Checklist

**Ideas**

✔ I said if I recommended the book, play, or film.

✔ I supported my opinion with reasons.

**Conventions**

✔ I used verbs of necessity such as *should, have to,* or *must.*

Trang Phan

    <u>Little House in the Big Woods</u>, by Laura Ingalls Wilder, is a really interesting book to read. It tells about life in Wisconsin in the 1800s.

    I liked learning how Laura's family worked to get and find food. Today we just go to the supermarket. But Laura's family had to grow their own vegetables and hunt wild animals in the woods. Laura and her sister had to make their own cheese and butter.

    I also liked finding out what people did for fun before television and computers. Laura's father played the fiddle, sang, and told wonderful stories.

    If you are looking for a good book to read, you should try this one.

87–88

## What You Will Learn

**Reading**

- Vocabulary building: *Context, phonics*

- Reading strategy: *Identify main idea and details*

- Text type: *Informational text (social studies)*

**Grammar**

Nouns

**Writing**

Write a persuasive article

These words will help you understand the reading.

### Key Words

confidential

delegates

merchants

tailors

cobblestone

curious

# Key Words

*One Hot Summer in Philadelphia* describes what life was like in Philadelphia during the Constitutional Convention.

## Words in Context  Audio

**1** Jane asked Toni to keep her secret **confidential** and not tell anyone.

**2** States sent several **delegates** to represent them at the Constitutional Convention.

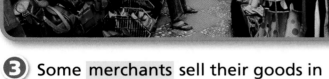

**3** Some merchants sell their goods in street markets.

**4** Tailors work hard to make sure people's clothes fit well.

**5** Cobblestone streets seem bumpy compared to most streets today.

**6** Sam and Sasha were curious about the goldfish in the bowl.

---

**Practice**

**Make flashcards to help you memorize the words.**

- Write a key word on the front.
- On the back, write the meaning.

## Make Connections

Have you ever visited a historical place? What was it like?
How do you think life was different when that place was built?

89

These words will help you
talk about the reading.

# Academic Words

## Academic Words

**circumstances**
conditions or
situations

**period**
particular length of
time

**physical**
having to do with
the body

## Words in Context  Audio

All of us should exercise to improve our **physical**
strength and health.

The article explained the **circumstances** that led
to the accident.

During the **period** when dinosaurs lived, there
were no human beings.

### Practice

**Write the sentences in your notebook. Choose
an academic word to complete each sentence.**

1. The late 1700s was an interesting ＿＿ of time.

2. Everyone on the soccer team was in good ＿＿
   condition.

3. In some ＿＿, such as a serious illness, one
   shouldn't go to school.

### Apply

**Ask and answer with a partner.**

1. If someone says he is in good **physical**
   condition, what does he mean?

2. What **circumstances** make it hard to study?

3. What was the most exciting **period** in your
   life? Why?

90

# Phonics

## Consonant Digraphs: *ch, sh,* and *th*

Listen as your teacher reads the words in the chart aloud.
Listen for the sounds of the letters. Then read the words aloud.

| ch | sh | th |
|---|---|---|
| **ch**arm | **sh**ip | **th**an |
| mer**ch**ants | **sh**ut | ga**th**ered |

### Rule

The letters *ch* blend together to make one sound. So do the
letters *sh* and the letters *th*. These digraphs can be at the
beginning, in the middle, or at the end of a word.

### Practice

**Read the sentences below with a partner.**

- List each word with *ch, sh,* or *th*.
- List six other words spelled with *ch, sh,* or *th*.

**Facts about Philadelphia**

1. Both George and Martha Washington slept there.
2. Many merchant ships docked there.
3. Teachers, butchers, and shoemakers lived there.
4. The Founding Fathers met there.
5. It's the home of cheese steaks.

91

**INFORMATIONAL TEXT**

Social Studies

### More About

How was life in the early days of our country?

**Audio** Listen to the Audio.
Listen for the general meaning. Think about the situation or context. Use this to help you understand the story.

### Reading Strategy

**Identify Main Idea and Details**

The **main idea** is what a selection is about. The **details** give you more information about the main idea.

- What is this selection about?
- What details are important?

Listen as your teacher models the reading strategy.

# One Hot Summer in Philadelphia

**by Ann Ponti**

Delegates from every state except Rhode Island went to Philadelphia in 1787 for the Constitutional Convention. There were no railroads or airplanes. Some delegates traveled for many days over dirt and cobblestone roads.

The weather was very hot that summer. Men and women dressed more **formally** in those days. Women wore one or more **petticoats** under long dresses or skirts. Men often wore suits made of wool. People buttoned their shirts all the way up, even in the summer. There was no air conditioning. People did not take off or loosen their clothing when they were hot.

---

**formally**    dressed up
**petticoats**    long skirts worn under skirts or dresses

**Crowds gathered outside Independence Hall in Philadelphia.**

It was hard
to get medical
care in the past.

The meetings in the State House were confidential. It was hot that summer, but the windows were kept closed. Guards kept watch to make sure that no one heard any secrets from the people in the State House. The delegates promised not to tell anyone what happened in their meetings.

The secrecy did not stop people from gathering in front of the State House. They knew important work was taking place. The locked windows and doors made the people curious.

The delegates had to be **tough** to get through the long, hot summer. If any of the delegates got sick or **fainted** from the heat, people called a doctor. It was important for the delegates to stay healthy.

Long ago, most people didn't go to the doctor unless they were very sick. There weren't a lot of medicines. People often drank herbal teas to feel better when they were sick. They also made some medicines from plants. Sometimes people didn't get better. Many people died from illnesses that are easy to treat today.

---

**tough**   able to deal with hard times

**fainted**   lost consciousness

**Before You Go On**   How did the heat affect people at the convention?

Water sometimes made people sick in the 1780s. People had no way of knowing if their drinking water was clean. To be safe, people didn't drink much plain water. They drank cider, milk, tea, and coffee. They could boil water for tea and coffee.

Houses did not have bathrooms. People used buckets to carry water from nearby wells to their houses. They filled washbowls and pitchers with water to clean their hands and faces. People didn't take baths very often. When they did, they would set a big wooden tub in front of the kitchen fire. After they filled the tub, a whole family would bathe in the same water. The person who went last didn't get very clean!

Like the well, the toilet was outside. It was in a separate building called an outhouse.

People used washbowls and pitchers to wash their hands and faces.

The 40,000 people who lived in Philadelphia in 1787 had come to the United States from all over the world. People from England and Germany lived next to people from Africa.

People in Philadelphia worked as bakers, teachers, merchants, tailors, and carpenters. They made bread, soap, furniture, and clothing. Their houses were small and close together. Rich people lived in large houses at the ends of the blocks. Poor people lived in houses on the side **alleys**.

People from all over the world lived as neighbors in Philadelphia.

Bakers and tailors sold their goods from their homes. Farmers used horses and wagons to drive their goods to market from farms around the city.

Life was harder in 1787 than it is today. But the people who lived in Philadelphia **witnessed** one of the most exciting times in U.S. history.

---

**alleys**   narrow streets

**witnessed**   saw

92–94

## Think It Over

1. **Recall**   Why did people drink mainly cider, milk, tea, and coffee?

2. **Comprehend**   What were the **circumstances** like inside the State House?

3. **Analyze**   What were some **physical** hardships of living in the United States during this **period**?

### Reading Strategy

**Identify Main Idea and Details**

- What was the main idea?
- What were some details?
- How did thinking about the main idea and details help you?

# Learning Strategies

## Main Idea and Details

Identifying the **main idea and details** can help you understand and summarize what you read. Ask yourself, "What was the reading about?" Your answer to the question is the main idea of the selection.

**Practice**

**Write a sentence based on the reading using each of the phrases below. Then state whether your sentence tells about a detail or the main idea of the selection.**

1. cobblestone roads
2. dirty water
3. hot weather
4. Constitutional Convention
5. closed windows

# Use a Main Idea and Details Chart

A Main Idea and Details Chart can help you understand and summarize what you read.

 **Practice** G.O. 141

Copy this Main Idea and Details Chart. Fill in the chart to show the main idea of the selection and some details that support it.

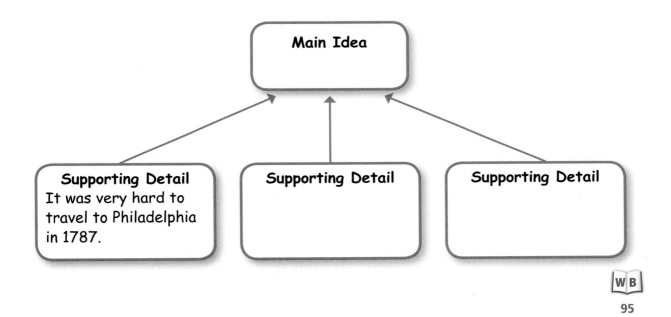

Main Idea

Supporting Detail
It was very hard to travel to Philadelphia in 1787.

Supporting Detail

Supporting Detail

W B
95

## Apply

Close your book and summarize the selection for a partner. Use the key words.

## Extension

**Utilize** Choose one supporting detail from your chart. Write your ideas about how that detail is different today. For example, today it is easy to travel to Philadelphia by car, bus, train, or airplane. Share your work with a partner or group.

# Grammar

## Nouns

A **singular noun** refers to *one* person, place, or thing. **Plural nouns** refer to *more than one*. Review the rules for plural nouns.

| | |
|---|---|
| Add an *-s* to most singular nouns. | soldier ⟶ soldiers |
| Words ending in consonant + *-y*, change the *-y* to *-ies*. | spy ⟶ spies |
| Words ending in *ch, sh, ss, x*, or consonant + *-o (except foreign words)*, add *-es*. | brush ⟶ brushes <br> tomato ⟶ tomatoes |
| Words ending in *-f* or *-fe*, change the *-f* or *-fe* to *-ves*. | wolf ⟶ wolves |

**Irregular plural nouns** change in form.

| | | |
|---|---|---|
| man ⟶ men | foot ⟶ feet | person ⟶ people |

In sentences, verbs must agree with singular and plural nouns.

| Singular Noun | The **child** | **visits** his aunt every day. |
|---|---|---|
| Plural Noun | The **children** | **visit** the city each year. |

**Collective nouns** are groups of persons or things. The noun refers to the group altogether.

| | | | | |
|---|---|---|---|---|
| audience | committee | crowd | group | society |
| class | company | family | public | team |

A collective noun is usually treated as a singular noun.

Our **team** **visits** other schools. *(the team as a single group)*

Complete the sentences with the correct simple present form
of the verb in parentheses. Write the sentences.

**Example:** (be) The delegates <u>are</u> in Philadelphia.

1. (come) A big crowd _____ every year.

2. (play) A lot of children _____ in the park.

3. (work) A tailor _____ at the department store.

4. (laugh) The audience _____ at the joke.

5. (sell) Some merchants _____ clothes.

6. (speak) Those women _____ French.

7. (be) The company _____ in Philadelphia.

8. (win) Our team _____ almost every game.

**Apply**

Work with a partner. Ask and answer about the collective noun
for each definition below. Use the collective noun in a sentence.

**Example:** A: What do you call a large group of people?

       B: A crowd. The crowd is very large.

- a large group of people
- a group of people watching a movie
- all the students in one classroom
- a mother, father, and their children
- a group of people who play a
  sport together

96

**Grammar
Check ✓**

How are collective
nouns different than
plural nouns?

# Writing

## Write a Persuasive Article

Ongoing
Writing
Skills
Practice

When you write a persuasive article, you give an opinion. Then you try to show your opinion is correct by supporting it with reasons.

### Writing Prompt

Write an article in which you try to persuade people to visit Philadelphia. Get your reader's attention with a strong opening. Support your argument with reasons. Pay attention to your subject-verb agreement with plurals and collective nouns.

## ❶ Prewrite

Do research and choose something about Philadelphia that you think is interesting. List reasons for visiting the city in a graphic organizer.

A student named Ken listed his ideas like this:

**Main Idea**
Visit Philadelphia to
see American history

**Detail**
Famous people lived
here, Congress
met here, and it
was the capital

**Detail**
See Independence Hall—
Jefferson and Franklin
wrote the Declaration of
Independence there

**Detail**
See the Liberty Bell—
it called citizens to
hear the Declaration

## ❷ Draft

Use your graphic organizer to help you write a first draft.

## ❸ Revise

Read over your draft. Look for places where the writing needs improvement. Use the Writing Checklist to help you identify problems. Then revise your draft.

## ❹ Edit

Check your work for errors in grammar, usage, mechanics, and spelling. Trade papers with a partner to get feedback. Use the Peer Review Checklist on page 404.

## ❺ Publish

Prepare a clean copy of your final draft. Share your paragraph with the class.

Here is Ken's article:

## Writing Checklist

**Organization**

✔ My opening grabs the reader's attention.

**Sentence Fluency**

✔ I used sentences of different lengths to make my article interesting to read.

Ken Watanabe

When you walk the streets of Philadelphia, you know you are in the birthplace of America. You can almost feel the presence of people such as Benjamin Franklin, Thomas Jefferson, and Betsy Ross. Congress met here during the Revolutionary War. Afterward, it was the capital of the country from 1790 to 1800. So if you're interested in American history, there is no better place to go!

Start your visit at Independence Hall. This is where a group of men, including Jefferson and Franklin, worked on the Declaration of Independence in 1776. Then cross the street to see the world famous Liberty Bell. When the Declaration of Independence was read for the first time, this bell called citizens to Independence Hall.

## What You Will Learn

**Reading**

- Vocabulary building: *Context, word study*

- Reading strategy: *Use prior knowledge*

- Text type: *Informational text (social studies)*

**Grammar**
Compound sentences

**Writing**
Write a persuasive poster

**These words will help you understand the reading.**

### Key Words

statesman

federal

liberty

surrender

veteran

republic

# Key Words

## Words in Context

**1** Benjamin Franklin was a famous **statesman**. He worked hard to make our country better.

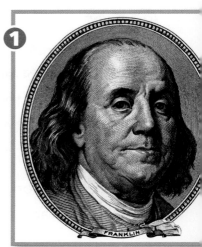

**2** The President, Congress, and Supreme Court make up the **federal** government.

**3** We are lucky to live in **liberty** in the United States. We have many freedoms that people in other countries do not.

**4** Only a general can surrender to officially end a war. The loser gives up and the fighting stops.

**5** A veteran deserves respect and honor for his or her service to our country.

**6** The United States is a republic. We elect officials to represent us in the government.

**Practice**

**Create a concept map for each new word.**

- Write the key word in the center.
- Around it, write words that relate to it.
- Connect the words using lines.

## Make Connections

What is one liberty that we have in our country? Why are liberties important? What would our lives be like if our liberties were taken away?

99

These words will help you talk about the reading.

## Academic Words

**cultures**
beliefs, way of life, and customs shared by a group of people

**expanded**
became larger in size or number

**impose**
force someone to have the same ideas you do

# Academic Words

## Words in Context

The class read about the many different **cultures** of many different countries.

The population of the country **expanded** as more food became available.

Ed tries to **impose** his opinions on others.

### Practice

**Write the sentences in your notebook. Choose an academic word to complete each sentence.**

1. The amount of time we spend on writing each week has _____ from one hour to three hours.

2. Our teacher doesn't want to _____ her ideas on us. She wants us to think for ourselves.

3. The restaurants in our town have food from many different _____ .

### Apply

**Ask and answer with a partner.**

1. What **cultures** do you know that have rice as an important part of their diet?

2. Has the number of chores you do at home **expanded** as you've gotten older?

3. Why do you think people try to **impose** their beliefs onto others?

# Word Study

## Synonyms and Antonyms

Read these sentences.

> Alaska is the largest state. The second biggest state is Texas.
> The smallest state is Rhode Island.

The words *largest* and *biggest* are synonyms. **Synonyms**
are words that have the same or almost the same meaning.
The words *largest* and *smallest* are antonyms. **Antonyms** are
words that have the opposite or almost the opposite meaning.

| Word | Synonym<br>Same Meaning | Antonym<br>Opposite Meaning |
|------|-------------------------|------------------------------|
| largest | biggest | smallest |

**Practice**

101

For each word below, find one synonym (S) and
one antonym (A) from the box.

| boring | few | interesting | loss |
|--------|-----|-------------|------|
| major  | many | unimportant | win |

1. important  S: _____ A: _____

2. fascinating  S: _____ A: _____

3. numerous  S: _____ A: _____

4. victory  S: _____ A: _____

### LITERATURE

#### Play

**More About** THE BIG QUESTION

How did we create one country out of many colonies?

**Listen to the Audio.**
Listen for the general meaning. Think about the situation, or context. Use this to help you understand the selection.

### Reading Strategy

#### Use Prior Knowledge

As you read, think about what you already know about the creation of the U.S. Constitution.

- What do you know about the Constitutional Convention?
- Who attended the Constitutional Convention?

Complete the first two columns of the KWL Chart on page 178.

Listen as your teacher models the reading strategy.

# One Out Of Many

## by Bob McCall

### Cast of Characters:

Benjamin Franklin ...... famous statesman and scientist

George Washington .... general in the American Revolution

Alexander Hamilton ... army officer and statesman

Bob ......................... boy, 10

Ned ......................... boy, 10

**Scene:** May, 1787. Philadelphia. Outside the State House. Benjamin Franklin and George Washington are sitting on a bench.

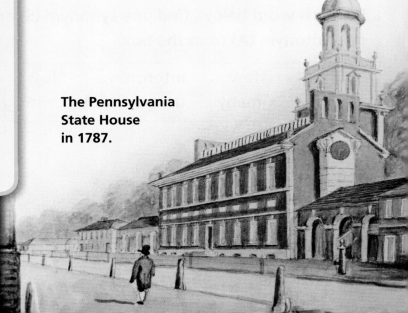

**The Pennsylvania State House in 1787.**

**Franklin**: It's too hot, Washington. Make them open the windows in there.

**Washington**: They don't want **rumors** to start. (*He sighs.*) This is going to be a very long summer.

*Bob and his friend Ned enter. They give the men glasses of water.*

**Washington**: Thank you, Bob.

**Franklin**: Thanks, Ned.

**Bob**: General Washington, what is this convention all about?

**Washington**: It's a kind of meeting.

**Ned**: But what is the meeting *for*?

**Washington**: We are here to write a constitution for the United States.

George Washington was at the convention.

---

**rumors**  information passed between people that may or may not be true

Before You Go On  What is the purpose of the convention?

**Ned**: Oh, a constitution! (*pause*) What's that?

**Franklin**: A constitution is a set of rules for a government.

**Bob**: I thought that we already had rules.

**Franklin**: We do. But they don't work.

**Ned**: Why not?

**Washington**: We are the United States. What does the word "united" mean?

**Ned**: It means "all together."

**Washington**: How many states do we have, Ned?

**Ned**: Thirteen.

**Washington**: It's like we have 13 separate countries. Does that sound united to you?

**Bob and Ned**: No, sir.

**Ned**: It's so hot! Why are the windows closed? Do you want to make King George's son the king of the United States? People say that's why the room is closed up tight.

**Franklin**: Washington, tell the boys we won't let that happen. I told you the windows should be open.

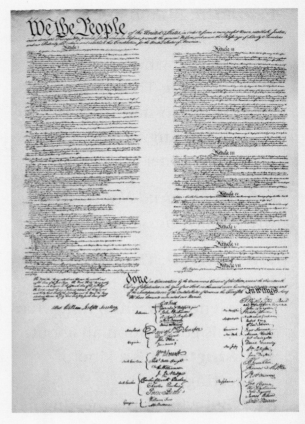

*Alexander Hamilton opens the door. He's very upset.*

**Hamilton**: Washington, you must stop Mr. Gerry from talking!

**Franklin**: That's why we're here, Hamilton, to talk.

**Washington**: Bob and Ned, this is Alexander Hamilton.

**Hamilton**: (*stiffly*) Oh. Good day, children.

**Ned and Bob**: Pleased to meet you!

**Hamilton**: Gerry says that a federal government will take power from the states.

**Franklin**: That's true.

**Hamilton**: But who cares about that?

**Franklin**: (*laughing*) Mr. Gerry, I guess.

*Hamilton groans and goes back into the convention.*

**Alexander Hamilton
wanted a strong
federal government.**

**Before You Go On** | **Why did Washington think the United States needed a constitution?**

**The British surrendered to George Washington at Yorktown.**

**Bob**: I hope Mr. Gerry talks for a week. I need this job.

**Washington**: Don't worry, Bob. The convention might last all summer.

**Ned**: All summer! You really think it will take them that long?

**Franklin**: Yes. People are afraid of government. They think it will take away their liberty.

**Ned**: We don't want that!

**Bob**: Make the government weak!

**Franklin**: What if we have to fight the British again?

**Bob**: Didn't they surrender?

**Washington**: Yes. But they might come back.

**Ned**: We just need a strong army then.

**Franklin**: Armies cost money. Yesterday, I saw an army veteran in great need. We must take care of the soldiers who fought in the war. France gave us a **loan**. We should pay them back. Where will we get the money?

**Bob**: Oh. Is that the only problem?

**Franklin**: No! There are many things to figure out. But first, we need a strong federal government.

**Washington**: But not so strong that we lose our freedom. Understand?

---

**loan**   something, usually money, that is borrowed and then returned

**Benjamin Franklin was a statesman and scientist.**

**Before You Go On**   What are some reasons for having a strong government?

**Scene:** About three months later. July 1787. Outside the State House.

**Ned**: What is the new government called?

**Franklin**: It's called a republic. The people who live in each state vote for **representatives** to run things. People will elect representatives every two years. The government will have three parts: The first branch is the legislature, or Congress—

**Bob**: The legislature makes the laws.

**Franklin**: Right. The second branch is the Supreme Court or judicial branch. This court will tell us what the laws mean if there are any questions. The third branch is the president or executive branch. He will make sure that people follow the laws.

**Ned**: He's like a king.

**Franklin**: No. He will only be president for four years. Then people will elect a new president.

**Bob**: So everything got done after all.

**Franklin**: There's still a lot to figure out.

**Bob**: Like what?

---

**representatives**   people chosen to speak or act for others

**Delegates sign the U.S. Constitution.**

**Franklin**: We need a list of rights. People's rights are things the government can't take away, like freedom to say what you think. Then each state has to agree on the list.

**Ned**: Are you happy with the new government, sir?

**Franklin**: People make governments, Ned. If the people do the right thing, our government will be fine. We still have big problems, such as slavery and rights for women. But you young people will have to figure those things out. We did the best we could.

**Ned**: Mr. Franklin, you did one very good thing.

**Franklin**: What was that?

**Ned**: When you came to Philadelphia, we had 13 separate states. But when you leave, we will have one country.

**Franklin**: "Out of many, one." That's good. We should put that on a coin.

102–104

## Reading Strategy

### Use Prior Knowledge

- How did your prior knowledge of the Constitutional Convention help you understand the reading?

- What new information have you learned about the Constitutional Convention?

## Think It Over

1. **Recall**   Who are the characters in this play?

2. **Comprehend**   What do the delegates believe that a new government might **impose** on the people?

3. **Analyze**   What problems of early American **culture** still existed when the U.S. Constitution was written?

# Learning Strategies

## Use a KWL Chart

A KWL Chart can be used to activate **prior knowledge.** It provides a plan for recording three kinds of information.

1. What you **know** about a topic before reading.

2. What you **want** to know or learn about the topic.

3. What you actually **learned** about the topic.

**Practice** | G.O. 145

**You completed the first two columns before. Now complete the final column.**

| CONSTITUTIONAL CONVENTION | | |
|---|---|---|
| WHAT I KNOW | WHAT I WANT TO KNOW | WHAT I LEARNED |
| | | |

1. What do you still want to learn about the U.S. government?

2. Where can you find more information?

# Use Prior Knowledge

When you activate **prior knowledge**, you use what you already know to learn more about something. For example, you can use what you now know about the U.S. Constitution to learn more about how the U.S. government was created.

Imagine that your next reading assignment is about the Bill of Rights, which is the list of rights that the government cannot take away. Copy the chart and complete it.

1. List three things you already know about the freedoms granted by the U.S. Constitution based on what you read in *One Out of Many.*
2. List three things you want to learn about the Bill of Rights.

| WHAT I KNOW | WHAT I WANT TO KNOW |
|---|---|
| 1. | 1. |
| 2. | 2. |
| 3. | 3. |

105

**Apply**

Close your book and retell the selection to a partner. Use the key words.

## Extension

**Utilize** Think about what else you want to know about the freedoms in our country. Choose a topic and do research on it. Make a poster on the topic. Use both text and pictures on your poster. Share your poster with the class.

# Grammar

## Compound Sentences

Two simple sentences, each with a subject and verb, can be joined to form a **compound sentence**.

| Simple Sentences |
| --- |
| The birds were singing. The sun was shining. |
| **Compound Sentence** |
| The birds were singing, **and** the sun was shining. |

Note that a compound sentence is composed of two **independent** clauses, each with a **subject** and **verb**.

| Independent Clause | | Independent Clause |
| --- | --- | --- |
| **It was** very late, | and | **I needed** to get home. |

To create a compound sentence, use the connecting words **and, but,** or **or.** Always use a **comma** before the connecting word. Use **and** for two equal sentences with similar ideas.

> He started playing guitar when he was five, **and** he still practices daily.

Use **but** for two equal sentences with different ideas.

> Tom forgot his umbrella, **but** Mia brought an extra umbrella.

Use **or** to show a choice between two equal sentences.

> We can win the tournament, **or** we can try again next year.

**Use the connecting words *and*, *but*, or *or* to combine the sentences.**

**Example:** Mr. Hamilton wanted a strong government.
Mr. Washington didn't.

Mr. Hamilton wanted a strong government, but
Mr. Washington didn't.

1. Ben Franklin wanted to talk with the windows open. George Washington wanted them closed.

2. His parents said he couldn't play the drums. He rebelled and joined a band.

3. Alexander Hamilton and George Washington wanted a strong federal government. Other leaders wanted the states to have more power.

4. Benjamin Franklin believed the government should take care of soldiers who had fought in wars. There wasn't enough money.

5. She can study foreign **cultures** in college. She can visit foreign countries instead.

6. He likes to play soccer. He likes to watch football.

**Work with a partner. Discuss what you found interesting about *One Out of Many*. Use compound sentences in your discussion.**

106

**Example:** A: It was interesting that they kept the windows closed during the convention, but they must have been so hot!

B: Yes, it had to be hot, but it was important that no one knew what they were talking about.

## Grammar Check ✓

What does a compound sentence consist of?

# Writing

## Write a Persuasive Poster

*Ongoing Writing Skills Practice*

When you write a persuasive poster, you need to catch your reader's attention right away. People usually take only a few minutes to study a poster. You need good headings and only the most important information.

### Writing Prompt

Create a poster in which you try to persuade people to move to your town. Think of good reasons why people would want to live there. Use compound sentences.

## ❶ Prewrite G.O. 141

Choose facts about your hometown that you think would make people want to move there. List them in a graphic organizer.

A student named Pat listed her ideas like this:

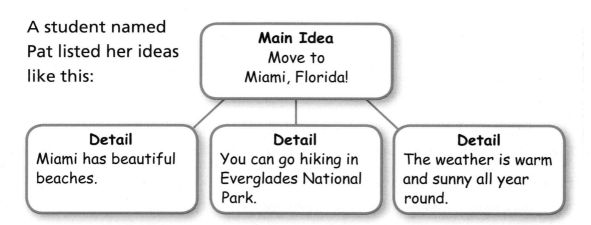

**Main Idea**
Move to Miami, Florida!

**Detail**
Miami has beautiful beaches.

**Detail**
You can go hiking in Everglades National Park.

**Detail**
The weather is warm and sunny all year round.

## ❷ Draft

Use your graphic organizer to help you write a draft.

## ❸ Revise

Read over your draft. Look for places where the writing needs improvement. Use the Writing Checklist to help you identify problems. Then revise your draft.

## ❹ Edit

Check your work for errors in grammar, usage, mechanics, and spelling. Trade papers with a partner to get feedback. Use the Peer Review Checklist on page 404.

## ❺ Publish

Prepare a clean copy of your final draft. Share your paragraph with the class.

Here is Pat's poster:

## Writing Checklist

**Organization**

✔ My headings grab the reader's attention.

**Sentence Fluency**

✔ I used sentences of different lengths.

**Conventions**

✔ I used compound sentences correctly.

Pat Vasquez

MIAMI, FLORIDA — YOUR NEW HOMETOWN

RECREATION

Miami has miles and miles of beaches, and you can go swimming even in the winter!

GREAT ATTRACTIONS

Everglades National Park is only one hour's drive away. You can go hiking, see amazing bird life, and take photos of alligators!

SUN! SUN! SUN!

The weather is warm in Miami all year round. Throw your winter coats away!

MIAMI, FLORIDA HAS IT ALL!

107–108

# Apply and Extend

## Link the Readings

Copy the chart into your notebook. Read the words in the top row. For each text selection, put an X under words related to that reading.

|  | Informational text | Literature | How people used to live | Fighting another country for land |
|---|---|---|---|---|
| **The Real Soldier** |  |  |  |  |
| **One Hot Summer in Philadelphia** |  |  |  |  |
| **One Out of Many** |  |  |  |  |

## Discussion

1. What challenges did the early Americans face when trying to create a new country?

2. What were the **circumstances** that the new Americans had to deal with in 1787?

3. Before they wrote a list of laws protecting people's rights, what did the delegates have to agree on **initially**? What were some reasons for having a federal government?

How do people create new countries?

> **Listening Skills**
>
> If you don't understand a word or phrase, you can ask "What does...mean?"

# Projects

**Your teacher will help you choose one of these projects.**

|  Written |  Oral |  Visual/Active |
|---|---|---|
| **Biography** | **Skit** | **Collage** |
| Research one of the people who helped form the country. Write a short biography of his or her life. | Write and perform a skit about a family during the American Revolution. | Use drawings, photos, and magazine clippings to create a collage that shows what freedom means to you. |
| **Letter** | **Presentation** | **Brochure** |
| Suppose you lived in Philadelphia in 1787. Write a letter to a friend telling about a day in your life. | Work as a group. Create a presentation that explains one important feature of the U.S. government. | Design a brochure that tells about historical sites in Philadelphia. Include illustrations and captions. |

*For more projects, visit*
*LongmanCornerstone.com*

# Further Reading

 ***The Swiss Family Robinson,*** Johann Wyss
In this Penguin Young Reader® version of the classic story, a family stranded on a tropical island works together to build a new home and learns how to live in a strange new land.

***The First Thanksgiving,*** Jean Craighead George
From the formation of Plymouth Rock many years ago to the Pilgrims' friendship with Squanto, readers learn valuable details about the first Thanksgiving.

**W B**

109–110

## Give a Speech

You are going to give a speech about living in the United States. You will listen as your classmates give their speeches.

### ❶ Prepare

**A.** Think about why you like living in the United States. You will write and give a speech about it. Your classmates will ask you questions afterwards.

**B.** Think of the main reasons you like living here. Think of details to support your main points. Now write your speech. Find effective visuals to use during your speech.

Example:

> ### Life in the United States
>
> I like living in the United States for many reasons. People are friendly, there are a lot of things to see and do, and I'm enjoying learning new things in a new country.
>
> When I first came to the United States, I was scared. I was leaving all my friends in Mexico, and many members of my family. I could speak hardly any English, and I didn't know if I would like it here. On my second day in the States, the Smiths came over. Their son, Steve, was studying Spanish. Steve is around my age, and we soon

### ❷ Practice

Practice your speech in front of your family or friends. If possible, record your speech. Then listen to it. How do you sound? Record it again and try to improve.

# ❸ Present

**As you speak,** do the following:
- Speak clearly and loudly enough for everyone to hear.
- Make eye contact with your audience.
- Be careful not to hide behind your visuals.

**As you listen,** do the following:
- Picture in your mind what the speaker is describing.
- Take notes.
- Think of questions to ask the speaker after the presentation.

# ❹ Evaluate

**After you speak,** answer these questions:
- ✔ Did you make eye contact with your audience and speak clearly?
- ✔ Did you express your ideas well?

**After you listen,** answer these questions:
- ✔ Did you understand the main points and details of the speech?
- ✔ Did you enjoy listening to the speech? Why or why not?

**Speaking Skills**

Speeches use formal language. Remember to use correct grammar and complete sentences, and to avoid slang.

**Listening Skills**

As you listen, use the visuals the speaker presents to help you enhance and confirm your understanding.

# Writing Workshop

## Write a Persuasive Essay

### Writing Prompt

Write an essay in which you express a clear, strong opinion and then try to convince the reader that your opinion is correct. Support your opinion with convincing reasons in a logical order. Include your opinion in the introduction, and restate it in the conclusion.

### ❶ Prewrite  G.O. 141

Review your previous work in this unit. Now choose a topic on which you have a strong opinion. Then think of reasons that support your opinion. List your ideas in a graphic organizer.

A student named David listed his ideas like this:

**Argument**
The mayor should declare a "clean our park" holiday.

**Reason**
People are always too busy on the weekend to pitch in and volunteer.

**Reason**
Litter is becoming a problem. The children's sandbox is dirty.

**Reason**
New grass can be planted, then people can have picnics.

### ❷ Draft

Use your graphic organizer to write a draft. Make sure your opinion is supported with good reasons.

## ❸ Revise

Read your draft. Use the Writing Checklist to help you identify problems. Then revise your draft.

Here is how David revised his essay:

## Six Traits of Writing Checklist

✔ **Ideas**
Are my ideas in a logical order?

✔ **Organization**
Do my introduction and conclusion state my opinion?

✔ **Voice**
Does my writing show enthusiasm?

✔ **Word Choice**
Do I avoid repeating words and phrases?

✔ **Sentence Fluency**
Did I use compound sentences?

✔ **Conventions**
Do my pronouns, subjects, and verbs agree?

---

David Lee

Let's Take a Holiday and Clean Up the Park.

Jefferson Park needs our help. It should be a place to relax, play, and enjoy nature. But lately it looks like the town garbage dump! I think we should ask the mayor to declare a town holiday—Jefferson Park Day.

Volunteers could clean up the litter that is now all over the park. If people could spend one whole day working together, we could do amazing things to Jefferson Park. We could clean out the sand box, so kids could have a safe place to play.

If we plant more grass, we could have picnics in the park. There are many place in the park with dirt instead of grass. Planting grass will make a huge improvement.

People is always too busy to volunteer, but if the mayor declares a town holiday, everyone could come together to fix up our park.

Please Mr. Mayor, declare a Jefferson Park Day. Then we can enjoy a clean, safe park with plenty of places to sit and enjoy a picnic lunch!

**Revised** to make a compound sentence.

**Revised** to make sentences flow better.

**Revised** to correct error in spelling.

**Revised** to correct error in grammar.

**Revised** to correct error in subject-verb agreement.

## ❹ Edit

Check your work for errors. Trade papers with a partner. Use the Peer Review Checklist to give each other feedback. Edit your final draft in response to feedback from your partner and your teacher.

## ❺ Publish

Make a clean copy of your final draft. Share your essay with the class.

**111-112**

## Peer Review Checklist

✓ The introduction states the author's opinion.

✓ The opinion is strong and clear.

✓ The supporting reasons are convincing.

## SPELLING TIP

Homophones are words th
sound alike but are spelled
differently, such as *whole*
and *hole*. It's important to
be aware of homophones
and make sure you have th
correct spelling.

**Listen to the sentences. Pay attention to the groups of words. Read aloud.**  Audio

1.  In *The Real Soldier*, a boy helps his father fight for independence.
2.  Delegates to the Constitution Convention attended confidential meetings in the State House in Philadelphia.
3.  The delegates decided on a republic where the people of each state elect representatives to run things.

**Work in pairs. Take turns reading the passage below aloud for one minute. Count the number of words you read.**

WB 113-114

| | |
|---|---:|
| Jacob wanted to be a soldier, like his father. His father | 11 |
| and other farmers in the area had promised to join General | 22 |
| George Washington if he needed help. | 28 |
| Jacob was getting some wood to bring into the house when | 39 |
| his mother rushed into the barn. "Redcoats are here," | 48 |
| she whispered. | 50 |
| Jacob was scared. He wondered if the British soldiers | 59 |
| knew that his father and the other farmers were Minutemen. | 69 |
| Emily was scared, too. She ran and hid in Star's stall. | 80 |
| Jacob wanted to hide with her, but his mother needed him. | 91 |
| Together, they walked into the yard to face the British. | 101 |
| Jacob was relieved when he heard what the Redcoats wanted. | 111 |
| This time, they only wanted food and supplies. Jacob | 120 |
| chose his words carefully. "My father has gone to the | 130 |
| market," he said. "We don't have anything here." Jacob | 139 |
| didn't tell the soldiers that the "market" was General | 148 |
| Washington's camp! | 150 |

# Test Preparation

## Taking Tests

You will often take tests that help show what you know.
Follow these tips to improve your test-taking skills.

### Coaching Corner

**Answering Test Items That Have Cloze Passages**

- Cloze items will ask you to fill in a blank.

- Sometimes you will be asked to complete a sentence. Other times you will be given a selection with some words left out.

- First read the questions and answer choices. Sometimes there is no question, just a list of words.

- Read the whole selection carefully. Try to think of words that might fit as you read.

- If you don't know what a word means, use the words around it to help you.

- If there is a question, read it carefully. Look for words like *best*, *least*, *main*, *most*, *most likely*, *not*, and *probably*.

- In your head, read the sentence with each answer choice. Choose the answer that makes the most sense.

**Read the following test sample. Study the tips in the box.**

115–116

**Read the selection. Then choose the correct words to fill in the blanks.**

1      There was once an armadillo who loved the sound of __1__. He decided he wanted to learn to sing. He asked the frogs, the crickets, and the birds in the forest if they would teach him to sing. They all said the same thing, "No, silly! Armadillos don't sing." The armadillo was very __2__. Why didn't the animals want to teach him to sing?

2      Then one day, an old man came walking in the __3__. The armadillo asked the old man if he could teach him how to sing. The old man picked up a stick and tapped the armadillo on its __4__. The shell-tapping made beautiful music! Soon all the animals in the forest came to listen to the old man and the armadillo make their beautiful songs.

1  **A** driving
    **B** singing
    **C** reading
    **D** fishing

2  **F** unhappy
    **G** joyful
    **H** athletic
    **J** musical

3  **A** forest
    **B** house
    **C** school
    **D** ocean

4  **F** foot
    **G** head
    **H** shell
    **J** door

**Tips**

✔ Make sure you read the whole selection and all the answer choices.

✔ Pay attention to the words in context. Some answer choices may make sense in one sentence. But they don't make sense when you read the whole selection.

# Your Environment

Deserts, mountaintops, tropical rain forests, and grasslands are all places where people live. Animals and plants live in these places, too.

## Reading

**1** | Science

**Biomes All Over the World**

**2** | Science

**Marine Food Web**

**3** | Article

**Save the Sea Turtles**

How do people
and environments
affect each other?

## Listening and Speaking

You will talk about your environment and
things you can do to protect it. In the
Listening and Speaking Workshop, you will
give a how-to presentation.

## Writing

You will practice expository writing. In the
Writing Workshop, you will write a compare-
and-contrast essay.

*Quick* **Write**

Write several sentences describing one thing
you do to protect your environment. Share
your work with a partner.

**VIEW AND RESPOND**

DVD

*Talk about the poster for this unit. Then
watch and listen to the video and answer
the questions at <u>LongmanCornerstone.com</u>.*

# What do you know about your environment?

## Words to Know

**Listen and repeat. Use these words to talk about the environment.**

 conserve energy

 reduce pollution

 protect wildlife

 conserve water

 recycle

 protect insects

## Practice

**Work with a partner. Ask and answer questions about the environment.**

| | |
|---|---|
| use fewer insecticides | take shorter showers |
| take the train or bus | protect forests |
| separate plastic, paper, and glass | turn off lights |

**Example:** A: What's a good way to <u>conserve energy</u>?

B: One good way is to <u>turn off lights</u>.

## Write

**Read the question. Write your response in your notebook.**

What are some things you do to protect the environment?

## Make Connections

Copy the sentences below into your notebook. Complete the sentences with the following words.

clean air

clean environment

fresh water

oxygen

1. Because _____ is an important part of the environment, we must conserve water in order to make sure we have enough of it.

2. Trees are an important part of our environment because they provide _____.

3. In order to have a _____, it's important to recycle.

4. Because cars are major contributors to pollution, we should ride the bus, take the train, or walk as much as possible so that we can have _____.

## What about you?

Talk with a partner. How you can help to protect the environment?

# Kid's Stories from around the World

**Germany**

**Bangladesh**

**Roth**

In Germany, we take recycling very seriously. Every city and town has bins where people can bring their used plastic and glass bottles, newspapers, cardboard, and aluminum cans. We hope this will mean a better future for everyone.

**Sharma**

Air pollution is a big problem in Bangladesh. In large cities, like Dhaka, we are just beginning to measure pollution that comes from cars and factories. We hope modern cars and factories will mean cleaner air for everyone.

Alaska

Brazil

**João**

In Brazil, where I live, rain forests grow along the Amazon River. Rain forests are home to many animals. The trees give off oxygen, which we all need to live. Some people have cut down trees to build homes or have cleared the land for farming. We need to stop cutting down trees. The whole world needs them.

**Ama**

I live on St. Paul Island in Alaska. Our rocky beaches get lots of garbage from boats that pass by. We get together and pick up trash, bottles, and cans. In September, children and adults from around the world do the same thing. It's called the International Coastal Cleanup.

## What about you?

1. What are some environmental problems in your area?

2. How do you help your environment? Share your story.

**Prepare to Read**

## What You Will Learn

**Reading**

- Vocabulary building: *Context, phonics*

- Reading strategy: *Visualize*

- Text type: *Informational (science)*

**Grammar**

Comparatives and superlatives

**Writing**

Compare and contrast

These words will help you understand the reading.

### Key Words

**biome**

**tundra**

**equator**

**desert**

**tropical**

**grasslands**

**ocean**

# Key Words

*Biomes All Over the World* describes the major biomes on Earth.

## Words in Context  Audio

**1** The Eden Project in Cornwall, England, has several man-made biomes. A biome is a group of plants and animals in a geographic area.

**2** The tundra is found at the North and South Poles. Plants do not grow very tall, because the ground is often frozen or covered with snow.

**3** The equator is an imaginary line that runs around the middle of our planet. It divides Earth in half.

**4** A desert is usually dry and hot.

**⑤** Most tropical rain forests are near the equator. They are usually hot and humid!

**⑥** Grasslands are large areas covered with grasses. Savannas and prairies are two types of grasslands.

**⑦** The ocean is the largest biome in the world. Oceans cover more than 70 percent of Earth's surface.

**Practice**

**Create a concept map for each new word.**
• Write the key word in the center.
• Around it, write words that relate to it.
• Connect the words using lines.

## Make Connections

Describe some of the plants and animals that live in your area.

**Speaking Skills**

If you can't think of the right word, try using a synonym.

117

These words will help you talk about the reading.

## Academic Words

**adapted**
changed to fit a new situation

**label**
use a word or phrase to describe something

**migrate**
move from one place to another

WB
118

# Academic Words

## Words in Context

Animals around the world have **adapted** to the places they live.

Map makers **label** each ocean on the map.

Many birds **migrate** south in winter to stay warm.

 **Practice**

**Write the sentence in your notebook. Choose an academic word to complete each sentence.**

1. In spring, some animals ____ north to find food.

2. My mother will usually ____ all the food she puts into the freezer.

3. Polar bears have ____ to living in very cold weather.

 **Apply**

**Ask and answer with a partner.**

1. Explain how to **label** a Venn diagram.

2. How have polar bears **adapted** to cold weather?

3. Why might animals **migrate** south in cold weather?

# Phonics

## Final *s* sound: *z, s, iz*

Listen. Identify whether the final *s* is pronounced *z, s,* or *iz*. Then read each word aloud.

| biomes | tops | pages |
|---|---|---|

### Rule

A final *s* is pronounced *z* after a vowel or a voiced consonant like *b, d, g, l, m, n, r,* or *v.* You can feel your throat vibrate when you say a vowel or voiced consonant. The final *s* is pronounced *s* after a voiceless consonant like *f, k, p,* or *t.* After words ending in *ch, sh, j, s, x,* or *z* sounds, the final *s* is pronounced *iz.*

### Practice

Work with a partner. Read each word aloud. Tell whether the final *s* sounds like *z, s,* or *iz.*

1. classes
2. was
3. mixes
4. cats
5. always

6. teaches
7. pages
8. goes
9. walks

**INFORMATIONAL TEXT**

Science

 **Listen to the Audio.**
Listen for the main points and important details.

### Reading Strategy

#### Visualize

Good readers often try to visualize, or see in their minds, what they are reading about.

- Use the descriptions in the text and the photos to create a mental picture of what you are reading.

Listen as your teacher models the reading strategy.

# Biomes
## All Over the World
### by Tiayana Markson

A biome is a **community** where certain kinds of plants and animals live. Earth has more than 30 different kinds of biomes. These photos show the most common ones.

Forests cover about one-third of the land on Earth's surface. Forests are filled with trees and plants. **Temperate** forests have different **seasons**. In the winter, these forests can be cold. In the summer, they can be hot. Temperate forests get a lot of sunlight. The sun helps plants grow.

Many animals live in the forest. All need to be able to survive in different seasons. Small animals, such as squirrels and skunks, can be found in the temperate forest. Large animals, such as black bears, also make their homes there.

**community**   group that lives together in the same place

**temperate**   never very hot or very cold

**seasons**   changes in weather that happen annually

A temperate forest is one kind of biome on Earth.

This tropical rain forest is located in South America.

Another kind of forest is the tropical rain forest. Tropical rain forests are in areas near the equator. All rain forests get a lot of rain every year. The rain helps plants grow. In fact, rain forests have more kinds of plants than any other biome. The trees grow so well that very little sunlight can get through the **canopy** of leaves. This makes the ground in the rain forest wet and dark.

The darkness inside the rain forest makes it a perfect home for animals such as bats and small insects. Many **exotic** birds, reptiles, and mammals live in rain forests.

---

**canopy**   cover

**exotic**   unusual and exciting

**Before You Go On**   Why is it dark inside a rain forest?

The **arctic** tundra is the coldest biome on Earth. Trees do not grow in the tundra. Winds are very strong. Ice covers the ground, and water freezes. Animals such as polar bears must be able to live in the cold. Most animals that live in the tundra have extra fat to keep them warm. Many birds and other animals **migrate** to a warmer **climate** for the winter.

In the summer, the weather is warm enough in the tundra for things to grow. Plants and flowers appear. These plants and flowers can live in colder temperatures. Animals that eat plants and grass can find more food during the summer.

---

**arctic**   very cold

**climate**   typical weather in an area

**Flowers appear on the tundra in the warmer months.**

**Polar bears like the snow and cold weather of the tundra.**

Mountains are on every **continent** on Earth. Most mountains have forests at the bottom of them. The higher you go up a mountain, the colder and windier it gets. The tops of very high mountains look like the tundra. Only small plants and flowers grow in these areas. The plants usually grow close to the ground, so the wind cannot knock them over. Animals that live on mountains, such as mountain goats and mountain lions, must be strong climbers.

Desert biomes have very little rain. Most plants cannot grow there. Deserts are either very hot or very cold. This makes it hard for anything to live there. Plants and animals that live in the desert have **adapted** to live with very little water.

---

**continent**    one of the main masses of land on Earth

The tops of many tall mountains are very cold and snowy.

Very few plants grow in the desert.

**Before You Go On**    What kind of climate does the tundra have?

Bison eat in this grassland in South Dakota.

There are few or no trees on grasslands. Average rainfall is somewhere between a temperate forest and a desert. The plants that live on grasslands do not get a lot of water year round. Grasses and wildflowers, though, get enough water to grow at least part of the year.

Prairies and savannas are two types of grasslands. Savannas are located near the equator. Animals such as zebras, elephants, and lions live on savannas. Prairies are in more temperate areas. Animals like bison, deer, and horses, live on prairies. Small animals and insects, such as rabbits, snakes, and grasshoppers, live there also.

People have turned most prairies into farms. The soil is good for planting **crops**. Farm animals can **graze** on the grass. But this means that there are not as many grasslands on Earth as there used to be.

---

**crops**   plants grown by a farmer and used for food

**graze**   feed on grass

The ocean biome is the largest biome on Earth. Oceans are huge bodies of water. They make up 70 percent of Earth's surface. Many kinds of animals and plants live in oceans. Fish, crabs, and clams spend their lives under water. Larger animals, such as whales, sharks, and dolphins, also live in the ocean. Blue whales live in the ocean. They are the largest known mammals on Earth. Ocean water is very salty. Animals that live in the ocean must be able to drink salt water.

Earth has many different biomes with a variety of plants and animals. Look around you. Which biome is most like the place where you live?

A scuba diver goes underwater to explore the ocean.

**W B**

120–122

## Reading Strategy

### Visualize

- What did you visualize when you read about temperate forests?

- What did you visualize when you read about the other biomes?

- How did visualizing as you read help you understand the selection?

## Think It Over

1. **Recall** What is the largest biome?

2. **Comprehend** When do birds **migrate** back to the tundra?

3. **Analyze** How would you **label** your biome? What animals have **adapted** to

# Animals
## and Their Biomes

### ▲ Desert
This roadrunner lives in the desert. It had to run very fast to catch its dinner!

### ▲ Temperate Forest
Squirrels are one of the many kinds of animals that live in temperate forests.

### ▲ Tundra
The arctic fox lives in the tundra. Its fur coat changes color with the seasons.

### ▲ Mountain
These llamas live in the Andes Mountains. Some llamas are wild, but people in the Andes also raise llamas for their fur and meat.

## ▲ Tropical Rain Forest

This poison arrow frog lives in the
tropical rain forests of South America.

## ▲ Ocean

Sharks live in the ocean.
They are an important part
of the marine food web.

## ◀ Savanna

The rhinoceros is one of
many animals that live
on the savanna. People
hunt rhinoceroses for
their meat and horns.

## ▲ Prairie

Prairie dogs are very social animals.
They live in underground burrows
called towns.

## Activity to Do

These pages use pictures and
words to tell about animals
and biomes.

- Pick any animal that
  interests you.

- Research that animal and
  its biome.

- Create two pages, using
  pictures and words, to
  describe that animal and
  its biome.

# Learning Strategies

## Visualize

Writers use words to help readers **visualize** what they are reading about. As you read, look for words that describe. These words will help you visualize what you are reading about.

**Describe one of the biomes, plants, or animals from the selection to a partner. Use as many adjectives as possible.**

• Have your partner guess what you are describing.
• After your partner guesses correctly, ask your partner to tell which details helped the most.
• Switch roles several times.

# Use a Compare and Contrast Chart

When you **compare**, you tell how two or more things are similar. When you **contrast**, you tell how two or more things are different. You can use a T-Chart like this one to help you identify things that are alike and different.

**Copy this chart. Compare and contrast the desert and grassland biomes. One example has been given.**

| How grasslands and deserts are similar | How grasslands and deserts are different |
|---|---|
| Both deserts and grasslands get little rain. | |

Reread the selection and take notes on the different biomes. Then close your book and use your notes to retell the selection to a partner.

123

## Extension

**Utilize**  Make a brochure about your biome. Write a brief description of your biome and the plants and animals that have **adapted** to living in it. Add photos or drawings.

# Grammar

## Comparatives and Superlatives

Use **comparative adjectives** to compare two things. Use **superlative adjectives** to compare three or more things.

| Adjective | Comparative | Superlative (the most) |
|---|---|---|
| a fast car ⟶ | a faster car **than** another ⟶ | **the** fastest car of all |

To form comparatives and superlatives of **one-syllable adjectives,** add -*er* or -*est* (or if ending in -*e*, add -*r* or -*st*). For adjectives ending in a vowel + consonant, double the consonant.

**tall** ⟶ **tall**er ⟶ **tall**est
**nice** ⟶ **nice**r ⟶ **nice**st
**big** ⟶ **big**ger ⟶ **big**gest

For adjectives with **two or more syllables,** add *more* or *most*. However, if a two-syllable adjective ends -*y*, change -*y* to -*i* and add -*est*.

**careful** ⟶ more **careful** ⟶ most **careful**
**busy** ⟶ **bus**ier ⟶ **bus**iest

A few adjectives have **irregular** comparative and superlative forms.

**good** ⟶ better ⟶ best          **little** ⟶ less ⟶ least
**bad** ⟶ worse ⟶ worst          **far** ⟶ farther ⟶ farthest

## Practice

Change each adjective to a comparative or superlative. Write the sentences.

**Example:** A bear is <u>fatter</u> than a horse. (fat)

1. The tundra is the ＿＿＿ biome of all. (cold)

2. A mountain's top is ＿＿＿ than its bottom. (windy)

3. The ocean is the ＿＿＿ biome on Earth. (large)

4. It is ＿＿＿ on the savanna than on the prairie. (hot)

5. A tropical rainforest is ＿＿＿ than a grassland. (dark)

6. A desert is ＿＿＿ than a grassland. (dry)

7. The ＿＿＿ mammal of all is the blue whale. (big)

8. Birds **migrate** to ＿＿＿ climates in winter. (warm)

## Apply

Work with a partner. Compare and contrast biomes and the plants and animals in them.

**Example:** A: I think the ocean is the most interesting biome.

B: Me, too. The ocean has the largest mammal, the blue whale.

W B
124

### Grammar Check ✓

When do you use comparatives and superlatives?

# Writing

## Compare and Contrast

Expository writing explains or informs. There are different ways to organize ideas in expository writing. One way is to compare and contrast— to tell how two things are similar and how they are different.

### Writing Prompt

Write a short essay in which you compare and contrast two biomes, such as a temperate forest and a tropical rain forest. Identify the subjects being compared. Then explain how they are alike and how they are different. Be sure to use comparatives and superlatives correctly.

## ❶ Prewrite

Choose two biomes to write about. List their similarities and differences in a Venn Diagram.

A student named Gabriella listed her ideas like this:

**Temperate Forest**
four seasons; most trees lose leaves and grow new leaves

**Same**
many different plants and animals

**Tropical Rain Forest**
hot; trees grow all year; more kinds of plants and animals

## ❷ Draft

Use your Venn diagram to write a draft. Use transitional words such as *similarly* and *also* to say how the biomes are alike, or *however* and *on the other hand* to say how they are different.

## ❸ Revise

Read over your draft. Use the Writing Checklist to help you identify problems. Then revise your draft.

## ❹ Edit

Check your work for errors in grammar, usage, mechanics, and spelling. Trade papers with a partner to get feedback. Use the Peer Review Checklist on Workbook page 404.

## ❺ Publish

Prepare a clean copy of your final draft. Share your paragraph with the class.

Here is Gabriella's essay:

## Writing Checklist

**Organization**

✔ The essay is organized to clearly show similarities and differences.

**Word Choice**

✔ I used transitional words.

**Conventions**

✔ I used comparatives and superlatives correctly.

Gabriella Marquez

A temperate rain forest and a tropical rain forest are alike in some ways. Both types of forests contain many trees and plants. Both also contain many different kinds of mammals and reptiles.

However, there are key differences between the two forests. Temperate forests grow where there are four seasons. Most trees in temperate forests lose their leaves in autumn, when temperatures become cooler. They grow new leaves in the spring.

A rain forest, on the other hand, is hot all year long. It also gets more rain than a temperate forest. This allows trees and bushes to grow all year. Also, the rain forest has a greater variety of plants and animals. More than half of all animals and plants on earth make their home in the rain forest.

125–126

## What You Will Learn

**Reading**

- Vocabulary building: *Context, phonics*
- Reading strategy: *Ask questions*
- Text type: *Informational text (science)*

**Grammar**

Indefinite pronouns

**Writing**

Explain a process

These words will help you understand the reading.

### Key Words

organisms

mammals

consumers

producer

predator

scavengers

decomposers

# Key Words

*Marine Food Web* describes the food web that exists in the world's oceans.

## Words in Context

**Audio**

**1** Both fish and coral are organisms, or living things.

**2** People, dogs, and whales are mammals. They give birth and feed their young with milk.

**3** Bears are consumers. They eat food, but they don't make their own like plants do.

**4** A plant is a  producer . It uses energy from the sun to make food.

**5** An orca, or killer whale, is a  predator . It hunts and eats other animals.

**6** Crabs are  scavengers . They search for and eat dead plants and animals.

**7** Bacteria are  decomposers . They break down dead plants, animals, and waste.

**Practice**

**Make flashcards to help you memorize the words.**
- Write a key word on the front.
- On the back, write the meaning.

## Make Connections

What are some  organisms  that live in the ocean? Are they  producers ,  consumers , or  decomposers ? After discussing these questions, write your response in your notebook.

WB
127

These words will help you talk about the reading.

### Academic Words

**primary**
most important

**role**
position or job someone or something has in a particular situation

**source**
where something comes from

# Academic Words

## Words in Context

Their **primary** concern is for the safety of their children.

A police officer's **role** is to make sure people obey laws.

The newspaper is my parent's main **source** of news.

### Practice

**Write the sentences in your notebook. Choose an academic word to complete each sentence.**

1. The _____ of Pat's pain was a broken bone.

2. Taking care of your health is your doctor's _____ job.

3. The mayor has played a major _____ in improving our city.

### Apply

**Ask and answer with a partner.**

1. What is the **primary** reason you go to school?

2. What **role** does your teacher play in your learning?

3. What is a **source** of fun for you during the school day?

# Phonics

## Consonant Clusters

Listen. Pay attention to the beginning consonant sounds. Then read each word aloud.

| *r*-blends | *l*-blends | *s*-blends |
|------------|------------|------------|
| bring      | black      | skin       |
| free       | float      | special    |
| predator   | please     | swim       |

### Rule

When *r*, *l*, or *s* come together with another consonant at the beginning of a word, the sounds of both letters usually blend together.

### Practice

1. Read page 224. Make a list of any *r*-blends, *l*-blends, and *s*-blends that you find.

2. Use the words in the box above to answer these clues.

   a. This word begins with an *r*-blend. It's an animal that hunts other animals.

   b. This word begins with an *l*-blend. It means "rest in or on top of water."

   c. This word begins with an *s*-blend. It's what covers your body.

   d. This word begins with an *s*-blend. It's something to do in hot weather.

129

## INFORMATIONAL TEXT
### Science

### More About

How do people and marine organisms affect each other?

**Audio** **Listen to the Audio.**
Listen for the main points and important details.

### Reading Strategy

### Ask Questions

Good readers ask themselves questions as they read. Here are questions to consider:

* What am I learning?
* What am I having trouble understanding?
* What do I need to reread?
* What do I need assistance with?

Listen as your teacher models the reading strategy.

# Marine Food Web

by Hiro Ishio

What is the difference between a food chain and a food web? A food chain shows one way that energy travels between producers, consumers, and decomposers. A food web shows many food chains that are connected to one another.

**Fish and coral**

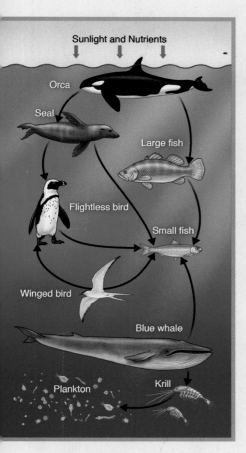

Sunlight and Nutrients

Orca

Seal

Large fish

Flightless bird

Small fish

Winged bird

Blue whale

Plankton

Krill

**This diagram shows a basic marine food web.**

The diagram shows a marine food web. The word *marine* means anything that has to do with the oceans or seas.

Food webs are very important to humans. Any change to one organism in a food web affects all the other organisms in the food web. Natural events, such as hurricanes and earthquakes, cause some major changes to food webs. Humans cause changes to marine food webs by overfishing or **pollution**. It is important to learn about food webs so that you can help to keep them **balanced**.

---

**pollution**   something that makes the air, water, or soil dirty

**balanced**   steady, secure

**commercial shrimp boat**

**Before You Go On**   What can cause changes to food webs?

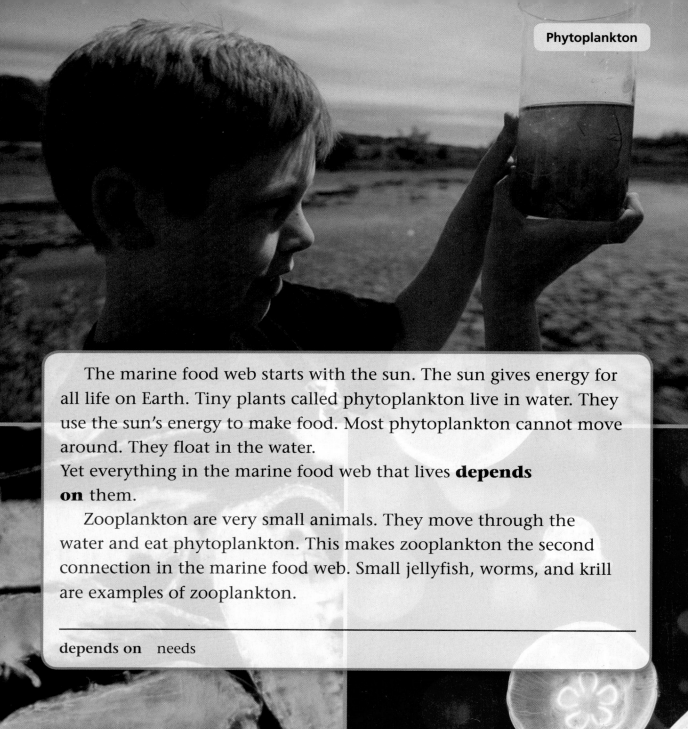

The marine food web starts with the sun. The sun gives energy for all life on Earth. Tiny plants called phytoplankton live in water. They use the sun's energy to make food. Most phytoplankton cannot move around. They float in the water.

Yet everything in the marine food web that lives **depends on** them.

Zooplankton are very small animals. They move through the water and eat phytoplankton. This makes zooplankton the second connection in the marine food web. Small jellyfish, worms, and krill are examples of zooplankton.

---

**depends on**   needs

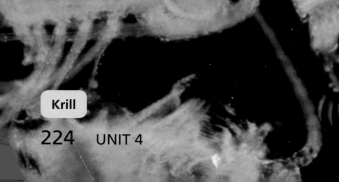

Krill

Jellyfish

School of fish

Hammerhead shark

Many small fish feed on plankton—both phytoplankton and zooplankton. These fish often swim in schools, or groups. This makes it harder for predators, such as sharks, to hunt them.

Some predators also eat plankton. Humpback whales feed on both small fish and plankton.

Humpback whales

**Before You Go On**

What is the **source** of phytoplankton's food?

Great white sharks

Large fish, such as sharks and tuna, eat smaller fish. Other animals that do not spend their entire lives in the water are also part of the marine food web. Penguins and elephant seals also eat fish.

Elephant seal

Penguins

Polar bears and orcas are at the top of the marine food web. This means they have no predators. They live on fish and other marine mammals.

Decomposers in the marine food web include bacteria and scavengers, such as lobsters. Decomposers eat the waste products of other organisms in the marine food web. They also eat dead animals and plants.

**WB**
130–132

## Reading Strategy

### Ask Questions

- What did you learn in this reading?
- What did you have trouble understanding?
- What sections did you reread or ask for assistance with?

## Think It Over

1. **Recall** Why do fish often swim in schools?
2. **Comprehend** What is the **role** of phytoplankton in the marine food web?
3. **Analyze** What are the three **primary** types of organisms in a food web?

# Learning Strategies

## Sequence

The order in which events take place in a process is called the **sequence**. After you read about a process, think about what happened first, second, third, and so on. Recognizing sequence can help you understand and remember the process better.

**( Practice )**

**Number the organisms in order of their place in the food web, beginning with the primary producer, phytoplankton.**

_____ phytoplankton          _____ polar bear

_____ lobster               _____ zooplankton

_____ small fish            _____ large fish

# Use a Sequence Chart

You can use a Sequence Chart to help you remember what happens first, next, and last in a process.

**Copy this chart. Complete it to show a sequence of events in a marine food web. Add more boxes as needed.**

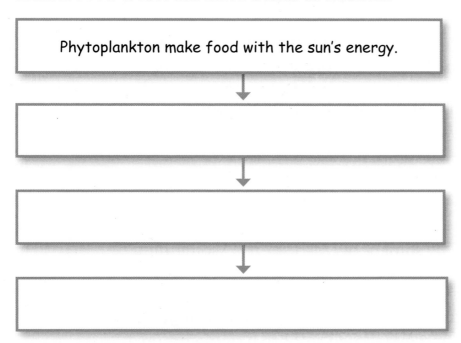

Phytoplankton make food with the sun's energy.

133

**Apply**

**Close your book and retell the selection to a partner.**

## Extension

**Utilize**  Work with a group. Plan and create a poster showing a food chain or web in your biome. Use photos or drawings. Listen carefully to your classmates and work cooperatively. Present your poster.

# Grammar

## Indefinite Pronouns

An **indefinite pronoun** is a word that takes the place of a noun in a sentence. It is not as specific as the pronouns *he, she, we, they,* or *it.* It can be used as a subject or object.

| Indefinite Subject Pronoun | Indefinite Object Pronoun |
|---|---|
| **Someone** called you. | I forgot **something** |

Look at the common indefinite pronouns below. Notice that they end in **-one**, **-body**, or **-thing**.

| Common Singular Indefinite Pronouns | | |
|---|---|---|
| anyone | anybody | anything |
| everyone | everybody | everything |
| someone | somebody | something |
| no one | nobody | nothing |

All of the indefinite pronouns above are considered **singular**. *Everyone, everybody,* and *everything* refer to a single group. A simple present verb must agree.

| Singular | **Everyone** at the party has a piece of cake. |
|---|---|

A few indefinite pronouns are **plural**. They are listed in the chart below.

| Common Plural Indefinite Pronouns | | | |
|---|---|---|---|
| (a) few | both | many | several |

| Plural | **Both** of the students have their books. |
|---|---|

## Practice

Complete the sentences with the correct simple present form of the verb. Write the sentences.

**Example:** <u>Does</u> anyone want to see a crab? (do)

1. Both _____ predators. (be)

2. No one _____ the answer. (know)

3. Many in the ocean food web _____ consumers. (be)

4. Something _____ to provide food for fish. (have)

5. A few _____ north in the summer for food. (travel)

6. Everybody _____ interested in going to the aquarium. (be)

7. Anything that _____ is part of the marine food web. (live)

8. Everything in the food web _____ on phytoplankton. (depend)

## Apply

Work with a partner. Make statements about what you learned in *Marine Food Web.* Use indefinite pronouns from the lists on the facing page. Then write your statements in your notebook.

134

**Example:** A: Everything is part of a food web.

B: Many living things are consumers, and some are producers.
Their role is to produce food.

### Grammar Check ✔

Name some indefinite pronouns that are singular. Name some that are plural.

# Writing

## Explain a Process

Ongoing Writing Skills Practice

Expository writing sometimes explains how something is made or how something happens. To do this, the writer presents a series of steps. The steps follow one another in a logical order.

### Writing Prompt

Write a paragraph that explains a process in nature. It might be a food web, or the migration habits of an animal, or how a plant grows. Be sure to use indefinite pronouns correctly.

## ❶ Prewrite  G.O. 144

Choose a process in nature to write about. Think about the steps in the process and how to present them in a logical order. List each step on a graphic organizer.

A student named Champey listed her ideas like this:

## ❷ Draft

Use your graphic organizer to write a draft. Keep in mind your purpose for writing—to explain a process in nature. Use sequence words such as *first, before, next, after, then* and *finally* to show the order in which things happen.

> **STEP 1:** First, rain or wind pushes the seed into the earth.

> **STEP 2:** Then the seed takes in water.

> **STEP 3:** Next, the first root grows from the seed and pushes into the soil. Tiny hairs from the root begin to take in water.

> **STEP 4:** Finally, after the root is long enough, the plant pokes its head above ground.

> **STEP 5:** When the plant grows leaves, it can make its own food from the sun.

## ❸ Revise

Read over your draft. Look for places where the writing needs improvement. Use the Writing Checklist to help you identify problems. Then revise your draft.

## ❹ Edit

Check your work for errors in grammar, usage, mechanics, and spelling. Trade papers with a partner to get feedback. Use the Peer Review Checklist on Workbook page 404.

## ❺ Publish

Prepare a clean copy of your final draft. Share your paragraph with the class.

Here is Champey's paragraph:

## Writing Checklist

**Ideas**

✓ I presented the steps in a logical order.

**Word Choice**

✓ I used sequence words.

**Conventions**

✓ I used indefinite pronouns correctly.

Champey Seng

Everyone knows that a seed has a tiny new plant inside of it. How does it grow? First, rain or wind pushes the seed into the earth. Then the seed takes in water. Next, the first root grows out from the seed. It pushes deep into the soil. Tiny hairs from the root begin to take in water from the ground. Finally, after the root has grown long enough, the plant pokes its head above ground. There is food inside the seed to keep the young plant growing. When the plant forms leaves, it is able to make its own food using light from the sun.

WB
135–136

### What You Will Learn

**Reading**

- Vocabulary building:
  *Context, word study*

- Reading strategy:
  *Identify fact and opinion*

- Text type:
  *Informational text (magazine article)*

**Grammar**
Transitional words

**Writing**
Organize ideas by cause and effect

These words will help you understand the reading.

**Key Words**

endangered

litter

pollution

illegal

conservation

protect

# Key Words

## Words in Context

**1** Many animals, such as the African elephant, are endangered. That is, they may soon not exist in the wild.

**2** When people litter, or throw garbage on the ground, I try to pick it up.

**3** Smoke from factories is one cause of air pollution.

**4** It is illegal, or against the law, to go too fast when you are driving down the road.

**5** Many people are concerned about the conservation of wildlife. They would like to create special places where animals will be safe.

**6** It is natural for a mother to protect her newborn baby from harm.

## Practice

**Make flashcards to help you memorize the words.**

- Write a word on the front.
- On the back, write a sentence, but leave a blank where the key word should be.

## Make Connections

Many people care for and own animals as pets. Do you or someone you know have a pet? What type of an animal is it? What care does this animal need?

WB
137

These words will help you talk about the reading.

## Academic Words

**contribute**
help make something happen

**cycle**
a number of related events that happen again and again in the same order

**enabled**
made it possible for something to happen

138

# Academic Words

## Words in Context

A flat tire could **contribute** to a bike accident.

The life **cycle** of a plant begins when a seed starts to grow and ends when the plant dies.

Practicing every night has **enabled** me to play a difficult piece on the piano.

### Practice

**Write the sentences in your notebook. Choose an academic word to complete each sentence.**

1. Reading books at home _____ her to become a better reader.

2. Each year the weather _____ repeats as the seasons change from spring to summer, to fall, and then winter.

3. Many things, from cars to factories, _____ to air pollution.

### Apply

**Ask and answer with a partner.**

1. Can you describe the life **cycle** of a butterfly?

2. How does your teacher **contribute** to your understanding of the world?

3. How has using graphic organizers **enabled** you to become a better writer?

# Word Study

## Commonly Confused Words

Words that sound the same, or almost the same, but have different spellings can cause problems for writers.

> • **It's** fascinating to watch sea turtles swim.
>
> • A turtle is protected by **its** hard shell.

**Practice**

**Work with a partner. Choose the correct word for each sentence.**

1. The turtle laid (its, it's) eggs in the sand.

2. Turtles are famous for (they're, their) long lives.

3. Sea turtles are usually larger (than, then) land turtles.

4. With (your, you're) help, sea turtles can be saved.

5. We saw the turtles swim (threw, through) the water.

6. Everyone was at the beach (except, accept) Carlos.

**INFORMATIONAL TEXT**

Magazine Article

### More About

THE BIG QUESTION

What can people do to save endangered wildlife?

 **Listen to the Audio.**

Listen for the main points and important details.

### Reading Strategy

#### Identify Fact and Opinion

A fact can be proven. An opinion is what someone thinks. As you read, ask yourself:

- Which statements can be proven?
- Which statements are opinions that can't be proven?
- What clue words show a statement is an opinion?

Listen as your teacher models the reading strategy.

# Save the Sea Turtles

## By Nina Hess

Sea turtles have been swimming in the oceans for millions of years, since long before dinosaurs. But now their lives are in danger, and if we don't take action to help them, they will die out forever.

## The Most Endangered Turtle

Five different **species** of sea turtles live in the warm waters of the Gulf of Mexico. The smallest are called Kemp's ridley turtles. They are the most endangered turtle species in the world.

---

**species** group of animals or plants whose members are similar and breed together to produce young

A Kemp's ridley turtle

Kemp's ridley turtles make nests along the beaches of Mexico near Rancho Nuevo. Each year, the females gather in the waters along the shore. Then all together, they crawl out of the water and dig nests in the sand. Each turtle lays about a hundred eggs and then returns to the ocean.

**Before You Go On** What **cycle** does a sea turtle follow to lay its eggs?

## What's Killing the Turtles?

In 1947, forty thousand Kemp's ridley turtles came ashore to lay eggs. By 1985, only about two hundred of these turtles came ashore. What happened to all the turtles?

Many years ago, people liked to eat turtles. Therefore, they killed them for meat and **collected** and ate their eggs. They also hung their shells on their walls. By the 1960s, the United States and Mexico **realized** that the Kemp's ridley turtles were in terrible danger. These governments passed laws making taking turtle eggs illegal.

---

**collected**   found and kept

**realized**   suddenly understood something

Kemp's ridley turtle

A turtle exclusion device allows turtles to get out of the nets while smaller animals like shrimp cannot.

Many turtles still died. Many choked on the plastic bags littering the ocean. Many more were trapped in shrimp fishing nets and drowned.

In 1989, the U.S. government passed a law requiring shrimp fishermen to use a special net with openings at the bottom and the top that allows larger animals like turtles and sharks to swim free. This law has helped a little. However, there are still major threats to the safety of Kemp's ridley turtles, especially pollution and litter. In 2010, for example, an oil rig exploded and caused 4.9 million gallons of oil to spill into the Gulf of Mexico. The spilled oil damaged the beaches where Kemp's ridley turtles nest and the water where they live.

**Before You Go On** What are some problems that **contribute** to the death of turtles?

Try not to disturb a nesting turtle or turtle eggs.

## How to Help

If you want to help the Kemp's ridley turtles, there are many ways you can get **involved** and make a difference.

First of all, talk to your parents, your friends, and your teachers about the turtles. Ask them to help you **support** turtle conservation. The more people who know about the problem, the more will get involved, and the sooner the turtles can get the help they need.

Never litter and be sure to pick up any trash you see, especially along the shore. And kick the plastic bag habit! Help your parents remember to bring reusable bags to the grocery store instead of using plastic bags.

---

**involved**   take part in something

**support**   help by giving time or money

If you see a turtle that has been damaged by oil, do not touch it. Protect the turtle from animals, **vehicles**, and people. If you are near the Gulf of Mexico, call the Wildlife Hotline at 1-866-557-1401 for help.

Finally, write a letter to the president asking him to create a marine **reserve** in the Gulf of Mexico. The marine reserve will be a place where turtles can swim free and fishing boats are not allowed. It will be the best way to make sure sea turtles will be around for millions more years to come.

---

**vehicles**   machines such as cars, buses, etc., that carry people or things

**reserve**   an area of land where wild animals are safe

140–142

## Reading Strategy

### Identify Fact and Opinion

- Name three statements that are facts that can be proven.
- Name three statements that are opinions.
- What clue words showed that the statements were opinions?

## Think It Over

1. **Recall**   How did the laws that were passed in the 1960s help **contribute** to saving sea turtles?
2. **Comprehend**   What are some things you can do to help sea turtles survive?
3. **Analyze**   How might a marine reserve **enable** sea turtle numbers to grow?

# Learning Strategies

## Identify Fact and Opinion

By **identifying facts and opinions** as you read, you can make better judgements about the content of a text. Remember that:

- Facts are points that are true and can be proven.
- Opinions are points that someone makes based on what they believe.

### Practice

**Tell whether each statement below is a fact or an opinion.**

1. Sea turtles have been swimming in the oceans for millions of years.
2. Five different species of sea turtles live off the Gulf Coast.
3. Kemp's ridley turtles are the most beautiful turtles in the Gulf of Mexico.
4. More laws should be passed to support turtle conservation .
5. Marine reserves can help protect marine creatures.
6. Shrimp fishermen care only about the number of shrimp they catch.

These animals are also on the critically endangered animal list.

# Use an Idea Web

An Idea Web can help you see how different ideas
in a story are connected.

**Copy this Idea Web. Complete it to show what you know
about ways to help save the** endangered **Kemp's ridley turtles.**

- Share your work with a partner.
- Discuss each idea and the affect it has on the
  sea turtles.

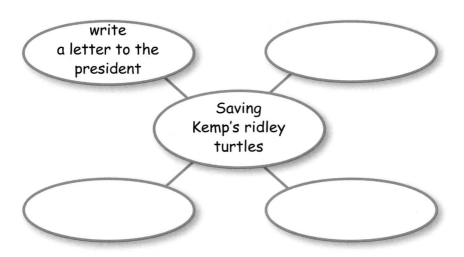

W B
194

## Apply

**Reread the selection and take notes.
Then close your book and retell the
selection to a partner.**

## Extension

**Utilize**   Work cooperatively
with a partner. Choose another
endangered animal. Do
research to find out why the
animal is endangered and how
you might help save it. Then
share what you learned with
the class.

# Grammar

## Transitional Words

**Transitional words,** are connecting words that show relationships between sentences. Some connecting words show **addition**.

| Also | In addition | As well as |
|---|---|---|
| Turtles have hard shells. In addition, they have sharp claws. | | |

Some connecting words show **contrast**.

| However | On the other hand | Instead |
|---|---|---|
| These turtles don't live on land. Instead, they live in the sea. | | |

Some are used to give an **example**.

| For example | For instance | Such as |
|---|---|---|
| Turtles have long lives. For example, one lived 250 years. | | |

Some tell a **result**.

| Therefore | As a result | For this reason |
|---|---|---|
| Turtles are endangered. Therefore, they should be protected. | | |

Remember to use a **comma** after introductory transitional phrases at the beginning of a sentence.

| I care about sea turtles. **As a result,** I work to protect them. |
|---|

**Practice**

Choose the best transitional word for each sentence. Write the sentences.

**Example:** Endangered animals <u>such as</u> Kemp's ridley turtles need our help! (instead, such as)

1. Plastic bags on the beach are ugly. _____ they can endanger a turtle's nest. (in addition, as a result)

2. Conservation does help turtles. _____ some say more efforts are needed. (however, such as)

3. People **contribute** to the problem. _____ littering and pollution hurt sea life. (in contrast, for instance)

4. Laws to conserve energy are being passed. _____ new technologies **enable** us to save more power, too. (for example, in addition)

5. Many people contributed money. _____ the organization can continue to protect wildlife. (in contrast, therefore)

**Apply**

Work with a partner. Use transitional words to make statements about saving sea turtles. Then write them in your notebook.

W B

144

**Example:** A: Sea turtles have been swimming in the ocean for millions of years. However, their lives are in danger these days.

B: Kemp's ridley turtles are endangered. However, laws have been passed to protect turtles.

**Grammar Check** ✓

Name some transition words that show addition, contrast, example, and result.

# Writing

## Organize Ideas by Cause and Effect

In expository text, writers often organize information by showing cause-and-effect relationships. A cause makes something happen. An effect is the result.

### Writing Prompt

Write a paragraph about an animal that is endangered or needs protection. Show causes and effects. Use transitional words.

### ❶ Prewrite  G.O. 148

Choose an animal to write about. Think about why the animal needs protection. List cause-and-effect relationships in a graphic organizer.

A student named Jorgé wrote about the ocelot, a small, endangered wildcat that lives in Central and South America, Mexico, Arizona, and Texas. He listed his ideas like this:

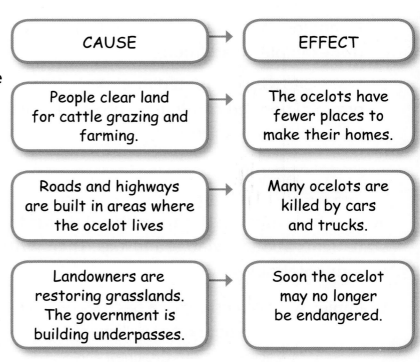

| CAUSE | → | EFFECT |
| --- | --- | --- |
| People clear land for cattle grazing and farming. | → | The ocelots have fewer places to make their homes. |
| Roads and highways are built in areas where the ocelot lives | → | Many ocelots are killed by cars and trucks. |
| Landowners are restoring grasslands. The government is building underpasses. | → | Soon the ocelot may no longer be endangered. |

### ❷ Draft

Use your graphic organizer to write a draft. Use transitional words and phrases such as *therefore, for this reason,* and *as a result.*

## ❸ Revise

Read over your draft. Use the Writing Checklist to help you identify problems. Then revise your draft.

## ❹ Edit

Check your work for errors in grammar, usage, mechanics, and spelling. Trade papers with a partner to get feedback. Use the Peer Review Checklist on Workbook page 404.

## ❺ Publish

Prepare a clean copy of your final draft. Share your paragraph with the class.

Here is Jorgé's paragraph:

## Writing Checklist

**Ideas**

✓ My ideas were clear.

**Organization**

✓ I organized my writing to show cause and effect.

**Conventions**

✓ I used transitional words.

Jorgé Martinez

The ocelot is a small wildcat with golden fur and black spots. For this reason, it is sometimes called "America's little leopard." About 200 years ago there were many ocelots living in the grasslands of Arizona and South Texas. Today, there are fewer than 100 left. The areas where they live are now covered with cattle ranches and farms. As a result, ocelots have fewer places to make their homes. Roads and highways are another problem for ocelots. More ocelots die from being hit by cars and trucks than from any other cause. However, there is hope. Many landowners are restoring grasslands to give ocelots a place to live. In addition, the government is building underpasses to help ocelots cross roads safely. Soon, the ocelot may no longer be endangered.

WB
145–146

# Apply and Extend

## Link the Readings

Copy the chart into your notebook. Read the words in the top row. For each text selection, put an X under words related to that reading.

|  | Informational text | Literature | Protecting animals | How animals survive |
|---|---|---|---|---|
| *Biomes All Over the World* |  |  |  |  |
| *Marine Food Web* |  |  |  |  |
| *Save the Sea Turtles* |  |  |  |  |

## Discussion

1. How do the different biomes **contribute** to our lives?

2. What **role** do humans play in changing marine food webs?

3. How have people's actions endangered Kemp's ridley turtles?
   How can people help **enable** the turtles to survive?

 How do people and environments affect each other?

> **Listening Skills**
>
> If someone is speaking too quickly, you can ask, "Could you speak a little more slowly, please?"

# Projects

**Your teacher will help you choose one of these projects.**

|  **Written** |  **Oral** |  **Visual/Active** |
|---|---|---|
| **List** | **Presentation** | **Poster** |
| Write a list that shows details about an interesting biome. Include the climate, along with animals and plants that live there. | Research an animal in your biome. Make a presentation that explains what the animal looks like, where it lives, what it eats, and its role in a food web. | Create a poster that shows the animals and plants in an interesting biome. Show how people can help the animals found there. |
| **Magazine Article** | **Song** | **Illustration** |
| Choose a biome. Write a magazine article that explains how people affect animals in that biome. Describe some of the things people can do to help those animals. | Work as a group. Write and perform a song that tells how people can help animals live safely in a biome, such as an ocean or a forest. | You read about a marine food web. Learn about another kind of food web. Create an illustration that shows how the food web's food chains are connected. |

 *For more projects visit*
 *LongmanCornerstone.com*

# Further Reading

 ***Rumpelstiltskin***
In this Penguin Young Reader® version of a classic fairytale, a queen must find out the name of a mysterious little man in time to save her family.

***Welcome to the Sea of Sand,*** Jane Yolen
Arizona's Sonoran Desert, the magnificent "sea of sand" home to a wide variety of animals, is described in an exciting way with colorful illustrations.

147-148

# Listening and Speaking Workshop

## Give a How-to Presentation

You are going to write and give a how-to presentation about staying safe in a dangerous situation. You will listen as your classmates give their presentations.

## ❶ Prepare

**A.** Choose a dangerous situation such as encountering a bear, shark, or rattlesnake, or being in a lightning storm, tornado, or hurricane, or getting lost in the wilderness.

**B.** Think about what you already know. Research answers to other questions you have. Then write your how-to presentation as step-by-step instructions. Find props to use in your presentation. Remember that your classmates will ask you questions after your presentation.

**Staying Safe in a Lightning Storm**

A lightning storm is very dangerous. More people die each year in lightning storms than in any other kind of weather. Here are the steps to take to keep you safe during a lightning storm.

If you are outside, try to find shelter in a building or a car. If you can't, put your feet together. Then crouch down near the ground and place your hands over your ears.

# ❷ Practice

Find a partner. Practice your presentation in front of your partner. Your partner will act out or mime your instructions to show he or she understands. Work with your partner to improve your presentation.

# ❸ Present

**As you speak,** do the following:
- Speak clearly and loudly enough for everyone to hear.
- Slow down and use your props to make important points.
- Use gestures and facial expressions.

**As you listen,** do the following:
- Think about or visualize what you are hearing.
- Take notes on the presentation.
- Think of questions to ask the speaker after the presentation.

# ❹ Evaluate

**After you speak,** answer these questions:
- ✓ Did you present each idea clearly?
- ✓ Did you use props to help make important points?

**After you listen,** answer these questions:
- ✓ Did you understand the main points and details of the presentation?
- ✓ What information did you find most interesting and useful?

**Speaking Skills**

How-to presentations are formal situations. Use formal sentence structures, grammar, and vocabulary. Don't use slang.

**Listening Skills**

Be an active listener. Listen carefully to the spoken words. Look at the speaker's gestures and visuals.

# Writing Workshop

## Write a Compare-and-Contrast Essay

Ongoing Writing Skills Practice

### Writing Prompt

Write an essay in which you compare and contrast two things based on facts and your own experience. You might compare two places you have visited, or two books you have read. Use signal words such as *both, also, however,* and *unlike* to point out similarities and differences. Include an introduction and conclusion.

### ❶ Prewrite

Review your previous work in this unit. Now choose a topic. Think about two things you have experienced or researched that you would like to compare and contrast. List details about the experience in a Venn Diagram.

DENVER

500,000 people, mountains, cold and snowy

SAME

Large cities, beautiful scenery, cold in winter

CHICAGO

2,700,000 people, lake front, hot and humid

### ❷ Draft

Use your graphic organizer to help you write a draft. Keep in mind your purpose for writing—to compare and contrast two things. Be sure to use signal words.

## ❸ Revise

Read over your draft. Look for places where the writing needs improvement. Use the Writing Checklist to help you identify problems. Then revise your draft.

## Six Traits of Writing Checklist

✔ **Ideas**
Did I describe my topic using facts and my own experience?

✔ **Organization**
Did I use good transition words between ideas?

✔ **Voice**
Did I show my knowledge about the subject?

✔ **Word Choice**
Did I use signal words to compare and contrast?

✔ **Sentence Fluency**
Did I use a variety of different sentence lengths and patterns?

✔ **Conventions**
Do my nouns, pronouns, and verbs agree?

---

Sofia Perez

### Denver and Chicago

My family moved from Denver, Colorado, to Chicago, Illinois, last year. Denver and Chicago are very different. **, but** They are also similar in some ways.

Chicago and Denver are both large cities, but Chicago is much larger. Denver **has** ~~have~~ a population of around 500,000, while Chicago has over two million people.

Both Chicago and Denver have interesting scenery. In Denver, you can see the **R**rocky **M**mountains, some of the tallest mountains in the world. Chicago is much fla**t**ter than Denver, and there are not any mountains. However, Chicago is on Lake Michigan. You can stand on the lake front and see water that stretches forever.

Chicago and Denver both get cold in winter, but it's even snowier in Denver. **On the other hand,** Summers in Chicago are much hotter and more humid. You have to use air-conditioning a lot more.

Both Denver and Chicago are interesting cities. I enjoy the ways they are similar and the ways they are different.

**Revised** to create a compound sentence.

**Revised** to correct error in subject-verb agreement.

**Revised** to correct error in capitalization.

**Revised** to correct error in spelling.

**Revised** to include signal words to connect the ideas.

## ❹ Edit

Check your work for errors. Trade papers with a partner. Use the Peer Review Checklist to give each other feedback. Edit your final draft in response to feedback from your partner and your teacher.

## ❺ Publish

Make a clean copy of your final draft. Share your essay with the class.

149–150

**Peer Review Checklist**

✓  The essay is informative.

✓  Signal words are used to compare and contrast

✓  All the information is related to the topic.

## SPELLING TIP

You can use a computer's spell check to check your spelling, but the computer can't tell if you mean *weather* or *whether*. You must still check your spelling carefully.

**Denver**

**Chicago**

**Listen to the sentences. Pay attention to the groups of words. Read aloud.**

1. Earth has many different biomes with a variety of plants and animals.

2. A food chain shows one way that energy travels between producers, consumers, and decomposers.

3. If you want to help the Kemp's ridley turtles, there are many ways you can get involved and make a difference.

| | |
|---|---|
| A biome is a community where certain kinds of plants | 10 |
| and animals live. Earth has more than 30 different kinds | 20 |
| of biomes. The most common are tropical rain forests, | 29 |
| tundra, mountains, grasslands, deserts, and oceans. | 35 |
| Mountains are on every continent on Earth. Most | 43 |
| mountains have forests at the bottom of them. The higher | 53 |
| you go up a mountain, the colder and windier it gets. | 64 |
| The tops of very high mountains look like the tundra. | 74 |
| Only small plants and flowers grow in these areas. | 83 |
| The ocean biome is the largest biome on Earth. Oceans | 92 |
| are huge bodies of water. They make up 70 percent of | 103 |
| Earth's surface. Many kinds of animals and plants live | 112 |
| in oceans. Fish, crabs, and clams spend their lives | 121 |
| under water. Larger animals, such as whales, sharks, | 129 |
| and dolphins, also live in the ocean. Blue whales live | 139 |
| in the ocean. They are the largest known mammals on Earth. | 151 |

**With your partner, find the words that slowed you down.**

- Practice saying each word and then say the sentence each word is in.
- Take turns reading the text again. Count the number of words you read.

# Test Preparation

## Taking Tests

You will often take tests that help show what you know. Follow these tips to improve your test-taking skills.

## Coaching Corner

**Answering Questions That Have Pictures or Graphics**

- Some test questions include pictures or graphics.

- You must read the text and look at the picture or graphic in order to answer one or more of the questions.

- Before reading the selection, look at the picture or graphic. Make sure you understand it.

- Next, preview the questions and answer choices.

- If there is text with the picture or graphic, read it next.

- After you read the selection, read the questions. Look at the graphic or picture again.

- Then choose the answer that comes closest to the answer in your head.

Read the following test sample. Study the tips in the box.

153–154

**Read the selection and the chart. Then answer the questions.**

1    When the female turtle is ready to lay her eggs, she comes out of the water and onto the beach. There, she digs a nest. The nest looks like a hole in the sand. She lays her eggs in the hole and covers them up with sand. Hiding the eggs makes it hard for predators to find the eggs and eat them.

2    The hatchlings, or baby turtles, are in great danger as soon as they hatch. Many animals and birds think the hatchlings are a tasty meal. The hatchlings run as fast as they can into the sea. With luck, they will grow up and have their own young.

| 1 | 2 | 3 | 4 | 6 |
|---|---|---|---|---|
| Female sea turtle arrives on the beach. | _____ _____ _____ | Female sea turtle returns to the sea. | Young sea turtles (called hatchlings) hatch. | Hatchlings go into the sea where they live and grow. |

1   Why do the baby turtles run into the sea after they hatch?
   A   Many birds and animals like to eat them.
   B   It is too hot for them to live on the beach.
   C   The male sea turtle wants to eat the hatchlings.
   D   The hatchlings are not in danger on the beach.

2   Look at the chart. Which of these belongs on the blank line?
   F   Female sea turtle swims and lays her eggs in the water.
   G   Female sea turtle digs a hole in the sand and lays eggs.
   H   The hatchlings dig holes in the sand to hide themselves.
   J   The hatchings grow up to be sea turtles and have babies.

**Tips**

✔ This item has a graphic and some text. Make sure you look at both before you try to answer the questions.

✔ You can eliminate answer choices that don't make sense. Then you can make a guess from the remaining answer choices.

# Sounds and Music

Playing instruments, listening, singing, and dancing are all ways we can appreciate sounds and music.

## Reading

### 1 | Social Studies

**Touching Sound with Evelyn Glennie**

### 2 | Social Studies

**A Song Map**

### 3 | Social Studies

**Elvis Presley
Austin: The Live Music Capital of the World**

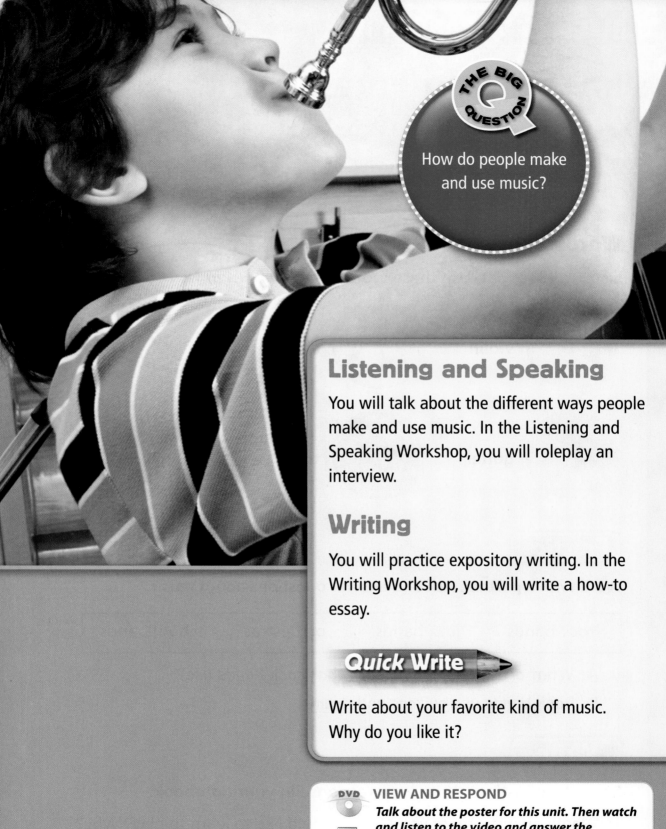

How do people make
and use music?

## Listening and Speaking

You will talk about the different ways people
make and use music. In the Listening and
Speaking Workshop, you will roleplay an
interview.

## Writing

You will practice expository writing. In the
Writing Workshop, you will write a how-to
essay.

### *Quick* Write

Write about your favorite kind of music.
Why do you like it?

**DVD** VIEW AND RESPOND
*Talk about the poster for this unit. Then watch
and listen to the video and answer the
questions at LongmanCornerstone.com.*

# What do you know about sounds and music?

## Words to Know

Listen and repeat. Use these words to talk about music.

 violin

 drum

 flute

 guitar

 trumpet

 cello

## Practice

Work with a partner. Ask and answer questions about music.

| rock bands | jazz bands | orchestras | school bands |
|---|---|---|---|

A: What are some instruments that <u>rock bands</u> use?

B: <u>Rock bands</u> use <u>guitars and drums</u>.

## Write

Read the question. Write your response in your notebook.

What's an instrument you play or would like to learn to play? Why?

## Make Connections

Copy the sentences below into your notebook. Complete the sentences with the following words.

 strumming

 striking

 blowing

 bowing

1. You play a guitar by _____ its strings with your hands and a guitar pick.

2. You play a drum by _____ it with drumsticks.

3. You play a flute by _____ across a hole at one end called the mouthpiece.

4. You play a drum by _____ its strings with a bow.

## What about you?

Talk with a partner. Talk about your favorite instruments. Why do you like them? Do you have any favorite musicians?

# Kids' Stories from around the World

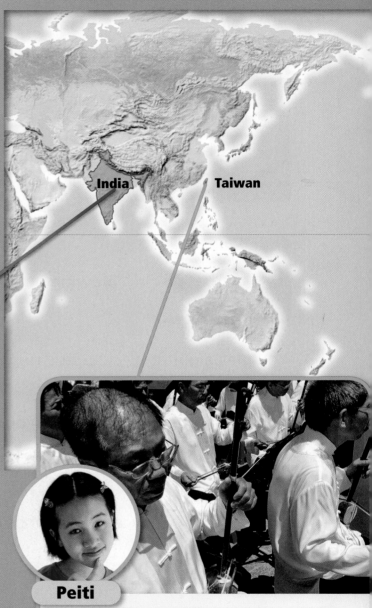

India          Taiwan

## Janak

Varanasi, India, is famous for its beautiful music. I am learning to play the *tabla* at school. One drum of the tabla is called the *daya*. It makes high sounds. The *baya* makes low sounds. These drums make the most beautiful sounds in Indian music.

## Peiti

I live in Taiwan. My parents play in the orchestra of the Ho-Lo Opera Troupe. In Taiwanese opera, the orchestra is divided into two parts. My mother plays the violin in the part of the orchestra called the *Wen Cheng*. My father plays the drums in the *Wu Cheng*. When I grow up, I hope to join the orchestra, too!

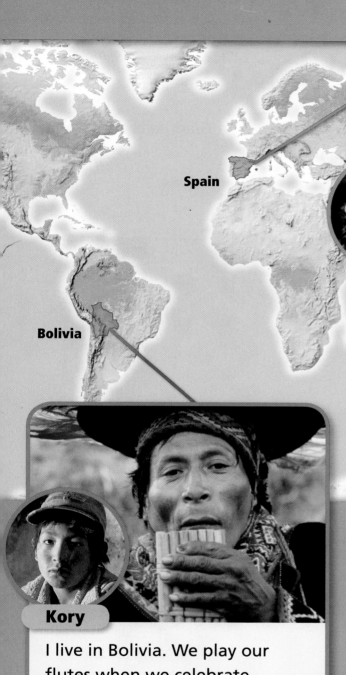

**Spain**

**Bolivia**

**Inez**

I live in Antequera, the heart of flamenco in Spain! I am going to school to be a flamenco singer. I am learning to dance. I am also learning to play the guitar and the *palillos*, or castanets. I want to share the rhythms of flamenco with the world.

**Kory**

I live in Bolivia. We play our flutes when we celebrate Carnival and other festivals. We carve the flutes carefully from wood. They make such beautiful sounds that people all over the world play them.

## What about you?

1. What kind of traditional music do people perform in the country you are from?

2. Do you have stories about traditional music where you are from? Share your story.

## What You Will Learn

**Reading**

- Vocabulary building: *Context, phonics*

- Reading strategy: *Identify main idea and details*

- Text type: *Informational (social studies)*

**Grammar**
Subordinating conjunctions

**Writing**
Problem and solution

These words will help you understand the reading.

### Key Words

- **instruments**
- **percussion**
- **vibrations**
- **notes**
- **composition**
- **award**

# Key Words

*Touching Sound with Evelyn Glennie* is about a world-famous musician.

## Words in Context   *Audio*

**①** Musicians play many different **instruments**.

**②** Drums are **percussion** instruments.

**③** Sounds travel as **vibrations** in the air. These vibrations enter the ear.

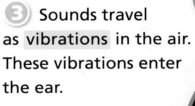

**4** Songwriters write music with musical notes . Each note stands for a sound.

**5** A song is one type of composition , or written musical piece.

**6** Musicians sometimes receive an award , or prize, for their work.

**Practice**

**Make flashcards to help you memorize the words.**

- Write a key word on the front.

- On the back, write a sentence, but leave a blank where the key word should be.

## Make Connections

Sit silently for one minute with your eyes closed. Then write a list of the different sounds you heard.

These words will help you talk about the reading.

### Academic Words

**achievements**
successful things a person does

**cease**
stop doing something

**perceive**
become aware of by using one's senses

# Academic Words

## Words in Context

Winning the game was one of my finest **achievements**.

I hope this rain will **cease** soon.

A dog can **perceive** sounds and smells that people cannot.

### Practice

**Write the sentences in your notebook. Choose an academic word to complete each sentence.**

1. Getting the highest grade on the test was a great _____.

2. Everyone needs to _____ talking before the presentation begins.

3. Although it was very dark, I could _____ a light in the distance.

### Apply

**Ask and answer with a partner.**

1. Which of your recent **achievements** are you most proud of?

2. Everyone has bad habits. What habit would you like to **cease**?

3. What senses do you use to **perceive** danger?

# Phonics

## Past -ed ending: id, d, t

The ending -ed is often part of past tense verbs. Listen.
Identify whether the final -ed is pronounced id, d, or t. Then
read the sentences aloud.

> Evelyn's performance was film**ed** for a documentary call**ed** *Touch
> the Sound*. The audience applaud**ed** when she finish**ed** playing.

### Rule

After words ending in *d* or *t*, the final -ed is pronounced *id*. It is
pronounced *d* after voiced consonants like *b, g, l, m, n, r,* or *v*. It
is pronounced *t* after voiceless consonants like *f, k, p, s,* or digraphs
like *sh* or *ch*.

### Practice

**Work with a partner.
Take turns.**

- Write five other words
  with the ending -ed.
- Ask your partner to
  read each word and
  tell whether the -ed is
  pronounced id, d, or t.

157

## INFORMATIONAL TEXT

### Social Studies

**More about**

How can you hear without using your ears?

 **Listen to the Audio.**

Listen for the main points and important details.

## Reading Strategy

### Identify Main Idea and Details

As you read, ask yourself:

- What is the selection about?
- What is the most important idea?
- What details help support the main idea?

Listen as your teacher models the reading strategy.

# Touching Sound with Evelyn Glennie

**by Trish Marx**

People walking through Grand Central Station in New York City often hear musicians performing. Musicians like to play there because of the large crowds.

One day, people gathered in Grand Central to hear Evelyn Glennie play her snare drum. She is the first percussionist in the world who made a career of performing as a **soloist.** Evelyn's performance was filmed for a **documentary** called *Touch the Sound.* The audience applauded when she finished playing.

Many people watching Evelyn did not know she couldn't hear the music she played. She is almost completely **deaf**.

---

**soloist**   musician who performs alone

**documentary**   movie about real people and events

**deaf**   unable to hear

**The marimbas are one of many instruments Evelyn Glennie plays.**

Evelyn grew up on a farm in Scotland. There was a piano in her home. As a young child, she asked her parents to let her take piano lessons. They let her take lessons when she was eight years old. Evelyn soon found out she had what musicians call "perfect pitch." She could hear the notes perfectly in her mind. This was good, because she was slowly losing her hearing.

Evelyn found that **hearing aids** kept her from being able to **perceive** sounds with the rest of her body. She stopped wearing them when she was 12 years old. Evelyn knew she could hear the correct music notes in her mind. She also used her body to feel the vibrations the instruments made. She learned to play many percussion instruments. This surprised her teachers, who thought Evelyn would not be able to play music once she lost her hearing.

**hearing aids**   small devices worn in the ear to make sounds louder

**Kettle drums are also called timpani.**

**Before You Go On**   **How does Evelyn perceive sounds?**

Evelyn loved the way music made her feel—sometimes happy, sometimes sad, but always alive.

She studied at the Royal Academy of Music after high school. She has had a successful **career** as a musician ever since.

On her Web site, Evelyn says, "Hearing is a special form of touch. Deafness does not mean that you can't hear. It only means that there is something wrong with the ears."

Evelyn uses her whole body to feel sounds. She often performs barefoot.

"Anything you can pick can create a sound," says Evelyn.

Evelyn plays well-known percussion instruments such as the snare, kettle, and bass drums. She also plays marimbas, xylophones, gongs, and the water drums pictured below. She has been filmed creating music using common objects, such as plates, pots and pans, bottles, pipes, and glasses filled with water.

---

**career**   job or profession

These are
water drums.

Evelyn performs in more than 100 concerts each year. She has won many awards for her music, including several Grammy Awards. These awards recognize high **achievement** in making and recording music. Evelyn has performed with some of the world's most famous musicians and orchestras. She writes and produces her own music. Many musicians have written compositions for her to play.

When she is not performing or writing music, Evelyn works hard to improve music education in schools in the United Kingdom. She also enjoys riding her motorcycle and making jewelry.

If you are **inspired** by Evelyn's life and music, learn more about your favorite instrument, and make your own music.

Evelyn performs more than 100 concerts each year.

---

**inspired**   given energy to do something

WB
158–160

## Think It Over

1. **Recall**   What instruments does Evelyn play?
2. **Comprehend**   Why did she cease wearing hearing aids?
3. **Analyze**   What are some of Evelyn's major achievements?

# Learning Strategies

## Main Idea and Details

The **main idea** is the most important idea in a selection. **Details** give information about the main idea. The details support the main idea by telling important facts.

**Practice**

**Read the sentences below.**

- Evelyn says hearing is a special form of touch.
- Evelyn could feel the vibrations the instruments made.
- Musicians play in Grand Central Station because of the large crowds.
- Evelyn Glennie's story proves that people can overcome challenges.

  **1.** Which sentence tells the main idea?
  **2.** Which two sentences tell important details to support the main idea?

# Use a Main Idea and Details Chart

Writers use details to help explain the main idea. A Main Idea and Details Chart can help you see a writer's plan.

Copy this Main Idea and Details Chart. Add the main idea from the previous page. Then reread the selection and add three new details.

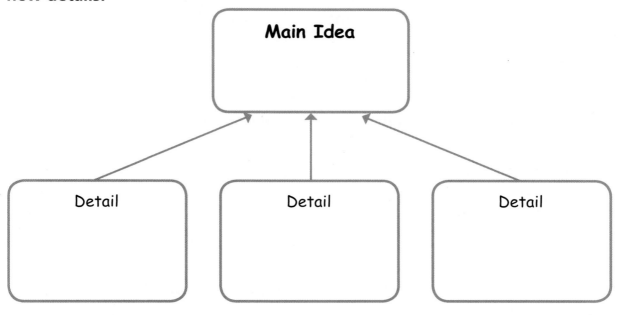

Close your book and retell the selection to a partner. Use the key and academic words.

161

## Extension

**Utilize** Make a brochure of different percussion instruments from around the world. Use pictures, photos, and text to describe the instruments. Share your brochure with the class.

# Grammar

## Subordinating Conjunctions

A **subordinating conjunction** is a connecting word used to combine a **subordinate (dependent) clause** with a **main clause**. Here are some subordinating conjunctions.

| | | | |
|---|---|---|---|
| after | because | once | until |
| although | before | since | when |
| as | if | though | while |

A **main** clause can stand on its own as a **complete thought**. But a **subordinate** (dependent) clause **cannot stand on its own**. It depends on the main clause for its meaning.

| Subordinate Clause | Main Clause |
|---|---|
| **Although** they were fresh, | the cupcakes didn't sell. |

In the example above, the subordinate clause isn't a complete sentence. But the main clause can stand alone as a complete sentence.

The subordinate clause can come at the beginning or end of a sentence. When it is at the **beginning** of the sentence, it is followed by a **comma**.

| Subordinate Clause | Main Clause |
|---|---|
| **While** she was swimming, | she saw a shark. |

| Main Clause | Subordinate Clause |
|---|---|
| He never walks anywhere | **because** he got a bike. |

**Practice**

Complete the sentences with a conjunction from the box below. Write the sentences.

| | |
|---|---|
| after | once |
| although | when |
| because | |

**Example:** <u>Although</u> she is deaf, Evelyn plays percussion instruments.

1. _____ hiring a new producer, the band won several awards .

2. _____ Ed is a beginner, he plays the drums well.

3. _____ they got new instruments , the band sounds better.

4. _____ we're outdoors, we perceive sounds differently.

5. _____ Pat can't read music, she can play the guitar.

6. _____ the train went by, I felt the vibrations .

7. _____ of his talent, he soon became famous.

8. They had good sailing _____ the wind was strong.

**Apply**

Work with a partner. Talk about things you like and dislike. Use sentences with subordinating conjunctions when you can.

**Example:** A: Although I enjoy watching baseball, I think I like soccer better.

B: I do, too. I like soccer better because it's a much faster, more exciting game.

**Grammar Check ✔**

What is the difference between a subordinate and a main clause?

WB
162

# Writing

## Problem and Solution

In expository text, writers often organize information by presenting a problem and offering solutions.

### Writing Prompt

Write a paragraph in which you present a problem and one or more possible solutions. Remember to use subordinating conjunctions, such as *because, although, while,* and *when,* correctly.

## ❶ Prewrite

Choose a problem to write about. List the problem and solutions in a graphic organizer.

A student named Ricky listed his ideas like this:

## ❷ Draft

Use your graphic organizer to write a draft. Keep in mind your purpose for writing—to present a problem and the steps needed to solve it. Use transitional words so that the ideas in your sentences flow smoothly.

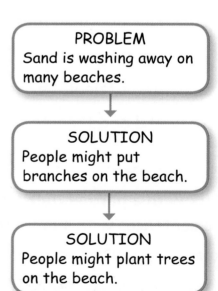

PROBLEM
Sand is washing away on many beaches.

SOLUTION
People might put branches on the beach.

SOLUTION
People might plant trees on the beach.

## ❸ Revise

Read over your draft. Look for places where the writing needs improvement. Use the Writing Checklist to help you identify problems. Then revise your draft.

## ❹ Edit

Check your work for errors in grammar, usage, mechanics, and spelling. Trade papers with a partner to get feedback. Use the Peer Review Checklist on page 404.

## ❺ Publish

Prepare a clean copy of your final draft. Share your paragraph with the class. Save your work for the Writing Workshop.

Here is Ricky's essay:

## Writing Checklist

**Organization**

✓ I clearly explained the problem and solutions.

**Sentence fluency**

✓ I used transitional words to make the ideas in my sentences flow smoothly.

**Conventions**

✓ I used subordinating conjunctions correctly.

Ricky Escobar

Sand is washing away on many beaches. After years of crashing waves and wind, some beaches are in danger of disappearing. What can we do to save these beaches?

One idea is to place large tree branches on the sand in winter to keep the sand from blowing or washing away. However, the branches might be washed out to sea when there are strong winds and storms.

Another, maybe better, solution is to plant trees along the beach. The roots would hold the sand in place, and the branches would help stop it from blowing away.

## What You Will Learn

**Reading**

- Vocabulary building: *Context, word study*

- Reading strategy: *Summarize*

- Text type: *Informational text (social studies)*

**Grammar**

Prepositions and prepositional phrases

**Writing**

Write a response to literature

These words will help you understand the reading.

### Key Words

- **code**
- **escape**
- **landmarks**
- **border**
- **riverbank**
- **tracks**

# Key Words

*A Song Map* is about *an* American folksong called *Follow the Drinking Gourd.*

## Words in Context  Audio

**1** The baseball player used a code to communicate with his teammates during a game.

**2** The boy opened the cage because he thought the bird wanted to escape.

**3** The big, old tree is one of the well-known landmarks in our area.

**4** The Rio Grande River is on the border between Texas and Mexico.

**5** In spring, wildflowers cover the riverbank . They grow right up to the edge of the water.

**6** When people or animals walk in the dirt or mud, they leave tracks . Can you guess who or what left these tracks?

## Practice

**Make flashcards to help you memorize the words.**

- Write a key word on the front.
- On the back, draw a picture that will help you remember the meaning.

## Make Connections

Can you make up a secret code? With a partner, pick signals to use for the key words on this page. Then share your code with another pair.

These words will help you talk about the reading.

### Academic Words

**instruct**
show or tell someone how to do a thing

**specific**
precise; exact

**symbols**
things that stand for or suggest something else

# Academic Words

## Words in Context

The teacher will **instruct** us on how to complete the assignment.

Set a **specific** time aside to do your homework.

On the U.S. flag, the stars are **symbols** of the fifty states.

### Practice

**Write the sentences in your notebook. Choose an academic word to complete each sentence.**

1. We should decide on a ＿＿ place to meet.

2. The Statue of Liberty is a ＿＿ of freedom.

3. I will ask my mother to ＿＿ me on how to bake brownies.

### Apply

**Ask and answer with a partner.**

1. What **specific** things do you do to prepare for a test?

2. What are two **symbols** found on road signs?

3. How would you **instruct** someone on the best way to learn vocabulary?

WB
166

# Word Study

## Figurative Language

**Figurative language helps you see in your mind what the author is describing.**

> When the sun comes back and the first quail calls, follow the drinking gourd.

In this line from a folksong, the "drinking gourd" is a symbol for the Big Dipper, a pattern of stars that points north. "When the sun comes back," it is spring, when days get warmer. That line could be rewritten as:

*At the first sign of spring, follow the Big Dipper north.*

Figurative language does not mean exactly what it says. It paints a word picture.

### Practice

**Work with a partner. Read each pair of sentences. Tell which sentence creates a better word picture.**

1. **a.** The leaves danced in the wind.
   **b.** The wind blew the leaves around.

2. **a.** At night, there are stars in the sky.
   **b.** The night sky wears a necklace of diamonds.

3. **a.** The sun creates light for Earth.
   **b.** The sun lights the world with its fire.

167

### INFORMATIONAL TEXT
#### Social Studies

**More About**

What messages can songs carry?

 **Listen to the Audio.**
Listen for the main points and important details.

## Reading Strategy

### Summarize

Summarizing a selection or a song can help you understand it.

* As you read this selection, think about what each section is mainly about.

Listen as your teacher models the reading strategy.

### by Ben McKenzie

Can a song also be a map? Some people think the song *Follow the Drinking Gourd* was really a secret code. Did the words in the song give **instructions** to slaves who were trying to escape? Did the song point the slaves toward freedom?

**Follow the Drinking Gourd**
*Stanza 1*
**When the sun comes back and the first quail calls,**
**Follow the drinking gourd.**
**For the old man is waiting for to carry you to freedom**
**If you follow the drinking gourd.**

The Big Dipper is a pattern of stars, or constellation, that points north. Could that be the drinking gourd? The sun comes back in the spring. Quail are birds that begin to call in the spring. Did this stanza tell slaves to leave when spring began and to follow the Big Dipper to the north?

Who was the old man waiting to carry them to freedom? Some people believe he was Peg Leg Joe, a former sailor who helped slaves. Peg Leg Joe used a wooden leg.

*Chorus*
**Follow the drinking gourd!**
**Follow the drinking gourd!**
**For the old man is waiting for to carry you to freedom**
**If you follow the drinking gourd.**
*Stanza 2*
**The riverbank makes a very good road,**
**The dead trees will show you the way,**
**Left foot, peg foot traveling on,**
**Following the drinking gourd.**

Some people say Peg Leg Joe marked trees and other landmarks along the riverbank. This helped the slaves make sure they were going in the right direction. These tracks, or marks, were often a mud or **charcoal** outline of a human left foot and another mark. Some people believe the other mark was Peg Leg Joe's wooden leg.

---

**charcoal**   black substance made of burned wood

**Before You Go On**   What did the song **instruct** slaves to do?

*Stanza 3*

**The river ends between two hills,**
**Follow the drinking gourd.**
**There's another river on the other side,**
**Follow the drinking gourd.**

As the slaves walked north, they were told to look for the place where the river ends between two hills. Many people think Woodhall Mountain in Mississippi is this landmark.

The Tennessee River is on the other side of the mountain. If slaves kept following the drinking gourd, they went north. They were closer to the states where they could be free.

Slaves found shelter across the river.

(Repeat Chorus)

*Stanza 4*

Where the great big river
meets the little river,
Follow the drinking gourd.
The old man is waiting for
to carry you to freedom,
If you follow the drinking gourd.

This map shows the directions in which slaves traveled.

The Ohio River is a big river that meets the Tennessee River on the border between Kentucky and Illinois. The song told slaves that the old man was waiting for them on the banks of the Ohio River. Some people believe Peg Leg Joe was there himself to lead the slaves to freedom. What do you believe? Is *Follow the Drinking Gourd* just a song? Or is it a secret map?

**W B**

168-170

## Reading Strategy

### Summarize

- Summarize the **instructions** that *Follow the Drinking Gourd* gave slaves.

- Summarize the reading selection.

- Did summarizing help you understand what you read? How?

## Think It Over

1. **Recall**   Who was Peg Leg Joe?

2. **Comprehend**   Why did the song **instruct** slaves to travel north?

3. **Analyze**   What are some **specific symbols** in the song? What do they mean?

# Learning Strategies

## Make Inferences

The slaves who used the song *Follow the Drinking Gourd* had to **make inferences**. They put the words of the song together with things they already knew to figure out what the clues meant.

**Practice**

**Write the letter of the inference that can be made from each statement.**

1. People escaping slavery often traveled at night.
2. The slaves crossed the Tennessee River in winter when it froze.
3. The slaves sang the song as they traveled.

> a. The Tennessee River was hard to cross in summer.
> b. The song was like a map.
> c. The slaves did not want to be seen.

# Use an Inference Chart

An Inference Chart can help you use what you know
to make inferences.

 G.O. 145

**We often make inferences based on what we hear.
Describe two sounds you hear frequently. Tell what you know
about each sound and what you infer.**

| Sound | What I Know | Inference |
|---|---|---|
| A song is playing over a microphone. | An ice cream truck plays that song. | The ice cream truck is coming. |
| | | |
| | | |

**Close your book and summarize
the selection to a partner.**

W B

171

## Extension

**Utilize** Find the words to
one or more verses of *The Star
Spangled Banner*. Discuss the
meaning of the words with a
partner. Listen carefully and
work cooperatively. Present
your interpretation to the class.

# Grammar

## Prepositions and Prepositional Phrases

Words such as *on*, *at*, and *in* are **prepositions**. A **preposition** is always followed by a **noun** or **noun phrase**. Together, they are called a **prepositional phrase**.

> The show is on Monday nights.
>
> I am waiting at the corner.

Some prepositional phrases are used to show **location**.

| | |
|---|---|
| on the table | between two hills |
| in the drawer | inside the house |
| above the door | by the driveway |
| under the desk | next to the shop |
| in front of the wall | on the left |

Some prepositional phrases are used to show **time**.

| | |
|---|---|
| at six o'clock | in 1995 |
| on Monday | until the summer |
| in December | by January first |

Some prepositional phrases are used to show **direction**.

| | |
|---|---|
| to the store | along the road |
| into the building | toward the school |

Some prepositional phrases are used to give **details**.

| | |
|---|---|
| by J.K. Rowling | without a coat |
| of gold | except the red one |

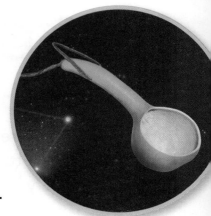

## Practice

Complete each prepositional phrase with a
preposition from the box. Write the sentences.

| | | | |
|---|---|---|---|
| above | at | except | on |
| along | between | from | toward |

**Example:** The drinking gourd pointed <u>toward</u> freedom.

1. The bird can escape _____ the cage.

2. The airplane flew _____ the city.

3. There is a border _____ Arizona and Mexico.

4. She was born _____ midnight.

5. They followed the tracks _____ the riverbank.

6. Everyone was there _____ Maya.

7. The slaves walked _____ the northern states.

8. Someone had carved symbols _____ the trees.

## Apply

Work with a partner. Play a guessing game.
Take turns giving clues that describe the
location of an object in the classroom. Have
your partner guess the object.

**Example:** A: It's near the board.

B: The teacher's desk?

A: No. It's above the
teacher's desk.

B: Is it the projector?

A: Yes, that's right.

## Grammar Check ✓

Name four types of
prepositions and give an
example of each.

W B

172

# Writing

## Write a Response to Literature

Ongoing Writing Skills Practice

When you write a response to literature, you introduce the plot, characters, and setting, and tell what you thought and felt about the book or story.

### Writing Prompt

Write a response to a book you have read. Tell whether you recommend it or not. Then give a brief introduction to the plot, characters, and setting. Tell why you did or didn't like the book. Be sure to use prepositional phrases correctly.

## ❶ Prewrite

Choose a book to write about. Think about whether or not you liked it, and why. Then list your response in a graphic organizer.

A student named Amanda listed her ideas like this:

## ❷ Draft

Use your graphic organizer to write a draft. Give reasons to support your opinion.

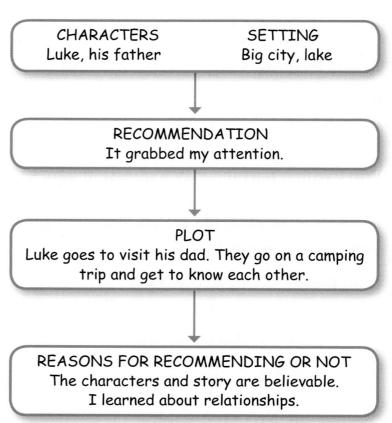

CHARACTERS
Luke, his father

SETTING
Big city, lake

RECOMMENDATION
It grabbed my attention.

PLOT
Luke goes to visit his dad. They go on a camping trip and get to know each other.

REASONS FOR RECOMMENDING OR NOT
The characters and story are believable.
I learned about relationships.

## ❸ Revise

Read over your draft. Look for places where the writing needs improvement. Use the Writing Checklist to help you identify problems. Then revise your draft.

## ❹ Edit

Check your work for errors in grammar, usage, mechanics, and spelling. Trade papers with a partner to get feedback. Use the Peer Review Checklist on Workbook page 404.

## ❺ Publish

Prepare a clean copy of your final draft. Share your paragraph with the class.

Here is Amanda's response to *The Lost Lake* by Allen Say:

## Writing Checklist

**Ideas**

✔ I introduced the plot, characters, and setting.

I gave reasons for my opinion.

**Conventions**

✔ I used prepositional phrases correctly.

Amanda Hong

The Lost Lake, by Allen Say, grabbed my attention and did not let go. It tells the story of Luke and his father. Luke goes to visit his father in the city, but his father is very busy. Then one day he takes Luke on a hike. On the hike. they build a strong relationship.

I think the author has created characters that act as real fathers and sons do. It is a very believable story. It reminded me of going camping with my father last summer. At that time, we got to know each other better. That's what happens to Luke and his father.

I learned about how relationships can change after reading this book. In fact, it helped me to understand my father a little better.

## What You Will Learn

**Reading**

■ Vocabulary building: *Context, phonics*

■ Reading strategy: *Identify author's purpose*

■ Text type: *Informational text*

**Grammar**
Present perfect

**Writing**
Write an article

These words will help you understand the reading.

### Key Words

country and western

rockabilly

emotions

career

tour

duet

# Key Words

## Words in Context

**①** Country and western is a type of popular music from the southern and western United States.

**②** Many artists combine rock and roll music and country music to come up with a style called rockabilly.

**③** People often show their emotions, or feelings, by the expressions on their faces.

**4** A career is the type of job or work that someone does. In a career with the post office, a mail carrier delivers letters as part of the job.

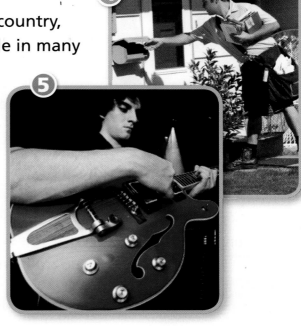

**5** Some musicians tour around the country, giving concerts for thousands of people in many different cities.

**6** When two singers sing together, they are performing a duet.

## Practice

**Create a concept map of each key word.**

- Write the keyword in the center.
- Around it, write words that relate to it.
- Connect the words using lines.

## Make Connections

What is your favorite type of music? What kinds of emotions do you feel when you listen to your favorite music? Why do you think people like different types of music?

These words will help you talk about the reading.

## Academic Words

**achieved**
worked to get a good result

**enormous**
very large

**status**
respect and importance given to someone

# Academic Words

## Words in Context  Audio

At the end of each week, it's good idea to stop and think about what you have **achieved**.

Music is of **enormous** importance to me.

Many actors have reached superstar **status**.

## Practice

**Write the sentences in your notebook. Choose an academic word to complete each sentence.**

1. The president of the United States has a very high _____ around the world.

2. I set goals, but I haven't _____ all of them.

3. Our class should be proud. It took an _____ amount of energy to put on the class play.

## Apply

**Ask and answer with a partner.**

1. What has your favorite athlete **achieved** in his or her career?

2. What is something you have done that took **enormous** effort to complete?

3. Who is someone you know of who has a very high **status**?

 WB

176

# Phonics

## Words with *ow, ou*

Listen. Pay attention to the vowel sounds.
Then read each word aloud.

how     loud     low

Which words have the same letters?
Which words have the same vowel sound?

### Rule

The diphthong /ou/ can be spelled as either *ow* or *ou*.
The long / ō / sound is sometimes spelled with *ow*.

Each word in the chart has the letters *ou* or *ow*. Read the
words. If one sound doesn't make sense, try the other.

| | | |
|---|---|---|
| about | how | owner |
| amount | know | powerful |
| around | known | prowl |

**Work with a partner. Use the words from the chart.**

1. List the words in which *ow* has the long /ō/ sound.

2. List the words in which *ow* or *ou* has the vowel sound in ***how***.

3. Add three more words to each list.

177

## Reading 3

### More About

**THE BIG QUESTION**

How does music reflect people's feelings and their way of life?

 **Listen to the Audio.**
Listen for the main points and important details.

### Reading Strategy

**Identify Author's Purpose**

Authors have a reason or purpose for writing. Ask these questions:

- Did the author write the text to entertain you?

- Did the author write the text to explain information (for example, about a science or social studies topic)?

- Did the author write the text to persuade? Is the author trying to make you think or do something?

Listen as your teacher models the reading strategy.

# Elvis Presley

## By Barbara Davis

In the early 1950s, a new kind of music was thrilling young people all across America. It was a **distinctive** blend of old-time country and western music mixed with rock and roll, jazz, and **blues**. This exciting new music that stirred people's emotions was called rockabilly. A young singer named Elvis Presley soon made the music and himself famous.

---

**distinctive**   having a special quality
**blues**   a slow sad style of music

Elvis Presley's unique appearance and singing style represented the excitement of rockabilly music. He shocked many people with his wild dance steps, but his young audiences loved his performances.

Elvis Presley was born in Tupelo, Mississippi, on January 8, 1935. From a young age, he attended church where gospel singing was an important part of the service. Elvis was eleven years old when he got his first guitar. He learned to play with the help of his uncle, Jimmy Smith, and his church pastor, Frank Smith. By the time Elvis was a teenager, his family had moved to Memphis, Tennessee. There, he learned rhythm and blues. This music was a large part of African American culture in the South.

When Elvis won a high school talent contest, he decided he wanted to be a professional singer. In 1953, he paid $4.00 to record two songs at a recording **studio**. This studio was owned by Sam Philips who also owned Sun Records, a well-known record label. However, Elvis did not meet Sam Philips in person until 1954. Sam loved Elvis's singing style and recorded him performing the song, "That's All Right." When the song was played on radio station WHBQ in Memphis, listeners responded enthusiastically. Elvis's musical career was born.

---

**studio**   place where music or TV shows are recorded

**Before You Go On**   What things had Elvis Presley **achieved** by the time he recorded the song, "That's All Right"?

By 1956, Elvis Presley was a national singing star. His style included rock and roll as well as rhythm and blues. Elvis continued to record hit after hit. In one year alone, he recorded eleven songs that went "gold." This means that at least 500,000 copies of each song were sold. This was an enormous achievement.

In 1956, Elvis also starred in his first movie, *Love Me Tender*. Many movies followed during Elvis's long career. In 1960, he even performed a duet on television with the famous singer and actor, Frank Sinatra.

Over the next 20 years, Elvis Presley recorded 94 gold singles and more than 40 gold albums. His musical style influenced many other musicians including The Beatles. Elvis's status in the music industry earned him the nickname, "The King of Rock and Roll." Elvis died in 1977. To this day, people travel to Memphis to tour Graceland mansion where he is buried.

**In 1986, Elvis Presley was inducted into the Rock and Roll Hall of Fame.**

# AUSTIN: THE LIVE MUSIC CAPITAL OF THE WORLD

**By Cliff Dean**

An important event in Austin's music history occurred in 1975. A 30-minute music show was taped at the University of Austin. Willie Nelson was there. The show presented Texas musicians, many of whom lived in Austin. That show, *Austin City Limits*, is now the longest running music show on television, and is seen in countries around the globe. Thousands of musicians, from the unknown to music legends, have been on the show, playing music from country and western to folk to rock. The *Austin City Limits* **scenery** is famous. The musicians play against a picture of Austin at night.

Partly because of *Austin City Limits*, Austin began to get a worldwide **reputation** as a music town. Many live music clubs opened, and Austin became a place that musicians from all over the world loved to visit and perform in. In the early 1990s, there were so many live music **venues** that Austin was named the Live Music Capital of the World. It continues to hold that title today.

---

**scenery**   the furniture and background used on a stage

**reputation**   the opinion people have of someone or something

**venues**   places where concerts, plays, meetings, etc., are held

**Before You Go On**   What helped Austin gain its **status** as a great place to hear live music?

For people living in Austin, as well as the many tourists who visit, Austin's live music is a special treat. Unlike listening to music coming from earphones or speakers, hearing music live really stirs the emotions. Musicians are free to create new songs and sounds for live audiences. There are often surprises in live performances, and if the audience responds well, the musicians may go out of their way to create a very memorable event.

And it is not only at clubs and concert halls that people can hear live music in Austin. There are many music festivals in the city. The most famous is the Austin City Limits Music Festival, a three-day event held outdoors in Austin's Zilker Park. Recent festivals have featured eight stages with up to forty bands playing each day.

**The Austin City Limits Music Festival is held every year and draws thousands of people to the city of Austin.**

Stevie Ray Vaughan was a famous blues musician.

Today, many Austin landmarks show how important music has been for the city. One such landmark is a large statue of a man in a big hat near Lake Austin. The statue is of the famous Austin guitar player Stevie Ray Vaughan. Vaughan played the **blues**, but with a special Texas flavor. The statue of Vaughan with his **trademark** hat stands as a reminder that many musicians have helped make Austin the live musical capital of the world. And at the same time, Austin has helped make the careers of many of our favorite performers.

---

**blues**   a slow, sad style of music

**trademark**   a special, recognizable feature

WB

178–180

## Reading Strategy

### Identify Author's Purpose

- Was the author's purpose in each reading to entertain, explain, or persuade?
- What information and words helped you understand the author's purpose?

## Think It Over!

1. **Recall**   What was Vaughan's trademark?
2. **Comprehend**   How did Elvis's early experiences affect his music?
3. **Analyze**   Why do you think Elvis Presley had such **enormous** success as a musician and performer?

# Learning Strategies

## Author's Purpose

Authors often write to inform, or give information to, their readers. Authors also write to entertain. Sometimes, authors write to persuade, or change the reader's mind.

**Practice**

**Copy this Author's Purpose Chart. Look back at the readings in Units 3 and 4. Identify the author's purpose for each selection.**

| Selection | To Entertain | To Inform | To Persuade |
|---|---|---|---|
| The Real Soldier | | | |
| One Hot Summer in Philadelphia | | | |
| One Out of Many | | | |
| Biomes All Over the World | | | |
| Marine Food Web | | | |
| Save the Sea Turtles | | | |

# Use a Venn Diagram

You can compare and contrast with a Venn Diagram by listing how two things are similar and how are they different.

 **Practice**  G.O. 142

**Copy and complete the Venn Diagram. Compare and Contrast the two readings in this selection**

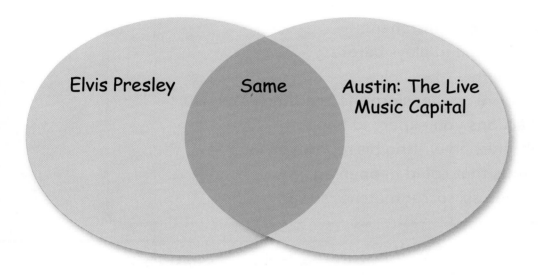

Elvis Presley | Same | Austin: The Live Music Capital

 **Apply**

**Close your book and retell the selection to a partner.**

## Extension

**Utilize** Imagine your class is going on two-day field trip to Austin. Research things to see and do in Austin. Choose several activities you think your class would enjoy. Create a brief presentation using visual aids. Share your ideas with the class.

# Grammar

## Present Perfect

Use the **present perfect** to talk about things that happened at an unspecified time in the past. Use it with time phrases such as *once, ever, never, before,* and *a few times.* Use it to talk about:

**Experiences or accomplishments**

   I have performed in plays **before**.

**Changes over time**

   You have grown taller since the **last time** I saw you.

**Unfinished actions you expect to happen**

   He hasn't finished writing his report **yet**.

**Multiple events that could happen again**

   We have won six soccer matches **so far**.

Form the present perfect with **have** or **has** and the **past participle**.

| **have/has** | **+ Past Participle** |
|---|---|
| She **has** | seen the show a **few times**. |

Most **past participles** are formed with **-ed**. Others are irregular.

| be ⟶ been | give ⟶ given | meet ⟶ met |
|---|---|---|
| buy ⟶ bought | got ⟶ gotten | see ⟶ seen |
| do ⟶ done | grow ⟶ grown | take ⟶ taken |
| find ⟶ found | hear ⟶ heard | win ⟶ won |

To talk about specific past events, use the **simple past**.

I **have been** to Houston. I went there last year. I liked it.

Complete each sentence with the present
perfect form of the verb in parentheses.
Write the sentences.

**Example:** They <u>have found</u> out about
Austin's music. (find)

1. I _____ country and western music before. (hear)

2. Live music _____ very popular in Austin. (grow)

3. Taylor _____ a lot in her singing career so far. (achieve)

4. They _____ her a music award. (give)

5. She _____ to Austin once. (be)

6. We _____ the band on tour a few times. (see)

**Apply**

Read the prompts below. Come up with a present
perfect tense statement about yourself for each one.
Then discuss your answers with a partner.

**Example:** A: I have been to a country
music concert.

B: Really? I haven't. When did you go?

182

- An experience
- An accomplishment
- How you have changed
- Something that has happened several times

## Grammar Check ✓

How do you
form the
present perfect?

# Writing

## Write an Article about a Musician

Ongoing Writing Skills Practice

When you write an article about a person, it's important to do research and give details about what makes the person special.

### Writing Prompt

Write an article about a favorite musician for a newspaper or magazine. Include interesting facts about the person and his or her career. Include a strong introduction and conclusion. Remember to use the present perfect correctly when you write.

## ❶ Prewrite

Choose a musician to write about. List details about the person in a graphic organizer.

A student named Desi listed his ideas like this:

> **MAIN IDEA**
> Miley Cyrus is one of the most exciting pop singers in the world.

| DETAIL | DETAIL | DETAIL |
|---|---|---|
| Miley is the daughter of Billy Ray Cyrus. She is in the TV series <u>Hannah Montana</u>. | Cyrus's music career began with <u>Meet Miley Cyrus</u>. It was #1. | Her second album, <u>Breakout</u>, was released in 2008. It was #1, too. |

## ❷ Draft

Use your graphic organizer to help you write a first draft. Include a strong introduction and conclusion.

## ❸ Revise

Read over your draft. Look for places where the writing needs improvement. Use the Writing Checklist to help you identify problems. Then revise your draft.

## ❹ Edit

Check your work for errors in grammar, usage, mechanics, and spelling. Trade papers with a partner to get feedback. Use the Peer Review Checklist on page 00.

## ❺ Publish

Prepare a clean copy of your final draft. Share your paragraph with the class.

Here is Desi's article:

## Writing Checklist

**Ideas**

✓ I included interesting facts.

**Sentence Fluency**

✓ I used a variety of sentence patterns.

**Conventions**

✓ I used present perfect correctly.

Desi Alvarado

Miley Cyrus has already had more success than people twice her age. She is one of the most exciting pop singers in the world. Cyrus is the daughter of the country singer Billy Ray Cyrus. Her road to fame began in 2006 when she won the title role in the <u>Hannah Montana</u> TV series.

Once the TV show was a success, Cyrus made her own album. <u>Meet Miley Cyrus</u> was released in 2007. It was a big success. The single from the album was called "See You Again." It made the Top 10. The album went to #1 on the charts.

In 2008, Cyrus made another album. It was called <u>Breakout</u>. It also went to #1! Miley Cyrus definitely has a bright future ahead of her.

W B
183–184

# Apply and Extend

## Link the Readings

Copy the chart into your notebook. Read the words in the top row. For each text selection, put an X under words related to that reading.

| | Informational text | Literature | Careers and achievements | History |
|---|---|---|---|---|
| **Touching Sound with Evelyn Glennie** | | | | |
| **A Song Map** | | | | |
| **Elvis Presley** | | | | |
| **Austin: The Live Music Capital of the World** | | | | |

## Discussion

1. How has music been important in Evelyn Glennie's life?

2. How was *Follow the Drinking Gourd* important to slaves? What were some **symbols** in the song?

3. How has music contributed to Austin's **status**? How does it shape the lifestyle of the people living there?

 How do people make and use music?

> **Listening Skills**
>
> If you don't understand something a speaker said, you can ask, "Could you explain that, please?"

# Projects

**Your teacher will help you choose one of these projects.**

|  **Written** |  **Oral** |  **Visual/Active** |
|---|---|---|
| **Slogans** | **Presentation** | **Mural** |
| Imagine you're starting a campaign to get people more interested in music. Write five interesting, snappy slogans that tell what is good about music. | Play a song from the country you are from. Explain who wrote and performed it, and what instruments are used. Summarize what it's about and tell why you like it. | Work with a group. Create a mural that shows how slaves might have used the Big Dipper and the song *Follow the Drinking Gourd* to guide them to freedom. |
| **Report** | **Song** | **Catalog** |
| Research and write a report about the life, career, and music of a singer, musician, or group you like. | Write a song that gives instructions. Use *Follow the Drinking Gourd* as an example. Then perform the song for your class. | Make a catalog that shows drawings and descriptions of some interesting musical instruments. |

# Further Reading

For more projects visit
*LongmanCornerstone.com*

 *Rumpelstiltskin*

In this Penguin Young Reader® version of a classic fairytale, a queen must find out the name of a mysterious little man in time to save her family. Could the song he sings hold the clue?

***What Charlie Heard,*** Mordicai Gerstein

As a child, Charlie Ives was fascinated by sounds of all kinds. Later, as an adult composer, he tried to recreate those sounds in his music.

185–186

## Roleplay an Interview

You are going to plan, write, and roleplay an interview with a celebrity. You will listen as your classmates roleplay their interviews.

### ❶ Prepare

**A.** Work with a partner. Choose a favorite celebrity, such as a singer, a sports star, or a TV or movie star. Decide which role you will play.

**B.** Discuss what questions the interviewer will ask. Research the answers and take notes. Work cooperatively and share information and ideas. Write your questions and answers on note cards. Find props and costumes to use.

> **Note Card #1**
>
> Q: David Archuleta, you were the youngest contestant on <u>American Idol</u>. Was that your first talent contest?
>
> A: No, it wasn't. I was sixteen when I was on <u>American Idol</u>. But when I was twelve, I was on <u>Star Search</u> and became the Junior Vocal Champion. Before that, when I was ten, I won the Utah Talent Competition in the children's division.

### ❷ Practice

Practice your interview with your props and costumes. Practice in front of your family or friends. If possible, record your interview. Then listen to it. How do you sound? Record it again and try to improve.

# ❸ Present

**As you speak,** do the following:

- Speak loudly enough for your audience to hear.
- Maintain eye contact with your partner.
- Act naturally. Speak with feeling and expression.

**As you listen,** do the following:

- Think about what you already know about the celebrity.
- Take notes on important details.
- Pay close attention. Your teacher will ask you questions after the roleplay.

# ❹ Evaluate

**After you speak,** answer these questions:

- ✓ Did you speak loudly enough for the audience to hear?
- ✓ Did you act naturally with feeling and expression?

**After you listen,** answer these questions:

- ✓ Did you understand all the questions and answers?
- ✓ Did the speakers use formal or informal language?
- ✓ Did you take good notes?

> **Speaking Skills**
>
> A celebrity interview can be a formal or informal situation. Use formal or informal language based on the situation you choose.

> **Listening Skills**
>
> Listen carefully for the main points and details. Use this to infer information that isn't stated directly.

# Writing Workshop

## Write a How-to Essay

### Writing Prompt

Write a how-to essay in which you explain how to do or make something. Include time-order connecting words such as *first, next*, and *then* to explain the order of the steps. You may also want to include tips on possible problems and how to solve them. Be sure to include an introduction and conclusion.

### ❶ Prewrite

Review your previous work in this unit. Now choose a topic. Think about something you know how to do and wish to explain to someone. List the steps of the process in a graphic organizer.

A student named Sonel listed his ideas in this graphic organizer:

### ❷ Draft

Use your graphic organizer to help you write a draft. Keep in mind your purpose for writing—to explain how to make or do something. Use time order words to explain each step clearly.

**INTRODUCTION:** Hurricanes are very dangerous. It's important to prepare.

↓

**STEP 1:** Make sure you have gas. Listen to radio reports.

↓

**STEP 2:** Check that you have supplies for your trip.

↓

**STEP 3:** Put boards on your windows.

↓

**CONCLUSION:** Prepare and you will protect yourself.

## ❸ Revise

Read over your draft. Look for places where the writing needs improvement. Use the Writing Checklist to help you identify problems. Then revise your draft.

## Six Traits of Writing Checklist

✔ **Ideas**
Is my explanation easy to understand?

✔ **Organization**
Are the steps I explained in time order?

✔ **Voice**
Does my writing show how I feel?

✔ **Word Choice**
Did I use time-order connecting words?

✔ **Sentence Fluency**
Did I use a variety of sentence patterns?

✔ **Conventions**
Did I use contractions correctly?

Here is how Sonel revised his essay:

Sonel Duval

### Preparing for Hurricanes

It's very important to plan ahead when you hear a hurricane is coming. With winds of up to 150 miles per hour, hurricanes can be dangerous killers. Here are some steps you can take to help you stay safe.

First, make sure your [you're] car is full of fuel. You must be ready to drive 20 to 50 miles to locate a safe place away from the storm. Listen to radio reports, to [ʌ] Learn what routes are safe to take out of town.

After that, check that you have supplies for your trip. These include cash, a flashlight, a first aid kit, [ʌ] and food and fresh water.

Finally, if you have time, put boards on your windows. This will help protect your windows. It will also [ʌ] prevent broken glass and flying objects from entering your house if the winds are strong.

Hurricanes are very dangerous storms. By preparing, you can protect yourself and your property.

**Revised** to correct error in mechanics.

**Revised** to correct error in spelling.

**Revised** to create a longer sentence.

**Revised** to correct error in mechanics.

**Revised** to make ideas flow more smoothly.

## ❹ Edit

Check your work for errors. Trade papers with a partner. Use the Peer Review Checklist to give each other feedback. Edit your final draft in response to feedback from your partner and your teacher.

## ❺ Publish

Make a clean copy of your final draft. Share your essay with the class.

### Peer Review Checklist

✔ The steps are clear.

✔ The steps are in a logical order.

✔ All the information is related to the topic.

### SPELLING TIP

Double-check your work for words that are commonly confused, such as *you're* and *your*, *there* and *their*, and *its* and *it's*.

**Listen to the sentences. Pay attention to the groups of words. Read aloud.**

1. Award-winning musician Evelyn Glennie believes that hearing is a form of touch.

2. *Follow the Drinking Gourd* contains a special message that helped slaves escape to freedom.

3. Elvis Presley's musical style was influenced by many different types of music.

**Work in pairs. Take turns reading aloud for one minute. Count the number of words you read.**

| | |
|---|---:|
| Evelyn loved the way music made her feel—sometimes happy, | 10 |
| sometimes sad, but always alive. | 15 |
| She studied at the Royal Academy of Music after high school. | 26 |
| She has had a successful career as a musician ever since. | 37 |
| On her Web site, Evelyn says, "Hearing is a special form of | 49 |
| touch. Deafness does not mean that you can't hear. It only | 60 |
| means that there is something wrong with the ears." | 69 |
| Evelyn uses her whole body to feel sounds. She often | 79 |
| performs barefoot. | 81 |
| "Anything you can pick can create a sound," says Evelyn. | 91 |
| Evelyn plays well-known percussion instruments such as | 99 |
| the snare, kettle, and bass drums. She also plays marimbas, | 109 |
| xylophones, gongs, and water drums. | 114 |
| She has been filmed creating music with common objects | 123 |
| such as pots and pans, bottles, pipes and glasses filled with water. | 135 |
| Evelyn performs in more than 100 concerts each year. She | 145 |
| has won many awards for achievement in making and | 154 |
| recording music. | 156 |

WB

189–190

# Test Preparation

## Taking Tests

You will often take tests that help show what you know. Follow these tips to improve your test-taking skills.

### Coaching Corner

**Answering Questions About a Selection**

- Many test questions ask you to answer questions about a selection. Some selections will be short. Some will be long.

- The selection can be fiction or nonfiction.

- Before you read the selection, preview the questions and answer choices. Knowing what the questions are will help you focus as you read.

- After reading the selection, try to answer each question in your head. When you read the choices, look for the one that is closest in meaning to the answer in your head.

- After you choose an answer, check the selection again. Make sure you can point to details in the selection that support your choice.

**Read the following test sample. Study the tips in the box.**

191–192

**Read the selection. Then answer the questions.**

1      The Austin City Limits Music Festival is a three-day event in Austin, Texas. It takes place every October. People from all over the world come to play their music at the festival. People can hear all kinds of music, including country and western, bluegrass, jazz, and reggae. This is a time when many bands can celebrate their musical achievements.

2      You can bring your own water, chairs, and umbrellas to the festival. You cannot bring your own food. You can buy food and drinks there. Make sure you don't put your chair too close to the stage. Tell your parents they cannot park near the festival. It might be easier to park downtown and take a bus to the shows.

1   Why can't you bring your own food to the music festival?

   **A** There is food available there.
   **B** It is a distraction to the musicians.
   **C** There is no eating during performances.
   **D** It will cause a littering problem.

2   In paragraph 1, <u>achievements</u> means —

   **F** accomplishments
   **G** punishments
   **H** celebrations
   **J** compositions

**Tips**

✔ You can review the selection to figure out the answer.

✔ Be careful. In Question 1, you are looking for something that you *can't* do.

# Visiting National Parks

Camping, hiking, exploring, and swimming are all things you can do in a national park.

## Reading

**1** | Social Studies

**Yosemite National Park**

**2** | Scrapbook

**My Trip to Yosemite**

**3** | Short Story

**A Night at Great Basin**

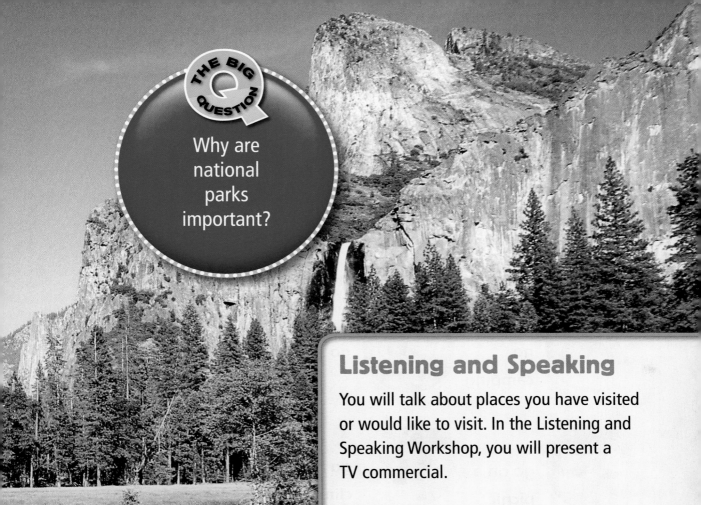

Why are national parks important?

## Listening and Speaking

You will talk about places you have visited or would like to visit. In the Listening and Speaking Workshop, you will present a TV commercial.

## Writing

You will practice skills needed for writing a research report. In the Writing Workshop, you will write a research report.

**Quick Write**

Write about an interesting place you have visited. Share what you wrote with a partner.

**DVD**

**VIEW AND RESPOND**

*Talk about the poster for this unit. Then watch and listen to the video and answer the questions at LongmanCornerstone.com.*

# What do you know about visiting national parks?

## Words to Know 🎧 Audio

Listen and repeat. Use these words to talk about outdoor activities.

 go camping

 go hiking

 go swimming

 go on a picnic

 go rock climbing

 go boating

### Practice

Work with a partner. Ask and answer questions about outdoor activities.

| at a lake | in the mountains | in a forest | at a beach |

**Example:** A: What outdoor activities can you do <u>at a lake</u>?

B: You can <u>go swimming, and boating, and go on a picnic.</u>

### Write

Read the questions. Write your responses in your notebook.

What's your favorite outdoor activity? When and where did you last do it?

## Make Connections

Copy the sentences below into your notebook. Complete the sentences with the following words.

**sunglasses and a hat**          **a flashlight and a first aid kit**

**a compass and
a map**          **a snack and a
canteen of water**

1. When you go boating, the sun can be strong, especially when it reflects off the water—so be sure to bring _____ .

2. When you go camping, don't forget _____ . You'll need to see at night, and you might get a cut or insect bite.

3. When you go hiking, it's important to bring _____ so that you don't get lost.

4. When you go rock climbing, you should bring _____ in case you get hungry or thirsty.

## What about you?

Talk with a partner. What outdoor activities do you like to do? What do you usually bring?

# Kids' Stories from around the World 🎵 Audio

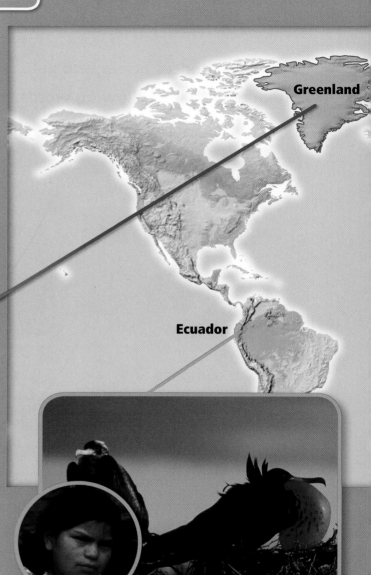

Greenland

Ecuador

### Victor

I live in Nuuk, Greenland. Did you know that Greenland is the world's largest island? My country is also home to the Northeast Greenland National Park, the largest national park in the world. The park covers an area of 370,000 square miles. Musk ox, polar bears, and walruses live there.

### Amaia

I live in Quito, Ecuador. My government set aside more than a million acres for the Galapagos National Park in 1959. People visit the Galapagos Islands to see birds and animals you can't find anywhere else in the world, such as frigates and giant tortoises.

India

Tanzania

**Pooja**

I live in India near the Jim Corbett National Park. The park was created more than 70 years ago. The wildlife there includes tigers, elephants, king cobras, wild boars, flying foxes, and nearly 600 species of birds. The park helps keep these animals safe from hunters.

**Jojo**

I live in Tanzania. The Serengeti National Park has one of the most diverse plant and animal collections in the world. These zebras are some of the many migratory animals that make their homes in the Serengeti. People come to study the plants and animals here.

## What about you?

1. Which one of these national parks would you most like to visit? Why?

2. Have you visited a national park? Share your story.

## What You Will Learn

- Vocabulary building:
  *Context, phonics*
- Reading strategy:
  *Make connections*
- Text type:
  *Informational
  (social studies)*

**Grammar**
Capitalization

**Writing**
Plan a research report

These words will help you understand the reading.

### Key Words

**tributaries**

**national parks**

**cliffs**

**sequoias**

**grove**

# Key Words

*Yosemite National Park* describes one of the most popular national parks in the United States.

## Words in Context

**1** A smaller river that joins a bigger river is called a tributary. The Missouri River has more than 50 **tributaries**. The Missouri River is a tributary of the Mississippi River.

**2** Yellowstone National Park is one of many **national parks** around the world. Is there a national park near where you live?

**3** It is exciting to walk along **cliffs**, but be careful not to walk too close to the edge.

**4** Sequoias are some of the biggest trees in the world.

**5** This grove of birch trees is in Acadia National Park in Maine.

**Practice**

**Make flashcards to help you memorize the words.**

- Write a key word on the front.

- On the back, write a sentence, but leave a blank where the key word should be.

## Make Connections

What national parks do you know of? If you could visit any of these national parks, which park would you choose? Why?

193

These words will help you talk about the reading.

### Academic Words

**factor**
one of several things that causes a result

**participate**
take part in

**region**
a large area

# Academic Words

## Words in Context

Why did my brother buy that car? One **factor** was its low cost.

The Yosemite **region** covers almost 1,200 square miles.

Students at our school **participate** in many different activities, such as soccer and band.

### Practice

**Write the sentences in your notebook. Choose an academic word to complete each sentence.**

1. This year I'll _____ in the school play.

2. The Southwest _____ includes Utah, New Mexico, and Arizona.

3. When buying a jacket, the most important _____ is fit.

### Apply

**Ask and answer with a partner.**

1. What **factors** are important to you when you choose a book to read?

2. What is a **region** in the United States that you would like to visit. Why?

3. What school activities did you **participate** in last year?

# Phonics

## Words with *v* and *w* 🎧 Audio

Listen as your teacher reads the words. Pay attention to how your teacher's lips move. Then read the words aloud.

| vase | verb | was | word |
|------|------|-----|------|

### Rule

- For words that begin with the letter *v*, narrow your lips, and put your upper teeth against your lower lip.
- For words that begin with a *w*, open your lips slightly.

### Practice

**Work with a partner. Read the words aloud.**

| waterfall | were | visit | valley |
|-----------|------|-------|--------|

1. Write three sentences using words with the *v* sound.

2. Write three sentences using words with the *w* sound.

3. Read your sentences aloud to your partner.

WB   PH

195

**INFORMATIONAL TEXT**

Social Studies

### More About

Why is it important to set aside land for national parks?

 **Listen to the Audio.**
First, listen for the main points. Then listen again for the important details. Take notes as you listen. Retell the selection to a partner.

### Reading Strategy

**Make Connections**

Think about your own life as you read.

* Have you visited places similar to Yosemite?

* What would you like to see and do if you visited Yosemite?

Listen as your teacher models the reading strategy.

# Yosemite National Park

by Vivian Ortiz

**Whether climbing, camping, or hiking, Yosemite has something for everyone.**

The Yosemite **region** of California takes up almost 1,200 square miles. It is known for its amazing waterfalls, deep valleys, and huge meadows. People have lived in the Yosemite region for 8,000 years. In the 1830s, people from other places visited. Some people built hotels and houses there. **Environmentalists** worried about this. They feared the land would be **ruined**.

**environmentalists**   people concerned about protecting the environment

**ruined**   spoiled or completely destroyed

**The Merced River is a great place to visit any time of the year**

The U.S. government stepped in to help, and in 1890, the area became known as Yosemite National Park. Rules were created to make sure the land was **preserved** for people to enjoy in the future. More than three million people visit the park each year.

Yosemite Valley is a popular **destination** for visitors. It has cliffs and rock formations, and many guests spend time visiting its waterfalls. Yosemite Valley is open all year. People often travel to the valley by car.

Yosemite National Park is also famous for its trees. Giant sequoias seem to reach the sky. The biggest group of giant sequoias is found in Mariposa Grove. Between November and March, the road to Mariposa Grove is closed to cars because of snow. Can you think of other ways to reach the grove? You can hike or ski!

---

**preserved**   kept unharmed and unchanged

**destination**   place someone is going to

**Rafting is a fun thing to
do on the Merced River.**

**Before You
Go On**   What can people see in the
Yosemite **region**?

Another great place to visit is Yosemite's Glacier Point. It is a high place where visitors can see many of the park's great features. You can see Yosemite Valley. You can see mountains too. Many people go hang gliding there. In winter, you'll need skis or snowshoes to reach it.

Have you ever tried to climb a climbing wall? In Yosemite National Park, people climb real rocks! El Capitan is a 3000-foot high (1000m) **vertical** rock formation. You can hike to the top of El Capitan on one of the trails in the park. Many people try to climb the face of the cliff itself. Climbing El Capitan is very dangerous. Only experienced rock climbers should try it. It is very difficult for park rangers to rescue climbers who get tired or hurt.

**There are easier ways to get to the top of El Capitan!**

---

**vertical**    pointing straight up and down

**Hang gliding is popular at Glacier Point. Half Dome is the tall peak in the background.**

**Yosemite Falls is the seventh highest waterfall in the world.**

Yosemite Falls are among the most **spectacular** waterfalls in the country, and are the seventh-highest in the world. The tributaries that form the falls lead to the Merced River. The best time to visit Yosemite Falls is in early spring, when the melting snow really makes the water roar.

The Hetch Hetchy Valley has a funny name, and it's really a fun place! Like Yosemite Valley, it has great views, and the Hetch Hetchy **Reservoir** supplies drinking water to people in San Francisco.

Yosemite National Park is a great vacation place— with all of its great features, there is something for everyone to enjoy.

**The natural beauty of Yosemite National Park brings more than three million visitors each year.**

---

**spectacular**   very impressive and exciting

**reservoir**   where water is stored before it is sent to people's homes

196–198

### Reading Strategy

#### Make Connections

- What places have you visited that are similar to Yosemite?

- What would you like to see and do if you visit Yosemite?

## Think It Over

1. **Recall**   Why is spring the best time to visit Yosemite Falls?

2. **Comprehend**   What different outdoor activities can people **participate** in at Yosemite?

3. **Analyze**   What **factors** led the U.S. government to create Yosemite National Park?

# Learning Strategies

## Make Connections

You can use your experience to help you understand what you read. **Experience** is something that you have done, seen, or taken part in.

As you read, ask yourself these questions:

- How are the people, places, and ideas familiar to you?
- What have you experienced that is similar to what you're reading about?
- Are the feelings described similar to your own?

**Reread the first paragraph on page 332 and look at the large photo.**

- Think about a similar experience you had.
- Think about how you felt.
- Write about a time when you saw an amazing view.

# Use a 5W Chart

You can use a 5W Chart to help you ask questions about what you read. If you can answer 5W questions, you will have a better understanding of the selection.

**Practice**

Write a question about *Yosemite National Park* in each box. Then ask a partner to answer your questions.

| Who? | Who likes to visit Yosemite National Park? |
|------|------|
| What? | |
| Where? | |
| When? | |
| Why? | |

**Apply**

Reread the selection and take notes. Then close your book and retell the selection to a partner.

199

## Extension

**Utilize** Choose a place you have visited or would like to visit. Create a 5W Chart with questions about that place. Try to find the answers to your questions. Then present your questions and answers to the class.

# Grammar

## Capitalization

Capitalize the first letter of **proper nouns**.

Names of specific people and things
John Adams, the Supreme Court, City Mall

Specific geographical names
South Africa, the Northeast, the Milky Way Galaxy

Days of the week, months, and holidays
Monday, January, President's Day

Historical events, documents, laws, and periods of time
World War I, the Constitution, the Renaissance

Nationalities, languages, and their adjectives
Spanish language, Swedish people, Mexican food

Names of groups, teams, awards, brands, and companies
National Library Association, Chicago Bears, Coca-Cola

Titles of books, newspapers, movies, and songs (but not prepositions or articles unless the first word of the title)
Alice in Wonderland, New York Times, Star Trek

Capitalize the first letter of **titles** when they come before names.

Senator Lumley, Mrs. Han, Doctor Jones

Capitalize **Acronyms** (organization names with initials said as letters).

the CIA, the FBI, NASA, the UN

**Rewrite the sentences. Use proper capitalization and punctuation.**

**Example:** i've never been to acadia national park in maine.

I've never been to Acadia National Park in Maine.

1. we visited the yosemite region of california

2. he can speak chinese and spanish

3. he read the book *james and the giant peach*

4. our class visited the white house in washington dc

5. there was a lot of snow on mount mckinley

6. the biggest group of sequoias is in mariposa grove

7. ms wilson loves to eat thai and vietnamese food

8. dr smith **participated** in the meetings at the un

**Apply**

**Work with a partner. Take turns dictating sentences to each other that contain proper nouns. The partner listening will write them down.**

**Example:** A says: The Empire State Building is in New York.

B writes: The Empire State Building is in New York.

200

**Grammar Check ✓**

Which words do you capitalize in a title?

# Writing

## Plan a Research Report

In a research report, you explain a topic that you have studied in depth. A good way to begin a research report is to narrow your topic and write a question to guide your research.

## Choose a Topic

Before you can write a research question, you need to choose a topic. Begin by thinking of a broad topic. Then ask yourself questions about this topic and do a little research. Your findings can give you ideas for a narrower topic. Once your topic is narrow enough, think of an open-ended question that you would like to answer. This question will guide your research and be the topic of your report.

### Task 1

To think of topic ideas, ask yourself some questions. What interests you? What would you like to learn more about? List your ideas, questions, and answers in a graphic organizer.

A student named Amy listed her ideas in this chart:

| BROAD TOPIC | Oklahoma History |
| --- | --- |
| QUESTION | What was one of the hardest times in Oklahoma history? |
| ANSWER | The Dust Bowl |
| QUESTION | What was the Dust Bowl? |
| ANSWER | A dry, dusty, difficult period during the 1930s. |

The answers Amy found to her question about Oklahoma history helped her decide to write about the Dust Bowl.

# Write a Research Question

Amy still needed to write a question to direct her research. She made a list of open-ended questions about the Dust Bowl.

1. What were the major causes of the Dust Bowl?
2. How did the Dust Bowl affect the farmers?
3. What did farmers do?
4. How did the Dust Bowl affect the population of Oklahoma?

## Task 2

Once you have narrowed your topic, write a list of open-ended questions. Then study the questions. Which one interests you the most? This question will direct the research for your report.

# Make a Research Plan

Amy chose the first question as the topic for her report. To create a research plan, she made a list of things she wanted to know about his topic. She listed them in a T-chart:

| What do I want to know? | Where can I find it? |
| --- | --- |
| 1. What did farmers do to contribute to the Dust Bowl? | World Book Encyclopedia Online: http://www.worldbookonline.com |
| 2. How did the weather contribute to the problem? | Book: The Dust Bowl by Anna Carver |
| 3. Were there other causes of the Dust Bowl? | Book: Causes of the Dust Bowl by Geoff Gregory |

## Task 3

Finally, create a research plan. Make a list of what you want to learn and where to look for it. Use a T-chart like the one above.

201–202

## What You Will Learn

**Reading**

■ Vocabulary building: *Context, word study*

■ Reading strategy: *Review and retell*

■ Text type: *Literary nonfiction (scrapbook)*

**Grammar**
Active and passive voice

**Writing**
Paraphrasing a source

These words will help you understand the reading.

### Key Words

cascade

meadow

peak

ascend

reflection

valley

# Key Words

*My Trip to Yosemite* is about Jay's summer trip to Yosemite National Park.

## Words in Context

**1** I love to watch the water cascade down the steps.

**2** A meadow in summer is one of the prettiest places to be. The grass is tall, and the flowers smell sweet.

**3** Sometimes, the peak of a high mountain stays covered with snow, even in summer.

**4** When you ascend to the top of a mountain, climbing the last few feet can be the most exciting.

**5** You can see this mountain's reflection, or image, in the lake.

**6** A valley often forms between mountains.

## Make Connections

Have you ever watched people climb mountains, go scuba diving, or explore the arctic on television or in a movie? Talk about whether you would like to do one of those activities.

These words will help you talk about the reading.

# Academic Words

| Academic Words |
| --- |
| **goal** something you want to achieve |
| **highlight** the most important or interesting part of something |
| **significant** important |

## Words in Context  Audio

Our team's **goal** is to win the next three games.

The fireworks are a **highlight** of a Fourth of July celebration.

My sister's wedding was a **significant** event for my family.

### Practice

**Write the sentences in your notebook. Choose an academic word to complete each sentence.**

1. Going up in the Empire State Building was a _____ of my trip to New York.

2. My uncle's graduation from college was a _____ event.

3. His _____ is to get As in all his classes this year.

### Apply

**Ask and answer with a partner.**

1. What's one **goal** you have this year?

2. What was one of the **highlights** of the last trip you took?

3. What was one **significant** event in your life this year?

# Word Study

## Greek and Latin Word Roots

Many English words come from Greek or Latin. For example, the word **circle** comes from the Latin root, **circ. Circ** means "round."

Half Dome is a mountain that looks like the top of a **circle.** The Latin root in each word below is in red.

| | |
|---|---|
| ani**m**al | **popu**lar |
| **cas**cade | **vac**ation |

**Practice**

**Complete each statement.**

1. The root *anim* means "life, spirit." So, an **animal** is _____.

   a. living       b. wild       c. dangerous

2. The root *vac* means "to be empty or free." During a **vacation,** you are likely to have _____.

   a. no time     b. free time    c. a good time

3. The root *popu* means "people." At a **popular** vacation spot, you're likely to see _____.

   a. plants      b. animals      c. people

4. The root *cas* means "fall." So, a **cascade** can be a _____.

   a. pool        b. lake         c. waterfall

WB
205

## LITERARY NONFICTION

### Scrapbook

**More About**

**THE BIG QUESTION**

What would you like to experience at a national park?

**Listen to the Audio.**
First, listen for the main points. Then listen again for the important details. Take notes as you listen. Retell the selection to a partner.

### Reading Strategy

#### Review and Retell

When you review and retell a selection, you pay attention to the most **significant** events and details. As you read:

* Ask yourself the 5W questions to help you remember the most important events and details.

Listen as your teacher models the reading strategy.

# My Trip to Yosemite

### by Jay Rabin

Hey Maria,

Check out my cool Yosemite scrapbook! I am going to show it to my friends at school.

Your friend,
Jay

▲ **Half Dome is one of the most famous mountains in Yosemite National Park.**

## August 8

On our first day, we drove to Glacier Point. Our **goal** was to **ascend** to the very top. We had a great view from there and saw the huge Yosemite Falls. We could see Yosemite **Valley** at the bottom. There were so many trees in the valley! We saw Half Dome mountain. It looks like the top of a circle. We passed rock climbers on the way down. People come from all over the world to climb rocks in Yosemite. It looked fun, but also a little scary!

**We saw these rock ▶ climbers. Yikes!**

◄ Yosemite Valley is one of the most popular places in Yosemite National Park.

Merced River is where visitors ▶ swim. People also go rafting down the river.

## August 9

The next day we saw Yosemite Valley again, but this time we saw it from the ground. We took a **mule** ride through the valley. Riding the mule was fun, but bumpy, and I was sore afterwards! Many people go on mule **tours** in Yosemite. There are trees and grass everywhere. We rode to Mirror Lake. When it is filled with water, you can see the reflections of mountains in it, like a mirror. We learned that the lake is slowly turning into a meadow. There is not much water there anymore, and it is mostly grass and plants. The lake was pretty, but the meadow is, too.

Later we went to a long river called the Merced River. The riverbank is like a beach, and many families were sitting on the sand. We swam in the water and watched people rafting.

---

**mule**   a cross between a horse and a donkey

**tours**   short trips through a place to see it

**Before You Go On**   What did Jay's family do on August 9?

## August 10

We wanted to see as many of the waterfalls in Yosemite as we could. There are eight major waterfalls that people visit. When it rains, many small waterfalls form. Yosemite Falls is the tallest waterfall in the United States. We took a tour and saw two other large waterfalls, Vernal Falls and Nevada Falls. They are not as tall as Yosemite Falls, but they are still amazing to see. We watched the water cascade down the sides of the mountains. We could see rainbows and felt the mist of water from the falls as we walked by.

We also hiked through the Mariposa Grove. It is a forest filled with very large old trees called sequoias. Many people think they are the biggest living things on our planet. They can grow to be over 200 feet tall. These trees are about 3,000 years old.

▲ **Wow! Look at how tall these trees are! They are also very old.**

▲ **There are hotels in Yosemite National Park, but we camped in our tent.**

▲ **My mom took this picture of Vernal Falls. Isn't the rainbow cool?**

▲ I heard people love to look at the mountains in the moonlight. Someday, when I am older, I will hike a mountain at night.

Hi Jay,
It looks like you had a really fun time. I can't wait to visit Yosemite again!
Talk to you soon,
Maria

## August 11

We slept outside in our tent. The park has a **campfire** set up for visitors to use. We swam in a lake just as the sun was going down, and then we warmed up by sitting around the fire. I was tired from all the walking, but I had seen many things for the first time on this trip. I had never seen rock climbers hanging off the side of a mountain! I had never seen waterfalls so high. I had never seen a forest filled with trees so tall and so **ancient**.

When the sun went down, we looked for the moon. It was high in the dark blue sky, high above the peak of the tallest mountain in Yosemite. When I was in my tent at night, I dreamed I was hiking through the valleys of Yosemite in the moonlight. This was a great vacation!

---

**campfire**   a fire made outdoors by people who are camping

**ancient**   very old

206-208

## Reading Strategy

### Review and Retell

Go back and review the selection.

- Retell what Jay did on August 10.
- Retell what Jay did on August 11.

## Think It Over

1. **Recall**   What **goal** did Jay mention in his August 10 entry?

2. **Comprehend**   What **significant** fact did Jay find out about Mirror Lake?

3. **Analyze**   What were the **highlights** of the trip to Yosemite for Jay?

# Learning Strategies

## Review and Retell

When you **review,** you re-read the selection and look for the main points and **significant** details. You can better remember the main points and important details if you **retell** them to a partner.

**Practice**

**Reread Jay's scrapbook entry for August 8. Look for the main event and three of the most important details. Then close your book and retell what Jay did on August 8 to a partner.**

August 8

   On our first day we drove to Glacier Point. Our goal was to ascend to the very top. We had a great view from there, and saw the huge Yosemite Falls. We could see Yosemite Valley at the bottom. There were so many trees in the valley! We saw Half Dome mountain. It looks like the top of a circle. We passed rock climbers on the way down. People from all over the world come to climb rocks in Yosemite. It looked fun, but also a little scary!

# Use a Main Idea and Details Chart

You can use a Main Idea and Details Chart to help you remember what you have read. You can then use your chart to retell the selection to a partner.

 G.O. 141

**Review Jay's entries for August 9, 10, and 11. Complete a Main Idea and Details Chart for each day.**

```
          ┌─────────────────────────┐
          │       Main Idea         │
          │                         │
          │                         │
          └─────────────────────────┘
           ↑          ↑          ↑
┌──────────┐  ┌──────────┐  ┌──────────┐
│  Detail  │  │  Detail  │  │  Detail  │
│          │  │          │  │          │
│          │  │          │  │          │
└──────────┘  └──────────┘  └──────────┘
```

**W B**
209

**Close your book and retell the selection to a partner.**

## Extension

**Utilize** Write a brief description about something you really liked or disliked about a place you have visited. Discuss your description with a partner or group.

# Grammar

## Active and Passive Voice

Written and spoken sentences can be in active voice or passive voice. In the **active voice**, the subject of the sentence acts on someone or something. It is usually better to use active voice in writing.

> **Active Voice**  A mountain lion  attacked  the boy.

In the **passive voice**, someone or something acts on the subject of the sentence. Use the passive voice when the action is more important that who did it.

> **Passive Voice**  The boy  was attacked  by a mountain lion.

Form the **passive voice** with *be* and the **past participle**. Remember that most past participles are formed by adding *-ed* to the verb, but some are irregular.

> **be + Past Participle**
> These trees are called sequoias.

> begin → begun   catch → caught   give → given   take → taken
> build → built    find → found     leave → left    tell → told

When you want to tell who or what did the action, include that information in a *by* phrase.

> **by Phrase**
> The park **was created** in 1890 by **the U.S. government.**

**Practice**

Rewrite each active voice sentence to make it passive voice.

**Example:** The tour guide took us to the waterfalls.

We were taken to the waterfalls by the tour guide.

1. My father took this picture.
2. A fire destroyed part of the forest.
3. Melting snow created all that cascading water.
4. Some people built hotels and houses.
5. The view from the tall peak surprised all of us.
6. Bears sometimes attack visitors to the park.
7. On the way down rock climbers passed us.
8. Each year more than three million people visit the park.

**Apply**

Write five passive voice sentences about an interesting place you have been. The questions below may help you. Then discuss your experience with a partner.

**Example:** A: Last year I was taken by my aunt and uncle to an old fort. It was built a long time ago.

B: Sounds fun! What did you do there?

WB
210

- Who were you taken by?
- Who or what built or made the place?
- When was it built or made?
- Were any pictures taken there?
- What were you surprised by?

**Grammar Check ✓**

How do you form the passive voice?

# Writing

## Paraphrasing a Source

When you put an author's ideas into your own words, you are paraphrasing. In this lesson, you will learn how to paraphrase information and ideas from the sources you use in your research.

### How to Paraphrase

Follow these steps to paraphrase ideas or information from a source:

1. Read the information in the reference source several times, so the important facts are clear in your mind.

2. Put the source away, and write what you learned in your own words.

3. Look at your source again. Make sure all the facts in your paraphrase are correct.

4. Finally, make a note of who wrote the book or article, as well as when it was published and by whom. If the information comes from a website, see if an author's name appears on the site, or copy down the URL. This is called a citation.

### Task

Begin research for the topic you chose in the last lesson. This will become the research report you will write in the workshop at the end of the unit. To practice paraphrasing, choose a paragraph from one of your sources. Express the ideas in your own words. List the text from the original source, your paraphrase, and the citation in a graphic organizer.

Amy listed some information she learned about the Dust Bowl in this chart:

| TEXT FROM SOURCE | PARAPHRASE | CITATION |
|---|---|---|
| The Dust Bowl was caused by several different factors that all seemed to come together at the same time. The reasons for this disaster didn't just happen overnight, they had been building up for at least a decade. | The Dust Bowl did not happen suddenly. There were many reasons why it occurred. These reasons had been building up for almost ten years. | Gregory. Geoff. <u>Causes of the Dust Bowl</u>. New York: Random House, 1999 |

Here is how Amy may use the information she found in her final research report. She included a citation of the source she used for the information.

Amy Ling

The Dust Bowl was a disaster that had devastating effects on American farmers. There were many causes that led to the Dust Bowl. The causes had been building up for almost ten years, beginning in the early 1920s. (Gregory)

**Prepare to Read**

## What You Will Learn

**Reading**

- Vocabulary building: *Context, phonics*

- Reading strategy: *Draw conclusions*

- Text type: *Literature (short story)*

## Grammar

Italics, underlining, and quotation marks

## Writing

Quoting a source

These words will help you understand the reading.

### Key Words

campsite

formation

incline

ranger station

rescue

encounter

# Key Words

## Words in Context

**1** My brother set up our campsite. We were going to spend the night there in a tent.

**2** The color and shapes of this unusual rock formation can be seen only in the Southwest.

**3** When a mountain has a steep incline, it is hard to climb.

**4**

**4** At the park, we checked in at the ranger station before we set out on the trails.

**5** The firefighters had to rescue a little girl from the burning house. They saved her life.

**6** When you go camping, you don't want to have an encounter with a hungry bear.

**Practice**

**Create a concept map for each key word.**
- Write the key word in the center.
- Around it, write words that relate to it.
- Connect the words using lines.

## Make Connections

Have you ever had an encounter with a wild animal? What happened? What would you do if you saw a bear in the woods?

213

These words will help you talk about the reading.

## Academic Words

**exhibit**
show a quality, sign, or emotion

**injured**
hurt

**deduce**
make a guess or judgment based on the information you have

# Academic Words

## Words in Context

Always try to **exhibit** good behavior.

No one wants to get **injured**, but accidents happen.

You can use details in a story to **deduce** what a character is thinking.

### Practice

**Write the sentences in your notebook. Choose an academic word to complete each sentence.**

1. You can take care of an ＿＿ ankle by wrapping a bandage around it.

2. If you see a broken window with a baseball nearby, you might ＿＿ that someone playing baseball broke it.

3. Even when he's afraid, my brother does not ＿＿ fear.

### Apply

**Ask and answer with a partner.**

1. What kinds of clues have you seen a TV detective use to **deduce** who has committed a crime?

2. What signs do you **exhibit** when you are mad?

3. How can you avoid being **injured** when running?

# Phonics

## Variant Vowel: oo *Audio*

Listen. Identify the two sounds the letters *oo* have. Then read the words aloud.

> **Words with Letters *oo***
>
> took   hook  |  too   food

### Rule

The /ŏŏ/ sound is the short sound of oo as in **took**.
The /ōō/ sound is the long sound of oo as in **too**.
If you come across a word you do not know, try reading it with the long sound first. It is more common.

### Practice

**Find each word with the letters *oo*. Sort the words into two lists based on how *oo* is pronounced.**

Dear Carlos,

Here's a picture of an old wooden schoolhouse. We saw it on the way to the beach. It was a little gloomy, but cool to see. It's proof we live in a better period! We had some good home-cooked food for lunch.

More soon,
Beatriz

Place
Stamp
Here

Carlos Reyes
10 Brook Lane
Salt Lake City,
Utah 84103

215

### LITERATURE

#### Short Story

**More About**

What experiences can people have at a national park?

**Listen to the Audio.**

First, listen for the main points. Then listen again for the important details. Take notes as you listen. Retell the story to a partner.

### Reading Strategy

#### Draw Conclusions

Good readers draw conclusions about things the author has not directly stated. By thinking about the details the author has given, you can **deduce** other information. Ask yourself:

- What conclusions can you draw about the characters?

- What conclusions can you draw about the situation the characters are in?

Listen as your teacher models the reading strategy.

# A Night at Great Basin

## By J.H. Diehl

As Miguel **staked** the corners of the tent to the ground, his little brother, Luis, jabbed a stick into the tall yellow grass at the edge of their campsite. "Yah! Yah!" he cried, "I'm hunting for scorpions–oops!"

The six-year-old tripped over his father's hiking boots, fell onto the still-flat tent, and burst out laughing. Miguel and the boys' father chuckled, too.

---

**staked**    pounded sticks into the ground that hold the tent in place

"Hey Dad," **observed** Miguel, "you bought Luis and me new boots for this trip, but yours are falling apart."

"Those are my lucky boots, from hikes I took as a teenager with your grandfather," his father answered, adding **affectionately**, "Luis, come help me snap these tent poles together."

When the tent was **erected**, their father showed the boys a book he had brought along: *Wildlife of Great Basin*. "There are scorpions here, but humans rarely see them. There are also bobcats and mountain lions, but most park visitors never see them either."

---

**observed**   saw or noticed something

**affectionately**   showing in a gentle way that you love someone

**erected**   made to stand up

**Before You Go On**   What can you **deduce** about the relationship among the three characters?

"OK," his father said, closing the book. "Let's get hiking before the sun sets."

For years, Miguel's father had talked about taking the boys camping in Great Basin National Park. He had finally arranged it and, this morning, the three of them had left their mother and their baby sister Isabel and driven 250 miles from their home in Salt Lake City.

"Yah! Yah!" Luis shouted, stirring up a pair of black tails in the bushes. The jack rabbits **scurried** away, and his father reminded Luis not to disturb wildlife.

---

**scurried**   moved quickly

The boys' father wanted to show them a rock formation he remembered along the trail. Looking up at the formation, he stepped off the path, slipped, and fell several feet down an incline. One of his old boots split apart, and he could not use his left leg. Miguel and Luis tried unsuccessfully to lift him. They waited for other hikers to come along, but none did.

Soon the pink sunset melted to darkness, the temperature dropped to sixty, and the sky filled with stars. Only a lonesome coyote howl broke the silence as the threesome **huddled** for warmth and eventually fell asleep.

---

**huddled**   moved close together

**Before You Go On**    What do you think will happen to the three hikers?

At daybreak, Miguel insisted on hiking back to the ranger station for help. His father said, "Thank you, son. I'm so sorry about this. Stay on the path, stay **alert**, and if you run into trouble, make noise."

Miguel did not feel like asking what his dad meant by trouble. As he walked, he sensed eyes observing him. He whirled around, but nothing was there. Suddenly the bushes rustled on his left, and Miguel spun around again. A young mountain lion stared straight at him.

Without thinking, Miguel hollered, "Yah! Yah!" and waved his arms wildly. The big cat, startled, paused only a second and then took off, disappearing into the **scrub**.

---

**alert**   giving all your attention to what is happening around you

**scrub**   low bushes that grow in dry country

Miguel ran the rest of the way to the ranger station. A first aid team was **notified** and sent out to rescue his father and transport him and Luis back to the station.

At the station, Miguel **related** his encounter with the lion, as his brother beamed with pride. "I shouted like Luis, and it worked!"

"You did *exactly* the right thing, son," said his father. "Thanks to you, we're all safe. I guess those *are* my lucky boots."

---

**notified** what happened in

**related** told about

216–218

## Reading Strategy

### Draw Conclusions

- What conclusions did you draw about the characters?

- What conclusions did you draw about the situations the characters were in?

- How did you reach those conclusions?

## Think It Over!

1. **Recall** Where were Luis, Miguel, and their father?

2. **Comprehend** What personal qualities does Miguel **exhibit** in the story?

3. **Analyze** How could the boys' father have been better prepared to avoid being **injured** and to handle the situation once it had happened?

# National Parks

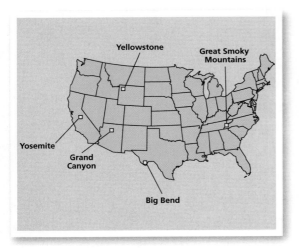

## ▲ National Park Map
This map shows the locations of the national parks on these pages.

## ▲ Big Bend National Park
Big Bend National Park is a large park in southwest Texas. Its southern boundary borders the Rio Grande River and Mexico. It includes dramatic mountain, desert, and river environments.

## ▲ Yosemite National Park
This national park in east-central California features a wide range of animals and plants. It is a World Heritage Site recognized for its groves of Giant Sequoia trees, waterfalls, and spectacular granite cliffs. It is an especially beautiful place for hiking. It attracts millions of visitors every year.

## ▲ Grand Canyon National Park

As one of the most famous and popular parks in the United States, the Grand Canyon has thousands of visitors every year. The canyon itself really is grand: it is 277 miles long (as the river winds), up to 18 miles wide, and a mile deep.

## ▲ Yellowstone National Park

Yellowstone is America's first national park, created in 1872. Crossing into parts of Montana, Wyoming, and Idaho, Yellowstone features a variety of landscapes and wildlife. It is famous for the hot water that shoots out of cracks in the rock, its tumbling waterfalls, and its wide open valleys. In Yellowstone, some people have had **encounters** with animals such as grizzly bears, bison, and wolves.

## ▲ Great Smoky Mountains National Park

In most years, Great Smoky Mountains National Park is the most heavily visited national park in the country, perhaps because people can see it by car and it is not too far from several big cities. Located in parts of North Carolina and Tennessee, this national park features ancient mountains. These mountains have been slowly wearing away over thousands of years, but they still provide amazing views.

## Activity to Do

These photos use pictures and words to tell about some national parks in the United States.

- Research a national park that interests you.

- Using pictures and words, create two pages telling about that park.

# Learning Strategies

## Draw Conclusions

When you **draw conclusions**, you use the information from the reading to **deduce** information and form your own ideas.

### Practice

**Read the paragraph.**

- What conclusions can you draw about the trail?
- Tell how you reached your conclusions.

> The boys' father wanted to show them a rock formation he remembered along the trail. Looking up at the formation, he stepped off the path, slipped, and fell several feet down an incline. One of his old boots split apart, and he could not use his left leg. Miguel and Luis tried unsuccessfully to lift him. They waited for other hikers to come along, but none did.

# Use a Story Map

You can use a Story Map to help you comprehend and remember a story.

**Practice**  G.O. 151

**Copy and complete this Story Map about *A Night at Great Basin*.**

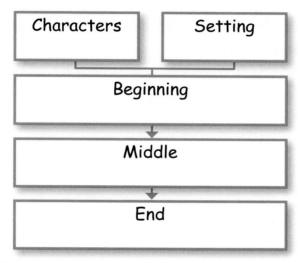

```
┌──────────────┐   ┌──────────────┐
│  Characters  │   │   Setting    │
└──────────────┘   └──────────────┘
       └──────┬──────────┘
       ┌──────────────────────┐
       │      Beginning       │
       └──────────────────────┘
                 ↓
       ┌──────────────────────┐
       │        Middle        │
       └──────────────────────┘
                 ↓
       ┌──────────────────────┐
       │         End          │
       └──────────────────────┘
```

**Apply**

**Close your book and retell the story to a partner.**

 W B
219

## Extension

**Utilize** With a small group, choose a scene from *A Night at Great Basin* that you'd like to perform. Find props and decide what actions you'll perform in the skit. Practice with your group, then perform the skit for the class.

# Grammar

## Italics, Underlining, and Quotation Marks

We use *italics*, <u>underlining</u>, and **"quotation marks"** to alert the reader to text that is different. Use *italics* or <u>underlining</u> for titles of **books, plays, newspapers, magazines, movies, TV shows**, and **CDs.**

> His favorite book is <u>Tales of a Fourth Grade Nothing</u>.
> They don't watch *Sesame Street* anymore.

Use *italics* or <u>underlining</u> for **foreign words** not common in English.

> Do you know what <u>carpe diem</u> means?

Use *italics* or <u>underlining</u> for **emphasis.**

> Report to the principal's office <u>immediately</u>.

Use **quotation marks** for titles of **short stories, songs, and poems.**

> The song "P.Y.T." is from the album <u>Thriller</u>.
> Poe's poem "The Raven" was published in 1845.

Periods and commas go inside quotation marks. Exclamation and question marks only go inside quotes if they are part of the title.

> The song "Who Let the Dogs Out?" was in *Rugrats in Paris: The Movie.*

**Rewrite each sentence using correct italics, underlining, or quotation marks. Write the reason you used that format.**

**Example:** Cesar Milan is on the TV show Dog Whisperer.

*Cesar Milan is on the TV show* <u>Dog Whisperer</u>*.*

1. The class sang What a Wonderful World for graduation.

2. I loved the book Murder on the Orient Express.

3. They'll get **injured** if they fight mano a mano.

4. They had an encounter with an alien in the movie E.T.

5. Dogs must be on a leash.

6. Do you know the song That's What Friends Are For?

7. I like the story The Legend of Sleepy Hollow.

8. Have you heard of the plays Hamlet or Romeo and Juliet?

**Apply**

**Work with a partner. Use the list below to ask and answer about your favorites. Write what your partner says, using correct italics, underlining, or quotations.**

220

| movie | newspaper | song | TV show |
| foreign word or phrase | book | play | magazine |

**Example:** A: *What's your favorite movie?*

B: *I really like Avatar.*

A writes: *He really likes* <u>Avatar</u>*.*

## Grammar Check ✓

How would you show the reader a book title? How about a foreign word?

## Quoting a Source

Including quotations from a source in a research report can be a powerful way of supporting your own ideas. In this lesson you will learn how to use quotations in this way.

## How to Include Quotations

Follow these steps to quote information directly from a source:

1.  Read the text you would like to quote. Think about why you wish to include it in your report. Does it support an idea better than you could in your own words?

2.  Write down the information word-for-word. It may be a sentence or an entire paragraph.

3.  Look at your original source again. Make sure you have copied the words correctly.

4.  Finally, make a note of who wrote the book or article, when it was published, and by whom. If the information comes from a website, see if an author's name appears on the site, or copy down the URL. This information is for the citation.

5.  When you write your report, surround the quoted text in quotation marks. Include your citation.

### Task

Continue the research for your report. To practice including quotations, look for information that supports a key point or idea in your report. Copy the text word-for-word. List the idea you want to support, the quotation, and the citation in a graphic organizer.

A student named Amy listed her idea, the direct quote she found, and her citation in this chart:

| INFORMATION SEARCH | DIRECT QUOTE | CITATION |
|---|---|---|
| Looking for information in which survivors of the Dust Bowl describe their experiences. | "For eight years dust blew on the southern plains. It came in a yellowish-brown haze from the South, and in rolling walls of black from the North. Simple acts of life, such as breathing or taking a walk, were no longer simple. My children wore dust masks to and from school." | Carver, Anna. <u>The Dust Bowl</u>. New York: History Press, 1999, page 126. |

Here is how Amy may use the information she found in her final research report. She included a citation of the source she used for the information.

Amy Ling

Many farms on the Great Plains were destroyed by dust and the long drought. Some people left their homes and traveled to California. They were looking for work. The ones who stayed found life very difficult: "For eight years dust blew on the southern plains. It came in a yellowish-brown haze from the South, and in rolling walls of black from the North. Simple acts of life, such as breathing or taking a walk, were no longer simple. My children wore dust masks to and from school." (Carver, p. 126)

# Apply and Extend

## Link the Readings

Copy the chart into your notebook.
Read the words in the top row. For each
text selection, put an X under words
related to that reading.

| | Informational text | Literature | Outdoor activities | Personal experiences |
|---|---|---|---|---|
| **Yosemite National Park** | | | | |
| **My Trip to Yosemite** | | | | |
| **A Night at Great Basin** | | | | |

## Discussion

1. What outdoor activities can people **participate** in at Yosemite National Park?

2. What were some of the **highlights** of Jay's trip to Yosemite and Luis's trip to the Great Basin?

3. What wildlife is able to live in the Great Basin?

THE BIG QUESTION Why are national parks important?

### Listening Skills

If you want to make sure you understood, you can ask "Do you mean...?" or "Are you saying?"

# Projects

**Your teacher will help you choose one of these projects.**

|  **Written** |  **Oral** |  **Visual/Active** |
|---|---|---|
| **Poem** | **Debate** | **Poster** |
| Write a poem about a place you have visited. Include details about the place and what people can do there. | Choose whether you would rather vacation at a national park or in a city. As teams, talk about the reasons for and against choosing each vacation spot. | Design a poster for a national park. Use photos or drawing to show what there is to do in the park. |
| **Brochure** | **Script** | **Blueprint** |
| Create a brochure for a national park. Include information about location, activities, and sights. Illustrate it with photos from the park's website. | Write a script a tour guide might use to show tourists around a national park. Be sure to include the park's most popular attractions. | Use your imagination to design a new national park. Draw a plan for the park that includes its features and activity areas. |

# Further Reading

 **For more projects visit** *LongmanCornerstone.com*

***Famous Sports,*** *Camron Fox*
This Penguin Young Reader® is a collection of great stories, facts, and quizzes about American football, basketball, athletics, and more.

***John Muir, America's Naturalist,*** Thomas Locker
Muir's study of nature in Yosemite National Park is featured in this biography of the famous scientist. Full-page paintings enhance the text.

223–224

## Present a TV Commercial

You are going to write and present a TV commercial about a special place. You will listen as your classmates present their commercials.

### ❶ Prepare

**A.** Work with two partners. Choose a special place such as an interesting city, national park, beach, or other tourist attraction.

**B.** Discuss the purpose of your commercial and who will watch it. Work cooperatively to research information about the place. Choose characters and roles. Now write your commercial. Be sure to describe the place well. Find props and costumes to use.

Carlsbad Caverns

Mom: [To the camera] If you need an idea for a great vacation, think about Carlsbad Caverns in New Mexico. Our family loved it. Just watch!

Sister: Mom, this is the coolest place!

Brother: Yeah! These caves are amazing.

Mother: It's hard to believe that this is in our own backyard, just outside of Carlsbad, New Mexico.

### ❷ Practice

Practice your commercial with your props and costumes. Practice in front of other classmates. If possible, record your commercial. Then listen to it. How do each of you sound? Record it again and try to improve.

# ❸ Present

**As you speak,** do the following:

- Use facial expressions and gestures.
- Show emotion through the tone of your voice.
- Pay attention to your partners so that you know when to say your lines.

**As you listen,** do the following:

- To help you understand, notice the actions of the actors and their props and costumes.
- Take notes on important details.
- Pay close attention. Your teacher will ask you questions after the presentation.

# ❹ Evaluate

**After you speak,** answer these questions:

- ✓ Did you use facial expressions and gestures?
- ✓ Did you show emotion through the tone of your voice?

**After you listen,** answer these questions:

- ✓ Did you understand the purpose of the commercial?
- ✓ Did you like the commercial? Why or why not?
- ✓ Did the actors use formal or informal language?

# Writing Workshop

## Write a Research Report

### Writing Prompt

Write the research report that you began earlier in this unit. Present a main idea, and include facts and details to support it. Gather information from a variety of sources, such as books, magazines, or online websites.

## ❶ Prewrite

Review the lessons in this unit. You have chosen and narrowed a topic. You have created a research plan. You have learned to paraphrase and quote directly from your sources.

### A. Taking Notes

Now it is time to do your research. As you do so, you will take notes on your findings. One of the most important things you need to do as you research is to keep track of your sources.

A good way to do this is to use note cards. Use one note card for each idea. Write a label for the idea at the top of the card. Then write your paraphrase or your quotation in the body of the card. Write the source, author, publisher, and page number at the bottom of the card.

You will use your cards when you plan your outline and write your report. You can also use them to put your sources in alphabetical order for your Works Consulted list.

Here is an example of a note card:

> ## DUST AFFECTS QUALITY OF LIFE
>
> "For eight years dust blew on the southern plains. It came in a yellowish-brown haze from the South, and in rolling walls of black from the North. Simple acts of life, such as breathing or taking a walk, were no longer simple. My children wore dust masks to and from school."
>
> Carver, Anna. The Dust Bowl. New York: History Press, 1999, page 126.

## B. Making an Outline

Use the labels on your note cards to sort the cards by ideas. Decide what order you would like to present the ideas in your report. Discard any note cards for ideas you decide not to use. Once you are satisfied with the arrangement of your ideas, create an outline.

> ## The Dust Bowl
>
> A. Introduction: The stage is set for disaster.
>    1. Farmers dig up grassland.
>    2. Soil is left without plants to keep it in place.
> B. Nature makes problems worse.
>    1. A drought dries the soil.
>    2. Winds sweep up the loose soil.
> C. People suffer.
>    1. Dust and drought destroy farms.
>    2. People are forced to leave their homes.
> D. Conclusion: Farmers suffer, but they also learn new methods.

# Writing Workshop

## ❷ Draft

Use your outline to help you write a first draft.

- Begin with a paragraph that clearly presents your topic.
- Use transition words to keep your ideas flowing smoothly.
- Include citations for paraphrases and quotations.

**Citing Sources** Use the following examples as models to help you cite your sources correctly:

---

**Book**

Pearson, Anne. Ancient Greece. New York: Dorling Kindersley, 2007.

**Magazine article**

Fitzgerald, Terrence. "March of the Caterpillars." Natural History September 2008: 28–33.

**Internet website**

"Small but WISE." Science News for Kids 6 January 2010. <http://www.sciencenewsforkids.org/articles/20100106/Feature1.asp>

**Encyclopedia article**

Lawson, Wendy. "Antarctica." World Book Encyclopedia. 2010 ed.

---

## ❸ Revise

Read over your draft. Look for places where the writing needs improvement. Use the Writing Checklist to help you identify problems. Then revise your draft.

## Six Traits of Writing Checklist

✔ **Ideas**
Does my first paragraph present the topic clearly?

✔ **Organization**
Are my ideas presented in a logical order?

✔ **Voice**
Is my tone appropriately formal?

✔ **Word Choice**
Did I use transition w
to connect ideas and
sentences?

✔ **Sentence Fluency**
Do I use a variety of
sentence patterns ar
sentence lengths?

✔ **Conventions**
Do my nouns, prono
and verbs agree?

Here is how Amy revised her report:

Amy Ling

## The Dust Bowl

The Dust Bowl was a disaster that had devastating a
effects on American farmers. There were many causes
that led to the Dust Bowl. The causes had been building up
for almost ten years, beginning in the early 1920s. (Gregory)
^Many farmers settled on the Great Plains. Throughout
the early part of the 1900s, they dug up hundreds of
acres of grassland to plant crops. When the crops were
harvested, the land was often left without crops or plants
of any kind. People did not know that plants kept the soil in
As a result,
place. The soil became loose.

Then, in the 1930s, a drought occurred. It lasted for many
years. The soil dried out and turned to dust. The strong winds
on the Great Plains swept up the loose soil. It turned into
huge clouds of dust. Parts of Texas, Colorado, New Mexico,
Kansas, and Oklahoma became known as the Dust Bowl.

Many farms in the area were destroyed by dust and the
and
drought. Some people left their homes, traveled to California.
They were looking for work. The ones who stayed found life
difficult: "For eight years dust blew on the southern plains. It
came in a yellowish-brown haze from the South, and in rolling
walls of black from the North. Simple acts of life, such as
breathing or taking a walk, were no longer simple. My children
wore dust masks to and from school." (Carver, p. 126)

The Dust Bowl caused hardship and tragedy for many
people. But it also taught farmers new farming methods and
Unfortunately,
ways to take better care of the land. It was a costly lesson.

**Revised** to correct a error in spelling.

**Revised** to clarify meaning.

**Revised** to add a transition.

**Revised** to correct errors in mechanics.

**Revised** to add a missing word.

**Revised** to correct error in mechanics.

**Revised** to add a transition.

**Works Consulted List**

Carver, Anna. <u>The Dust Bowl</u>. New York: History Press, 1999.

Gregory, Geoff. <u>Causes of the Dust Bowl</u>. New York: Random House, 1999.

Lookingbill, Brad D. "Dust Bowl." <u>World Book Student</u>. 5 Jan. 2011. <http://www.worldbookonline.com/student/article?id=ar170200>

## ❹ Edit

Check your work for errors. Trade papers with a partner. Use the Peer Review Checklist to give each other feedback.

## ❺ Publish

Make a clean copy of your final draft. Share your report with the class.

### Peer Review Checklist

- ✔ Ideas are presented in a logical order.
- ✔ Transition words are used to link one idea to the next.
- ✔ The main ideas are supported by facts and details.

225–226

**Listen to the sentences. Pay attention to the groups of words. Read aloud.**  Audio

1. Objects of natural beauty in Yosemite National Park make it a great vacation place with something for everyone to enjoy.
2. People come to Yosemite from all over the world to climb rocks, ride mules, and see waterfalls cascade down the mountains.
3. Miguel helps to rescue his brother and father during a camping trip in Great Basin National Park.

| | |
|---|---|
| The Yosemite region of California takes up almost 1,200 | 9 |
| square miles and is known for its amazing waterfalls, deep | 19 |
| valleys, and huge meadows. People have lived in the | 28 |
| region for 8,000 years. In the 1830s, people from | 37 |
| other places visited, and some built hotels and houses | 46 |
| there. Environmentalists worried about this and feared | 53 |
| the land would be ruined. | 58 |
| The U.S. government stepped in to help, and in 1890, | 68 |
| the area became known as Yosemite National Park. Rules | 77 |
| were created to make sure the land was preserved for | 87 |
| people to enjoy in the future. More than three million | 97 |
| people visit the park each year. | 103 |
| Yosemite Valley is a popular destination for visitors. | 111 |
| It has cliffs and rock forms, and many guests spend | 121 |
| time visiting its waterfalls. Yosemite Valley is open | 129 |
| all year. People often travel to the valley by car. | 139 |
| Yosemite National Park is also famous for its trees. | 148 |
| Giant sequoias seem to reach the sky. | 155 |

227–228

# Test Preparation

## Taking Tests

You will often take tests that help show what you know.
Follow these tips to improve your test-taking skills.

## Coaching Corner

### Answering Test Items That Have Cloze Passages

- Cloze items ask you to fill in a blank.

- Sometimes you will be asked to complete a sentence. Other times you will be given a selection with some words left out.

- First read the questions and answer choices. Sometimes there is no question, just a list of words.

- Read the whole selection carefully. Try to think of words that might fit as you read.

- If you don't know what a word means, use the words around it to help you.

- If there is a question, read it carefully. Look for words like _best_, _least_, _main_, _most_, _most likely_, _probably_, and _not_.

- In your head, read the sentence with each answer choice. Choose the answer that makes the most sense.

Read the following test sample. Study the tips in the box.

229–230

**Read the selection. Then choose the correct words to fill in the blanks.**

1      How did the hot springs in Big Bend National Park form? If you could __1__ down through the Earth's crust, you would see that the rocks in the crust get __2__ the further down you go. The water that is near or touching the hot rocks also gets hot and comes up to the surface. When the water does this, it becomes a hot spring.

2      In areas near volcanoes, like in Yellowstone National Park, the water comes in contact with molten rock called magma. The water that touches magma becomes so hot it __3__. Steam rises above Earth's crust in the form of a geyser. Old Faithful is one of the most famous __4__ in the world!

1  **A**  hear
    **B**  travel
    **C**  swim
    **D**  meet

2  **F**  heavier
    **G**  lighter
    **H**  hotter
    **J**  colder

3  **A**  boils
    **B**  flows
    **C**  freezes
    **D**  melts

4  **F**  waterfalls
    **G**  hot springs
    **H**  earthquakes
    **J**  geysers

**Tips**

✓ Read the answer choices first. That way you will know what to look for as you read the selection.

✓ If you don't know what some words mean, use the words around them to help you.

# Handbook

## How to Learn Language

Learning a language involves listening, speaking, reading, and writing. You can use these tips to make the most of your language learning.

### LISTENING

**1.** Listen with a purpose.

**2.** Listen actively.

**3.** Take notes.

**4.** Listen to speakers on the radio, television, and Internet.

### SPEAKING

**1.** Think before you speak.

**2.** Speak appropriately for your audience.

**3.** Practice reading aloud to a partner.

**4.** Practice speaking with friends and family members.

**5.** Remember, it is okay to make mistakes.

### READING

**1.** Read every day.

**2.** Use the visuals to help you figure out what words mean.

**3.** Reread parts that you do not understand.

**4.** Read many kinds of literature.

**5.** Ask for help.

### WRITING

**1.** Write something every day.

**2.** Plan your writing before you begin.

**3.** Read what you write aloud. Ask yourself whether it makes sense.

**4.** Check for spelling and grammar mistakes.

## How to Study

**Here are some tips for developing good study habits.**

- **Schedule a time for studying.** It is easier to develop good study habits if you set aside the same time every day to study. Once you have a study routine, it will be easier for you to find time to prepare for larger projects or tests.

- **Create a special place for studying.** Find a study area where you are comfortable and where you have everything you need for studying. If possible, choose an area that is away from telephones or television. You can play music if it helps you to concentrate.

- **Read the directions first.** Make sure you understand what you are supposed to do. Ask a partner or your teacher about anything you do not understand.

- **Preview the reading.** Look at the pictures, illustrations, and captions in the reading. They will help you understand the text.

- **Learn unfamiliar words.** Try to figure out what unfamiliar words mean by finding context clues in the reading. If you still can't figure out the meaning, use a dictionary.

- **Take notes.** Keep notes in a notebook or journal of important things you want to remember from the reading.

- **Ask questions.** Write any questions you have from the reading. Discuss them with a partner or your teacher.

# How to Build Vocabulary

**Use these ideas to help you remember the meanings of new words.**

**Keep a Vocabulary Notebook**  Keep a notebook of vocabulary words and their definitions. Test yourself by covering either the word or the definition.

**Make Flashcards**  On the front of an index card, write a word you want to remember. On the back, write the meaning. Use the cards to review the words with a partner or family member.

**Say the Words Aloud**  Use your new words in sentences. Say the sentences to a partner or a family member.

# How to Use a Book

**The Title Page**  The title page states the title, the author, and the publisher.

**The Table of Contents**  The table of contents is at the front of a book. The page on which a chapter begins is next to its name.

**The Glossary**  The glossary is a small dictionary at the back of a book. It will tell you the meaning of a word, and sometimes how to pronounce it. Use the glossary the same way you would use a dictionary.

**The Index**  The index is at the back of a book. It lists subjects and names that are in the book, along with page numbers where you can find information.

**The Bibliography**  The bibliography at the back of a book or chapter lets you know the books or sources where an author got information.

# How to Use a Dictionary and Thesaurus

## The Dictionary

You can find the **spelling, pronunciation, part of speech**, and **definitions** of words in the dictionary.

Pronunciation    Part of Speech

Definitions

**let•ter** /let´ər/ noun ① one of the signs that you use to write words: *A, B, and C are the first three **letters** in the English alphabet.*

② a written message that you put into an envelope and send to someone: *I wrote a **letter** to my friend in Texas.*

Example Sentence

## The Thesaurus

A thesaurus is a specialized dictionary that lists **synonyms**, or words with similar meanings, and **antonyms**, or words with opposite meanings. Words in a thesaurus are arranged alphabetically. You can look up the word just as you would look it up in a dictionary.

**Main entry**: sad
**Part of speech**: adjective
**Definition**: unhappy
**Synonyms**: bitter, depressed, despairing, down, downcast, gloomy, glum, heartbroken, low, melancholy, morose, pessimistic, sorry, troubled, weeping
**Antonyms**: cheerful, happy

# How to Take Tests

**Taking tests is part of going to school. Use these tips to help you answer the kinds of questions you often see on tests.**

## True-False Questions

- If a statement seems true, make sure it is *all* true.
- The word *not* can change the meaning of a statement.
- Pay attention to words such as *all*, *always*, *never*, *no*, *none*, and *only*. They often make a statement false.
- Words such as *generally*, *much*, *many*, *sometimes*, and *usually* often make a statement true.

## Multiple Choice Questions

- Try to answer the question before reading the choices. If your answer is one of the choices, choose it.
- Eliminate answers you know are wrong.
- Don't change your answer unless you know it is wrong.

## Matching Questions

- Count each group to see whether any items will be left over.
- Read all the items before you start matching.
- Match the items you know first.

## Fill-In-the-Blank Questions or Completions

- Read the question or incomplete sentence carefully.
- Look for clues in the question or sentence that might help you figure out the answer.
- If you are given possible answers, cross each out as you use it.

## Short Answers and Essays

- Take a few minutes to organize your thoughts.
- Give only the information that is asked for.
- Answer as clearly as possible.
- Leave time to proofread your response or essay.

## How to Read Maps and Diagrams

Informational texts often use maps, diagrams, graphs, and charts. These tools help illustrate and explain the topic.

### Maps

Maps show the location of places such as countries, states, and cities. They can also show where mountains, rivers, lakes, and streets are located. A compass rose on the map shows which way is north. A scale shows how miles or kilometers are represented on the map.

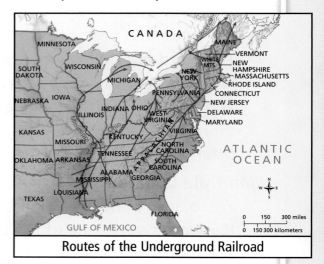

Routes of the Underground Railroad

### Diagrams

Diagrams are drawings that explain things or show how things work. Some diagrams show pictures of how objects look on the outside or on the inside. Others show the different steps in a process.

This diagram shows the steps of the Scientific Method. It helps you understand the order and importance of each step.

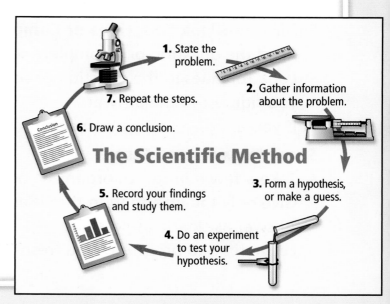

1. State the problem.
2. Gather information about the problem.
3. Form a hypothesis, or make a guess.
4. Do an experiment to test your hypothesis.
5. Record your findings and study them.
6. Draw a conclusion.
7. Repeat the steps.

**The Scientific Method**

# How to Read Graphs

Graphs show how two or more kinds of information are related or alike. Three common kinds of graphs are **line graphs**, **bar graphs**, and **circle graphs**.

## Line Graph

A **line graph** shows how information changes over a period of time. This line graph explains how the Native American population of Central Mexico changed over 120 years.

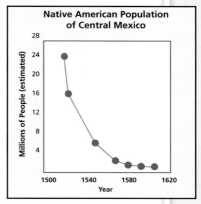

## Bar Graphs

We use **bar graphs** to compare information. For example, this bar graph compares the populations of the 13 United States in 1790.

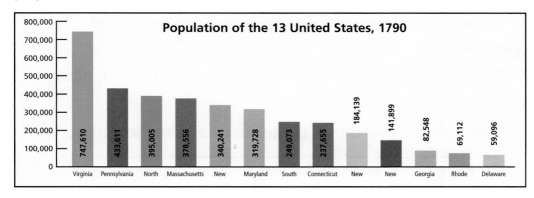

## Circle Graphs

A **circle graph** is sometimes called a pie chart because it looks like a pie cut into slices. Circle graphs are used to show how different parts of a whole compare to each other.

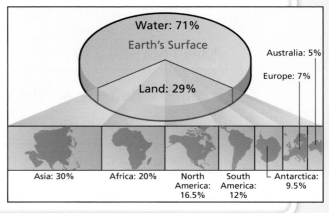

## Parts of Speech

In English there are nine **parts of speech**: nouns, articles, pronouns, verbs, adjectives, adverbs, prepositions, conjunctions, and interjections.

### Nouns

Nouns name people, places, or things.

A **common noun** is a general person, place, or thing.

> person       thing       place
> The **student** brings a **notebook** to **class**.

A **proper noun** is a specific person, place, or thing.

> person       place       thing
> **Joe** went to **Paris** and saw the **Eiffel Tower**.

### Articles

**Indefinite articles** are *a* or *an*. They refer to a person, place, or thing.

Use *an* before a word that begins with a vowel sound.

> I have **an** idea.

Use *a* before a noun that begins with a consonant sound.

> May I borrow **a** pen?

*The* is called a **definite article**. Use *the* to talk about specific people, places, or things.

> Please bring me **the** box from your room.

## Pronouns

**Pronouns** are words that take the place of nouns or proper nouns.

| proper noun | pronoun |
| --- | --- |

Ana is not home. **She** is babysitting.

|  | **Subject Pronouns** | **Object Pronouns** |
| --- | --- | --- |
| **Singular** | I, you, he, she, it | me, you, him, her, it |
| **Plural** | we, you, they | us, you, them |

A **subject pronoun** replaces the subject of a sentence. A **subject** is who or what a sentence is about.

subject     subject pronoun (singular)
**Dan** is a student. **He** goes to school every day.

**Object pronouns** replace a noun or proper noun that is the object of a verb. An **object** receives the action of a verb.

object                          object pronoun (singular)
Lauren gave **Ed** the notes. Lauren gave **him** the notes.

Possessive pronouns replace nouns or proper nouns. They show who owns something.

|  | **Possessive Pronouns** |
| --- | --- |
| **Singular** | mine, yours, hers, his |
| **Plural** | ours, yours, theirs |

## Verbs

**Verbs** express an action or a state of being.

An **action verb** tells what someone or something does or did.

| Verbs that Tell Actions You Can See | Verbs that Tell Actions You Cannot See |
|---|---|
| dance        swim | know        sense |

A **linking verb** shows no action. It links the subject with another word that describes the subject.

| Examples of Linking Verbs | | |
|---|---|---|
| look | smell | is |
| are | appear | seem |

A helping verb comes before the main verb. They add to a verb's meaning.

| | Helping Verbs |
|---|---|
| **Forms of the verb *be*** | am, was, is, were, are |
| **Forms of the verb *do*** | do, did, does |
| **Forms of the verb *have*** | have, had, has |
| **Other helping verbs** | can, must, could, have (to), should, may, will, would |

## Adjectives

**Adjectives** describe nouns. An adjective usually comes before the noun it describes.

> **tall** grass          **big** truck

An adjective can come *after* the noun it describes. This happens in these kinds of sentences.

> The bag is **heavy**. The books are **new**.

## Adverbs

**Adverbs** describe the action of verbs. They tell *how* an action happens. Adverbs answer the question *Where?, When?, How?, How much?,* or *How often?*

Many adverbs end in *-ly*.

> easily          slowly

Some adverbs do not end in *-ly*.

> seldom          fast          very

In this sentence, the adverb *everywhere* modifies the verb *looked*. It answers the question *Where?*

>       verb     adverb
> Nicole looked **everywhere** for her book.

## Prepositions

**Prepositions** show time, place, and direction.

| Time | Place | Direction |
|---|---|---|
| after | above | across |
| before | below | down |

In this sentence, the preposition *above* shows where the bird flew. It shows place.

> preposition
> A bird flew **above** my head.

In this sentence, the preposition *across* shows direction.

> preposition
> The children walked **across** the street.

A **prepositional phrase** starts with a preposition and ends with a noun or pronoun. In this sentence, the preposition is *near* and the noun is *school*.

> ⌐ prepositional phrase ¬
> The library is **near the new school**.

## Conjunctions

A **conjunction** joins words, groups of words, and whole sentences. Common conjunctions include *and*, *but*, and *or.*

The conjunction *and* joins two proper nouns: *Allison* and *Teresa*.

> proper     proper
> noun      noun
> Allison **and** Teresa are in school.

The conjunction *or* joins two prepositional phrases: *to the movies* and *to the mall*.

> prepositional    prepositional
> phrase        phrase
> They want to go to the movies **or** to the mall.

The conjunction *but* joins two independent clauses.

> independent clause    independent clause
> Alana baked the cookies, **but** Eric made the lemonade.

## Interjections

**Interjections** are words or phrases that express emotion.

Interjections that express strong emotion are followed by an exclamation point.

> **Wow!** Did you see that catch?

A comma follows interjections that express mild emotion.

> **Gee**, I'm sorry that your team lost.

# Sentences

## Clauses

**Clauses** are groups of words with a subject and a verb.

- An **independent clause** can stand on its own as a complete sentence.
- A **dependent clause** cannot stand alone as a complete sentence.

## Sentences

A simple sentence is an independent clause. It has a subject and a verb.

> subject   verb
> The dog barked.

A **compound sentence** is made up of two or more simple sentences, or independent clauses.

> ⌐ independent clause ¬      ⌐ independent clause ¬
> The band has a lead singer, but it needs a drummer.

## Sentence Types

**Declarative sentences** are statements. They end with a period.

> We are going to the beach on Saturday.

**Interrogative sentences** are questions. They end with a question mark.

> Will you come with us?

**Imperative sentences** are commands. They end with a period or an exclamation point.

> Put on your life jacket. Now jump in the water!

**Exclamatory sentences** express strong feeling. They end with an exclamation point.

> I swam all the way from the boat to the shore!

# Punctuation

## End Marks

End marks come at the end of sentences. There are three kinds of end marks: periods, question marks, and exclamation points.

## Periods

- Use a period to end a statement (declarative sentence).
- Use a period to end a command or request (imperative sentence).
- Use a period after a person's initial or abbreviated title.
- Use a period after abbreviations.

## Question Marks and Exclamation Points

- Use an exclamation point to express strong feelings.
- Use a question mark at the end of a question.

## Commas

**Commas separate parts of a sentence or phrase.**

- Use a comma to separate two independent clauses linked by a conjunction.
- Use commas to separate the parts in a series. A series is a group of three or more words, phrases, or clauses.
- Use a comma to set off introductory words or phrases.
- Use commas to set off an interrupting word or phrase.
- Use a comma to set off a speaker's quoted words.
- Use commas to set off the name of the person being addressed in a letter or speech.

## Semicolons and Colons

**Semicolons** can connect two independent clauses. Use them when the clauses are closely related in meaning or structure.

**Colons** introduce a list of items or important information. Also use a colon to separate hours and minutes when writing the time.

## Quotation Marks

Quotation marks set off direct quotations, dialogue, and some titles.

* Commas and periods always go inside quotation marks.
* If a question mark or exclamation point is not part of the quotation, it goes outside the quotation marks.
* Use quotation marks to set off what people say in a dialogue.
* Use quotation marks around the titles of short works of writing.

## Apostrophes

**Apostrophes** can be used with singular and plural nouns to show ownership or possession. To form the possessive, follow these rules:

* For singular nouns, add an apostrophe and an *s*.
* For singular nouns that end in *s*, add an apostrophe and an *s*.
* For plural nouns that do not end in *s*, add an apostrophe and an *s*.
* For plural nouns that end in *s*, add an apostrophe.
* Apostrophes are also used in contractions, to show where a letter or letters have been taken away.

## Capitalization

There are five main reasons to use capital letters:

* to begin a sentence
* to write the pronoun *I*
* to write the names of proper nouns
* to write a person's title
* to write the title of a work (artwork, written work)

## Modes of Writing

**Narrative Writing** is used to tell a story. Here are some types of narrative writing.

- Autobiography is the story of a person's life, told by the person.
- Biography is the story of a person's life told by another person.
- A short story is a short fictional narrative.

**Descriptive Writing** paints a picture of a person, place, thing, or event.

**Expository Writing** gives information or explains something. Here are some types of expository writing.

- Compare and Contrast writing analyzes the similarities and differences between two or more things.
- Cause and Effect writing explains why something happened and what happens as a result.
- Problem and Solution writing describes a problem and offers one or more solutions to it.
- How-to writing explains how to do or make something.

**Persuasive Writing** is writing that tries to convince people to think or act in a certain way.

**Functional Writing** is writing for real-world uses. Here are some types of functional writing.

- You might fill out a form to sign up for lessons, take a field trip, or apply for a library card.
- You might create an invitation to a holiday party.

# The Writing Process

**The writing process is a series of steps that helps you write clearly.**

### Step 1: Prewrite

When you prewrite, you explore ideas and choose a topic. You identify your audience, and you choose your purpose for writing.

To choose a topic, try one or more of these strategies.
- **List** many ideas that you might want to write about.
- **Freewrite** about some ideas for five minutes.
- **Brainstorm** a list of ideas with a partner.

To identify your audience, think about who will read your writing. What do they already know? What do you need to explain?

To identify your purpose for writing, ask:
- Do I want to entertain my audience?
- Do I want to inform my audience?
- Do I want to persuade my audience?

Now, decide on the best form for your writing. Gather and organize the details that will support your topic.

### Step 2: Draft

You start writing in this step. Put your ideas into sentences. Put your sentences into paragraphs. Begin to put your paragraphs in order. Don't worry too much about grammar and spelling. You will have a chance to correct any errors later.

## Step 3: Revise

This is the time to look at your ideas and the organization of your writing. Read your first draft. Ask yourself:

- Are the ideas presented in the best order?
- Is there a clear beginning, middle, and end?
- Does each paragraph have a main idea and supporting details?

Decide what changes you will make. Then revise your draft.

## Step 4: Edit/Proofread

This is the time to look at word choice, sentence fluency, and writing conventions. Reread your paper. Proofread for mistakes in spelling, grammar, and punctuation. Correct any mistakes you find.

When you edit and proofread your draft, use these proofreading marks to mark the changes.

| Editing/Proofreading Marks | | |
|---|---|---|
| **To:** | **Use This Mark:** | **Example:** |
| add something | ∧ | We ate rice, bean$_\wedge^s$ and corn. |
| delete something | ℓ | We ate rice, beans, and corns. |
| start a new paragraph | ¶ | ¶ We ate rice, beans, and corn. |
| add a comma | ⌣ | We ate rice, beans and corn. |
| add a period | ⊙ | We ate rice, beans, and corn⊙ |
| switch letters or words | ∼ | We ate rice, baehs, and corn. |
| change to a capital letter | a̲ | we ate rice, beans, and corn. |
| change to a lowercase letter | A̸ | WE ate rice, beans, and corn. |

## Peer Review Checklist

### Ideas

☐ Is the content interesting and thoughtful?
☐ Is the main idea clearly stated?
☐ Are the main ideas supported by facts and details?
☐ Do the ideas flow from one to the next?

### Organization

☐ Are the ideas in an order that makes sense?
☐ Are the ideas connected by transitions and other connecting words?

### Voice

☐ Does the writing have energy and personality?

### Word Choice

☐ Has the writer chosen precise words?

### Sentence Fluency

☐ Do the sentences flow smoothly?
☐ Are the sentences varied in type and length?

### Conventions

☐ Do the subjects of sentences agree with the verbs?
☐ Do the pronouns agree with the words they refer to?
☐ Are the verb tenses appropriate and consistent?
☐ Is the possessive case (apostrophe -s) used correctly?
☐ Are negatives and contractions used correctly?
☐ Are the punctuation and capitalization correct?
☐ Is the writing free of spelling errors?

## Step 5: Publish

Once you have revised and proofread your paper, share it with others. Look at these publishing ideas.

- Post your paper on the bulletin board.
- Photocopy your paper. Hand it out to your classmates and family members.
- Attach it to an email and send it to friends.
- Send it to a school newspaper or magazine for possible publication.

Once you have shared your work with others, you may want to put it in your portfolio. A portfolio is a folder or envelope in which you keep your writing. If you keep your work in a portfolio, you can look at what you have written over a period of time. This will let you see if your writing is improving. It will help you become a better writer.

## Build Your Portfolio

You may want to keep your completed writing in your portfolio. It is a good idea to keep your drafts, too. Keep comments you receive from your teacher or writing partner, as well.

## Reflect on Your Writing

Make notes on your writing in a journal. Write how you felt about what you wrote. Use these questions to help you get started.

- What new things did you learn about your topic?
- What helped you organize the details in your writing?
- What helped you revise your writing?
- What did you learn about yourself as you wrote?

# Rubric for Writing

A rubric is a tool that helps you assess, or evaluate, your work. This rubric shows specific details for you to think about when you write. The scale ranges from 4 to 1, with 4 being the highest score and 1 being the lowest.

| 4 | Writing is clearly focused on the task. <br> Writing is well organized. Ideas follow a logical order. <br> Main idea is fully developed and supported with details. <br> Sentence structure is varied. Writing is free of fragments. <br> There are no errors in writing conventions. |
|---|---|
| 3 | Writing is focused, with some unnecessary information. <br> There is clear organization, with some ideas out of order. <br> The main idea is supported, but development is uneven. <br> Sentence structure is mostly varied, with some fragments. <br> Writing conventions are generally followed. |
| 2 | Writing is related to the task but lacks focus. <br> Organization is not clear. Ideas do not fit well together. <br> There is little or no support for the main idea. <br> No variation in sentence structure. Fragments occur often. <br> Frequent errors in writing conventions. |
| 1 | The writing is generally unfocused. <br> There is little organization or development. <br> There is no clear main idea. <br> Sentence structure is unvaried. There are many fragments. <br> Many errors in writing conventions and spelling. |

# Writing and Research

Sometimes when you write, you need to do research to learn more information about your topic. You can do research in the library, on the Internet, and by viewing or listening to information media.

### Library Reference

**Encyclopedias** contain basic facts, background information, and suggestions for additional research.

**Biographical references** provide brief life histories of famous people in many different fields.

**Almanacs** contain facts and statistics about many subjects, including government, world history, geography, entertainment, business, and sports.

**Periodicals** are past editions of magazines. Use a periodical index to find articles on your topic.

**Vertical files** contain pamphlets on a wide variety of topics.

**Electronic databases** provide quick access to information on many topics.

## Citing Sources

When you do research, you read what other people wrote. The material you research is called the source or reference. When you tell who wrote the material, this is called citing the source. It is important to cite each source you use when you write.

In your paper, note each place in which you use a source. At the end of the paper, provide a list that gives details about all your sources. A bibliography and a works cited list are two types of source lists.

- A **bibliography** provides a listing of all the material you used during your research.

- A **works cited list** shows the sources you have quoted in your paper.

---

**Plagiarism**

Plagiarism is presenting someone else's words, ideas, or work as your own. If the idea or words are not yours, be sure to give credit by citing the source in your work. It is a serious offense to plagiarize.

---

Look at the chart of the Modern Language Association (MLA). Use this format for citing sources. This is the most common format for papers written by middle and high school students, as well as college students.

## MLA Style for Listing Sources

| | |
|---|---|
| **Book** | Pyles, Thomas. *The Origins and Development of the English Language*. 2nd ed. New York: Harcourt Brace Jovanovich, Inc., 1971. |
| **Signed article in a magazine** | Gustaitis, Joseph. "The Sticky History of Chewing Gum." *American History* Oct. 1998: 30–38. |
| **Filmstrips, slide programs, videocassettes, DVDs** | *The Diary of Anne Frank*. Dir. George Stevens. Perf. Millie Perkins, Shelly Winters, Joseph Schildkraut, Lou Jacobi, and Richard Beymer. Twentieth Century Fox, 1959. |
| **Internet** | *National Association of Chewing Gum Manufacturers*. 19 Dec. 1999. <http://www.longmancornerstone.com> [Indicate the date you found the information.] |
| **Newspaper** | Thurow, Roger. "South Africans Who Fought for Sanctions Now Scrap for Investors." *Wall Street Journal* 11 Feb. 2000. |
| **Personal interview** | Smith, Jane. Personal interview. 10 Feb. 2000. |

## Internet Research

The Internet is an international network of computers. The World Wide Web is a part of the Internet that lets you find and read information.

To do research on the Internet, you need to open a search engine. Type in a keyword on the search engine page. **Keywords** are words or phrases on the topic you want to learn about. For example, if you are looking for information about your favorite musical group, you might use the band's name as a keyword.

To choose a keyword, write a list of all the words you are considering. Then choose a few of the most important words.

**Tips**
- Spell the keywords correctly.
- Use the most important keyword first, followed by the less important ones.
- Open the pages at the top of the list first. These will usually be the most useful sources.

###  How to Evaluate Information from the Internet

When you do research on the Internet, you need to be sure the information is correct. Use the checklist to decide if you can trust the information on a Web site.

✓ Look at the address bar. A URL that ends in "edu" is connected to a school or university. A URL that ends in "gov" means it is a site posted by a state or federal government. These sites should have correct information.

✓ Check that the people who write or are quoted on the site are experts, not just people telling their ideas or opinions.

✓ Check that the site is free of grammatical and spelling errors. This is often a hint that the site was carefully designed and researched.

✓ Check that the site is not trying to sell a product or persuade people.

✓ If you are not sure about using a site as a source, ask an adult.

## Information Media

Media is all the organizations that provide news and information for the public. Media includes television, radio, and newspapers. This chart describes several forms of information media.

| Types of Information Media | |
|---|---|
| Television News Program | • Covers current news events<br>• Gives information objectively |
| Documentary | • Focuses on one topic of social interest<br>• Sometimes expresses controversial opinions |
| Television Newsmagazine | • Covers a variety of topics<br>• Entertains and informs |
| Radio Talk Show | • Covers some current events<br>• Offers a place for people to express opinions |
| Newspaper Article | • Covers one current event<br>• Gives details and background about the event |
| Commercial | • Presents products, people, or ideas<br>• Persuades people to buy or take action |

## How to Evaluate Information from Various Media

Because the media presents large amounts of information, it is important to learn how to analyze this information. Some media sources try to make you think a certain way instead of giving you all the facts. Use these techniques to figure out whether you can trust information from the media.

✓ Sort facts from opinions. A fact is a statement that can be proven true. An opinion is how someone feels or thinks about something. Make sure any opinions are supported by facts.

✓ Be aware of the kind of media you are watching, reading, or listening to. Is it news or a documentary? Is it a commercial? What is its purpose?

✓ Watch out for bias. **Bias** is when the source gives information from only one point of view. Try to gather information from several points of view.

✓ Discuss what you learn from different media with your classmates or teachers. This will help you determine if you can trust the information.

✓ Read the entire article or watch the whole program before reaching a conclusion. Then, develop your own views on the issues, people, and information presented.

# How To Use Technology in Writing

## Writing on a Computer

You can write using a word processing program. This will help you when you follow the steps in the Writing Process.

- When you write your first draft, save it as a document.
- As you type or revise, you can move words and sentences using the cut, copy, and paste commands.
- When you proofread, you can use the grammar and spell check functions to help you check your work.

## Keeping a Portfolio

Create folders to save your writing in. For example, a folder labeled "Writing Projects—September" can contain all of the writing you do during that month.

Save all the drafts of each paper you write.

## Computer Tips

- Rename each of your revised drafts using the SAVE AS function. For example, if your first draft is "Cats," name the second draft "Cats2."
- If you share your computer, create a folder for only your work.
- Always back up your portfolio on a server or a CD.

# Glossary

## A

**achieved** worked to get a good result (p. 296)

**achievements** successful things you have done p. 268)

**adapt** change to fit a new situation (p. 202)

**affected** produced a change in someone's thinking (p. 42)

**aid** help (p. 88)

**ascend** move higher (p. 340)

**assist** help someone (p. 10)

**attach** connect one object with another (p. 104)

**awards** prizes you get for doing something well (p. 266)

**aware** know about or having knowledge of (p. 74)

## B

**benefit** receive help from (p. 10)

**biome** community of plants, animals, and insects—like a rain forest or a desert (p. 200)

**border** the dividing line between two places—like countries or states (p. 280)

**bore** carried something (p. 8)

## C

**campsite** a place where people can camp (p. 354)

**career** a job that you know a lot about and want to do for a long time (p. 294)

**carry** take something somewhere (p. 24)

**cascade** small waterfall (p. 340)

**cattle** large animals kept for their meat, milk, and skins (p. 72)

**cease** stop (p. 268)

**challenge** something hard to do that tests strength, skill, or ability (p. 104)

**charge** run toward something quickly (p. 24)

**circumstances** conditions or situations (p. 154)

**clever** able to use your intelligence to do something, especially in a slightly dishonest way (p. 102)

**cliffs** areas of high steep rock (p. 326)

**cobblestone** small round stone set in the ground to make a street (p. 152)

415

**code** words, letters, or numbers used to send secret messages (p. 280)

**colonies** areas that are controlled by other countries (p. 136)

**commit** say that you will definitely do something (p. 88)

**compositions** stories, poems, pieces of music, etc. that you have written (p. 266)

**confidential** not intended to be shown or told to other people (p. 152)

**conservation** protection of animals or plants (p. 234)

**consumers** organisms that feed on others in a food chain (p. 218)

**contribute** give money or help to a cause (p. 236)

**cooperate** work together with someone else to get something done (p.8)

**cottage** small house in the country (p. 24)

**country western** popular music in the style of music from the southern and western U.S. (p. 294)

**courageous** brave (p. 86)

**cultures** societies that have their own beliefs, customs, and way of life (p. 168)

**curious** wanting to know or learn about something (p. 152)

**cycle** a number of related events that happen again and again (p. 236)

**damage** harm something (p. 40)

**deduce** use information you have to understand something or form an opinion about it (p. 356)

**delegates** people who are chosen to speak, vote, and make decisions for a group (p. 152)

**desert** large area of land where it is hot and dry (p. 200)

**duet** song or piece of music for two people (p. 294)

**eager** having a strong desire to do something (p. 102)

**emergency** unexpected and dangerous situation (p. 86)

**emotions** strong feelings (p. 294)

**enabled** made it possible for something to happen (p. 236)

**encounter** an occasion when you meet someone or something without planning to (p. 354)

**endangered** a type of animal or plant that might soon not exist (p. 234)

**enormous** very large (p. 296)

**equator** imaginary line around the middle of Earth (p. 200)

**escape** get out of a place (p. 280)

**establish** start or set up a company, system, situation, rules, etc. (p. 42)

**exhibit** show signs of a certain behavior, quality, emotion (p. 356)

**expanded** became larger in size or number (p. 168)

**factor** reason (p. 328)

**fastened** attached something firmly to another object or surface (p. 102)

**federal** relating to the central government of a country that controls a group of states (p. 166)

**goal** something you want to achieve (p. 342)

**grains** the seeds of a crop such as wheat, rice, or corn used as food (p. 8)

**grasslands** large areas of land covered with wild grass (p. 200)

**grateful** thankful (p. 8)

**grove** piece of land with trees growing on it (p. 326)

**herd** a group of animals of the same kind (p. 72)

**highlight** the most important or interesting part of something (p. 342)

**hiking** taking a long walk in the country or in the mountains (p. 354)

**identify** tell what something or someone is (p. 26)

**illegal** not allowed by law (p. 234)

**impose** force someone to think the way you do (p. 168)

**incline** a slope (p. 354)

**infer** make a guess based on knowledge or facts (p. 138)

**initially** first; at the beginning (p. 138)

**injured** got hurt (p. 356)

**inspect** look carefully at or investigate (p. 138)

**instruct** tell someone how to do something (p. 282)

**instruments** objects used for making music (p. 266)

**intervene** try to stop an argument, problem, or war (p. 86)

**label** word or phrase that describes something (p. 202)

**landmarks** things that help you recognize where you are, such as a famous building (p. 280)

**liberty** freedom (p. 166)

**license** official document giving the right to do something, such as a drive (p. 42)

**littering** leaving pieces of waste paper, etc., on the ground in a public place (p. 234)

**major** big or important (p. 26)

**mammals** animals that drink their mothers' milk when they are young—like a cow, lion, or human (p. 218)

**marvelous** very good (p.8)

**meadow** field with wild grass and flowers (p. 340)

**mechanic** someone whose job is to repair vehicles or machines (p. 40)

**merchants** people who buy and sell large quantities of goods (p. 152)

**migrate** move from one place to another (p. 202)

**militia** citizens who are trained to be soldiers in emergencies (p. 136)

**Minutemen** armed fighters for American independence in the Revolutionary War (p. 136)

**motivate** encourage someone with a reason to do something (p. 74)

**motive** reason for doing something (p. 10)

**national parks** large areas of land throughout the United States that the government has set aside for nature (p. 326)

**notes** particular sounds in music, or the signs for these sounds (p. 266)

## O

**occur** take place or happen (p. 26)

**ocean** very large area of water (p. 200)

**organisms** living things (p. 218)

## P

**participate** join an activity (p. 328)

**pasture** land covered with grass, used for cattle and sheep to feed on (p. 72)

**peak** pointed top of a hill or mountain (p. 340)

**peeked** quickly looked at something (p. 24)

**perceive** see, feel, or recognize (p. 268)

**percussion** drums and other musical instruments which you play by hitting or shaking them (p. 266)

**period** piece of time (p. 154)

**physical** having to do with the body (p. 154)

**pilot** someone who flies an aircraft (p. 40)

**pollution** a substance that makes the air, water, or soil dirty or dangerous (p. 234)

**predator** animal that kills and eats other animals (p. 218)

**pretended** did something to make someone believe that something was true when it was not (p. 102)

**primary** most important (p. 220)

**producer** an organism that makes its food (p. 218)

**protect** prevent someone or something from being harmed or damaged (p. 234)

**punishment** the act of making someone suffer because he or she has done something wrong (p. 102)

## R

**ranger station** the building a ranger—someone whose job is to watch and take care of a forest or area of public land—works in (p. 354)

**Redcoats** British soldiers who fought in the Revolutionary War (p. 136)

**reflection** what you see in a mirror or on the surface of water (p. 340)

**refugees** people who have to leave their own countries, especially because of war (p. 86)

419

**region** area or location (p. 328)

**related** of the same family (p. 72)

**republic** a government with an elected head of state (p. 166)

**rescue** save someone from danger (p. 354)

**riverbank** land on the sides of a river (p. 280)

**rockabilly** a style of music that combines rock and country (p. 294)

**role** the way something or someone is involved (p. 220)

**rule** have power in a country and control it (p. 136)

—— S ——

**scarce** not enough of something (p. 24)

**scattered** thrown in different directions (p. 102)

**scavengers** animals that feed on dead animals and animal waste (p. 218)

**secure** to get something, using a lot of effort (p. 104)

**sequoias** very tall trees that grow near the coast in Oregon and California (p. 326)

**share** have or use something together with other people (p. 24)

**significant** important (p. 342)

**similar** almost the same, but not exactly (p. 74)

**skywrite** write a message in the sky using smoke from an airplane (p. 40)

**solo** done alone, without anyone else helping you (p. 40)

**source** where something comes from (p. 220)

**specific** precise; exact (p. 282)

**statesman** a political leader who is wise and respected (p. 166)

**status** respect and importance given to someone (p. 296)

**sufficient** enough (p. 88)

**surrender** stop fighting because you know you cannot win (p. 166)

**survive** continue to live in spite of difficulties (p. 72)

**symbols** things that stand for or suggest something else (p. 282)

**tailors** people whose job is to make suits, coats, etc. (p. 152)

**teamwork** ability of a group to work well together, or the effort the group makes (p. 86)

**tend** take care of someone or something (p. 72)

**tour** a planned trip by a group of musicians in order to play in several different places (p. 294)

**tracks** marks made on the ground by an animal, person, or vehicle (p. 280)

**tradition** a belief or custom that has existed for a long time (p. 40)

**training** process of being taught how to do a particular job (p. 86)

**tributaries** rivers or streams that flow into a larger river (p. 326)

**tropical** coming from the hottest and wettest part of the world (p. 200)

**tundra** large flat lands in northern areas where it is very cold and there are no trees (p. 200)

**valley** area of lower land between two lines of hills or mountains (p. 340)

**veteran** someone who has been a soldier in a war (p. 166)

**vibrations** continuous slight shaking movements (p. 266)

**virtue** good quality of someone's character (p. 8)

# Index

# Credits

**ILLUSTRATORS: Julie Downing** 28-33, 56 **Soud** 12-17 **Gary Torrisi** 76-79 **Doris Ettlinger** 139, 140-145, 184 **Richard Dani Jones** 106-109,114,120 **Lindy Burnett** 110-113 **Daphne Gillam** 170, 172 (top) **Gary Torrisi** 172 177 (bottom) **Daphne Gillam** 239 **Ward** 200 **Daniel Mather** 260, 298-300, 393, 305, 510 **Janice Skivington-Wood** 358-363

**COVER:** Terry Kovalcik

**ICONS:** Bill Melvin

**LETTER LOGOS:** Jan Bryan-Hunt

**UNIT 1** 2 bottom right, Courtesy of the Library of Congress; 5 top left, © Dana White/PhotoEdit Inc.; 5 bottom left, PhotoEdit Inc.; 5 top right, © Steve Gorton/Dorling Kindersley; 5 bottom right, © David Young-Wolff /PhotoEdit Inc.; 6 left, © Mark Richards/PhotoEdit Inc.; 6 right, © Danilo Balducci/Peter Arnold; Inc.; 6 right, (Clara) © David Young-Wolff/PhotoEdit Inc.; 7 left, © Cindy Miller Hopkins/Danita Delimont Photography; 7 left, (Mert) © Michele Molinari/Danita Delimont Photography; 7 right, © Michael Dunning/Photo Researchers Inc.; 8 top, © David Young-Wolff/PhotoEdit Inc.; 8 middle, © Peter Anderson/Dorling Kindersley; 8 bottom, © Richard Morrell/CORBIS; 9 top, © Charlotte Thege/Peter Arnold Inc.; 9 middle, © Gary Ombler/Dorling Kindersley; 9 bottom, Lawrence Migdale; 10 Stephen Coburn/Shutterstock; 11 Dorling Kindersley; 18 © Christopher and Sally Gable/Dorling Kindersley; 19 © Chad Ehlers/Stock Connection; 23 VanHart/Shutterstock; 24 top, © Don Mason/CORBIS; 24 middle, Taxi/Getty Images; 24 bottom, © G.Baden Gerhard Steiner/CORBIS; 25 top, National Geographic Image Collection; 25 right, © Nelly Boyd/Robert Harding World Imagery; 25 bottom, © Martin Harvey/Peter Arnold Inc.; 26 Photos.com, a division of Getty Images; 27 © David Young-Wolff/PhotoEdit Inc.; 34 © Ralph Talmont/Aurora and Quanta Productions; 35 © Jerry Mason/Photo

Researchers Inc.; 37 Photos.com, a division of Getty Images; 39 Rich Legg/iStockphoto; 40 top, Carlos E. Santa Maria/Shutterstock; 40 center, Tracy Whiteside/Sutterstock; 40 bottom, Photos.com, a division of Getty Images; 41 left, Crosseyedphoto/iStockphoto; 41 right, james steidl/iStockphoto; 41 bottom, Photos.com, a division of Getty Images; 42 Fancy Collection/SuperStock; 43 © Susan Montgomery/Shutterstock; 44-49 background, konradlew/iStockphoto; 44, 45, 46, 47, 48, 50, 51 Courtesy of the Library of Congress; 53 Photos.com, a division of Getty Images; 55 Mighty Sequoia Studio/Shutterstock; 58 Jani Bryson/iStockphoto; 59 Artemis Gordon/iStockphoto; 62 graphicola/iStockphoto.

**UNIT 2** 66-67 Anton Vengo/Superstock; 69 top left, © Dave King/Dorling Kindersley; 69 bottom left, © Mark Richards/PhotoEdit Inc.; 69 top right, © Annabella Bluesky/Photo Researchers Inc.; 69 bottom right, PhotoEdit Inc.; 70 left, © A. Ramey/Stock Boston; 70 left, (Charlene) © Simon Greig/Shutterstock; 70 right, Ryanís Well Foundation; 70 right, (Sophie) © Mark Richards/PhotoEdit Inc.; 71 left, Victor Englebert; 71 left, (Panut) © Claire Liembach/Robert Harding World Imagery; 71 right, Picture Desk/Kobal Collection; 71 right, (Dai) © David Young-Wolff/PhotoEdit Inc.; 72 top, Birute Vijeikiene/Shutterstock; 72 bottom, Jean Frooms/Shutterstock; 73 top, Orientaly/Shutterstock; 73 center, Mytho/Shutterstock; 73 bottom, David Dohnal/Shutterstock; 74 Eric Isselée/Shutterstock; 75 Kitch Bain/Shutterstock; 80 Graeme Shannon/Shutterstock; 81 Paul Banton/Shutterstock; 83 dibrova/Shutterstock; 85 Tobkatrina/Dreamstime; 86 top, © Dwayne Newton/PhotoEdit Inc.; 86 bottom, © Vince Streano/NY/CORBIS; 87 top left, © Blair M. Seitz Creative Eye/MIRA; 87 top right, © Bill Aron/PhotoEdit Inc.; 87 bottom, AP World Wide Photos; 88 Samrat35/Dreamstime; 89 National Geographic Image Collection; 90 MSF Sygma/CORBIS; 91 Kieran Doherty/